WHAT YOUR COLLEAGUES AI

These exceptional books are overflowing with worthwhile activities. Going well beyond sharing ideas, they illuminate how manipulative(s) can be used to support mathematical thinking. A particularly important feature of this book is the ongoing discussion of making connections among representations. With such intentionality and engagement in multiple representations, we can ensure that every child become confident and competent in mathematics.

Jennifer Bay-Williams
Professor and Author
University of Louisville, KY

Every math teacher knows that using manipulatives is a good idea. Now, with *Mastering Math Manipulatives*, every math teacher can now how to use them best. It unpacks how different manipulatives work, provides rich tasks for using them, and teaches how to maximize their effectiveness. It includes virtual manipulatives! This is a must-have for every math teacher!

John SanGiovanni
Mathematics Supervisor
Howard County Public Schools, MD

I highly recommend *Mastering Math Manipulatives*. Manipulatives play a vital role in developing a solid conceptual understanding of the math, even at the middle school level. Not only do the authors share wonderful ideas of how to use a variety of manipulatives; they also share reasons why that manipulative is effective for the given topic as well as ways to further develop that concept. This resource is great for those who are new to using manipulatives as well as those who are experienced in using them.

Kevin Dykema
Mathematics Teacher, Mattawan Middle School, Mattawan, MI
President-Elect, National Council of Teachers of Mathematics, 2021–2023

I expected to like this book, but I flat out *love* it! Whether you are a veteran teacher, a new teacher just starting your journey, or a parent trying to help your child at home, this book is a wonderful and practical resource. While manipulatives are clearly the star here, solid instructional strategies supported by just the right amount of research provide a strong supporting cast. Each chapter features a manipulative and includes ideas for organization, classroom management, distance learning, homemade alternatives, and multiple lessons highlighting the use of the manipulative. This is a book you will use all year long!

Donna Boucher
Math Coach's Corner

Sara Delano Moore and Kimberly Rimbey have written a robust and immensely helpful guide to using manipulatives for profound student learning. In short, they have done all the deep, hard work laying out for us the intellectual and pedagogical queries we need to examine when considering using particular manipulatives—or even in deciding to use manipulatives at all! And they have done so with insight on matters of attitude and mindset, the availability of student support, fair accessibility, the role of the virtual, and more. Practical. Readable. Concrete. This is a winner of a guide.

James Tanton
Founder of the Global Math Project

Sara Delano Moore and Kimberly Rimbey masterfully show us why something we know works actually works—that manipulatives are powerful and essential tools to help children learn mathematics. This book serves as a guide to help teachers in their classrooms and in their PLCs effectively make judicious use of manipulatives. Moore and Rimbey empower teachers to use sound learning theories to select the most appropriate manipulative for a particular topic and task. Mathematics educators can use this book to sharpen their mathematical knowledge for teaching and mathematics leaders can use this book as a reference for building curriculum framework documents and engaging in deep collegial coaching conversations. The best part? Students will benefit from a much deeper understanding of *why* the mathematics works as it does. Every mathematics teacher needs a highly dog-eared version of this book in their professional library!

Paul Gray
President, NCSM: Leadership in Mathematics Education, 2021–2023
Chief Curriculum Officer, Cosenza & Associates, LLC

I thought I was aware of most everything I needed to know about the use of manipulatives in teaching mathematics at the elementary level—but Sara Delano Moore and Kimberly Rimbey proved me wrong. *Mastering Math Manipulatives: Hands-On and Virtual Activities for Building and Connecting Mathematical Ideas* makes a significant contribution in several ways: First, it consistently links the various representations in a useful visual that reminds the reader what mental connections students should be making from this experience. The use of multiple representations is critical to support all students particularly those with special needs in mathematics as per the new IES Practice Guide. The book also is practical and full of "I can use this tomorrow" examples across multiple content areas. An important read.

Karen S. Karp
Professor and Author
Johns Hopkins University, MD

As a mathematics coach and consultant I have visited dozens of math closets, those dusty corners of every school where you can find the tools you need to unlock hands-on, student-centered learning in your classroom. *Mastering Math Manipulatives* takes you to those places, yes, but it also takes you to the future with connections to virtual manipulatives, exploring the strengths and limitations of each. In this book you will find seasoned, practical advice and the kind of targeted lessons and directions you need to feel confident enough to dust off those tools and put them to good use. As I like to say, "Put your pencils down and get thinking!"

Kimberly Morrow-Leong
Mathematics Education Specialist and Fifth-Grade Teacher

What a tremendous resource for teachers of mathematics! Sara Delano Moore and Kimberly Rimbey provide helpful tips and practical strategies for incorporating hands-on and virtual manipulatives into daily lessons. This book identifies a wealth of versatile manipulatives that can be used across grade levels and math domains, offers tips for planning and management, and shares sample lessons. And it includes critical discussions about making connections between varied representations to deepen students' understanding of the math skill or concept. The organization of the book is easy to follow and allows teachers to jump in and out as needed to find just what works for their students. If you are looking for useful tips and effective strategies for incorporating hands-on and virtual manipulatives into your math teaching, this is the book for you!

Sue O'Connell
Author, Speaker, Consultant/Quality Teacher Development

It's always so gratifying to find a book filled with the answers to the questions we have asked over and over again. There is widespread belief in the power of concrete materials but the questions I hear are "Which manipulatives are best?", "Where and when do I fit them in?", "How do I best use them?", and "Why are these essential tools for learning?" This wonderful book answers each of these questions with clarity and classroom tested examples. Whether you teach, coach, or administrate in Grades 4 to 8, there is no doubt that the ideas and activities found in this book will strengthen the teaching and significantly enhance the learning of mathematics of your students.

Steve Leinwand
Principal Researcher
American Institutes for Research, Washington DC

We educators spend a great deal of time researching, exploring, and consolidating all the elements that combine to support students as they develop and connect mathematical understandings. It is very exciting to have this uniquely comprehensive resource that unites what is critical and necessary for rich and engaging mathematics instruction, explicitly connecting the research base and mathematics concepts and processes with essential math manipulatives. Distinct and detailed visuals and clearly articulated activities are presented in a consistent format that is accessible to new and experienced teachers.

Kathleen M. Morris
Administrative Coordinator, Elementary/Title I Mathematics
Prince William County Public Schools, VA

Mastering Math Manipulatives is the perfect support to help teachers move beyond using manipulatives for play during recess. This book provides additional ideas and strategies for supporting students who are struggling by helping them learn and grow mathematically. The practical examples included in the book are helpful for pre-service teachers as well.

Cindy Beaman
Math Coordinator
Grand Island Public Schools, NE

Hands-on strategies are essential for student learning, and often natural for teachers in other contents. However, when it comes to math, the connection of hands-on tools to content and activity often seems fuzzy at best. There is finally the resource to connect the tool, the task, and the conceptual understanding together! These manipulatives-based activities provide the foundation for understanding that is essential for mathematics to make sense instead of being memorized. This book is a must for every teacher of mathematics!

Nanci Smith
Author, Consultant, and Associate Professor, Mathematics Department Chair,
and Director of Masters of Education Program
Arizona Christian University
Glendale, AZ

This book is a great resource for assisting educators in teaching mathematics for understanding. It offers preservice teachers a foundation for their future teaching by giving them opportunities to learn math concepts more deeply and conceptually by using physical (or virtual) manipulatives. In-service teachers will find this book a valuable resource to enhance their mathematics curriculum. I applaud the authors for addressing issues of access to manipulatives (physical and virtual) as well as providing helping parents and caregivers understand the importance of manipulatives and how they can assist their children at home.

Shelly M. Jones
Professor, Central Connecticut State University
New Britain, CT

Mastering Math Manipulatives
Grades 4–8
The Book at a Glance

Each chapter focuses on a different manipulative and begins with an introduction to the featured manipulative including images and descriptions and information about homemade and virtual alternatives. The introduction is followed by a set of activities intended to illuminate the range of usefulness for each tool. Each activity includes:

Materials and Organization include everything that you'll need to gather and think about ahead of time.

Mathematical Purpose centers on the math students will encounter through this activity.

Activity Resources include downloadable activity sheets and recording sheets you'll use during the lesson as well as brief demonstration videos.

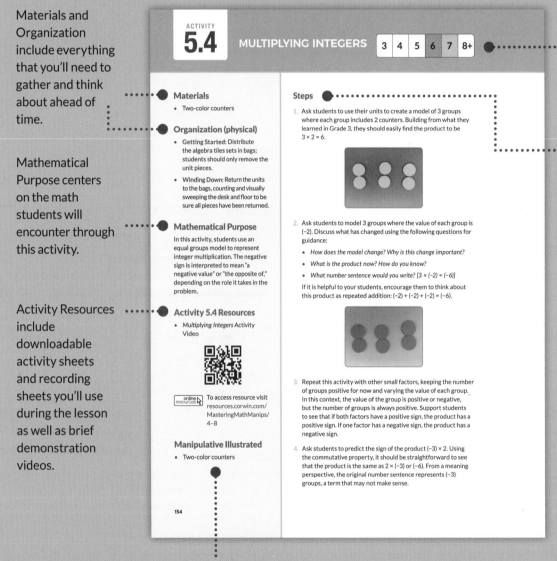

Grade-Level Bands indicate the grade levels that the activity generally addresses. The darker the color, the more relevant it is to that grade.

Steps are provided for each activity, including guiding questions and illustrated examples.

Manipulative Illustrated names the exact tool used in the activity and the URL for any virtual tools used.

Talk with students about the idea that (−3) can also mean "the opposite of three," where opposite refers to the additive inverse. From this perspective, (−3) × 2 can be read as "the opposite of 3 × 2" or "the additive inverse of 6" or (−6). From an action perspective, (−3) × 2 means to make 3 groups of +2 and then flip the 3 groups over to find the additive inverse, or opposite, of the value. This is modeled in the accompanying video. Practice this until students are comfortable with the process.

5. With this understanding in mind, explore the product of (−3) × (−2). In this case, it is helpful to think of this expression as "the opposite of three groups when each group has a value of negative two." This long-winded description shows the efficiency of mathematical notation and can be readily modeled with the unit tiles. Students should create 3 groups, each including 2 negative (red) tiles. They then flip over all the tiles to find the opposite. The resulting product is +6, seen visually in the absence of red tiles. Repeat the process with other combinations of small factors to help students develop fluency with this interpretation of multiplying negative factors.

Why This Manipulative?

The units from algebra tiles (or two-color counters) are helpful tools for modeling both meanings of the negative symbol incorporated here. By placing them red or not-red side up, students show the sign of the number, an adjective-like descriptor indicating the "negative" kind of 3 in the same way an adjective tells the reader to focus on the yellow dress. By flipping them over, to show the opposite side, students signal the operator interpretation of the negative symbol, toggling between a value and its additive inverse (Stephan & Akyuz, 2012). Making sense of multiplication where both factors are negative is a challenging topic, most straightforward when these two interpretations of the negative sign are used for the two purposes of the factors in an equal groups structure.

Developing Understanding

Not all multiplication situations are equal groups situations, and the interpretation of negative values varies depending on the context. The use of an equal groups structure here is designed to support students' emerging understanding of how the product of two negative factors could be positive. This helps develop computational fluency; it does not eliminate the need to understand the meaning of individual multiplication situations when the computations appear in context.

As with subtraction, be careful with the language used to express these number sentences. Using different terms to represent the three meanings of the negative sign (*negative*, *subtract*, or *opposite*) helps clarify for students the sometimes confusing use of the same symbol for three different mathematical ideas.

Featured Connection

This lesson incorporates the Name Your Model strategy for connecting physical representations with symbolic representations. As the video shows, students hear verbal descriptions of mathematical operations, create physical models of those operations, and then name the models with symbolic equations.

Source: Lesh, Post, & Behr (1987).

Why This Manipulative? focuses on the specific features of the selected tool and why its unique characteristics make it useful for illustrating the math concept.

Developing Understanding provides insight and guides you to think about ways in which you will develop student understanding throughout the activity.

Featured Connection provides further explanation for how to connect the concrete representations to other modes of mathematical representation including visual, symbolic, verbal, and contextual.

MASTERING MATH MANIPULATIVES

Grades 4–8

MASTERING MATH MANIPULATIVES

Hands-On and Virtual Activities for Building and Connecting Mathematical Ideas

Grades 4–8

Sara Delano Moore

Kimberly Rimbey

A JOINT PUBLICATION

FOR INFORMATION:

Corwin

A SAGE Company

2455 Teller Road

Thousand Oaks, California 91320

(800) 233–9936

www.corwin.com

SAGE Publications Ltd.

1 Oliver's Yard

55 City Road

London, EC1Y 1SP

United Kingdom

SAGE Publications India Pvt. Ltd.

B 1/I 1 Mohan Cooperative Industrial Area

Mathura Road, New Delhi 110 044

India

SAGE Publications Asia-Pacific Pte. Ltd.

18 Cross Street #10–10/11/12

China Square Central

Singapore 048423

President: Mike Soules

Associate Vice President and Editorial Director: Monica Eckman

Publisher: Erin Null

Content Development Editor: Jessica Vidal

Senior Editorial Assistant: Caroline Timmings

Production Editor: Rebecca Lee

Copy Editor: Melinda Masson

Typesetter: Integra

Proofreader: Susan Schon

Indexer: Integra

Cover/Graphic Designer: Scott Van Atta

Marketing Manager: Margaret O'Connor

Printed in the United States of America.

Library of Congress Control Number: 2021942201

This book is printed on acid-free paper.

21 22 23 24 25 10 9 8 7 6 5 4 3 2 1

CONTENTS

Visit the companion website at
resources.corwin.com/MasteringMathManips/4–8
for downloadable resources.

ACTIVITIES (BY TOPIC)

VIDEO LIST (BY ACTIVITY NUMBER)

ABOUT THE AUTHORS

 **Sara Delano Moore** serves as Vice President for Content and Research and chair of the Mathematics Advisory Board at ORIGO Education. A fourth-generation educator, Sara emphasizes in her work the power of deep understanding and multiple representations for learning mathematics. Her interests include building conceptual understanding to support procedural fluency and applications, incorporating engaging and high-quality literature into mathematics and science instruction, and connecting mathematics with engineering design and computational thinking in meaningful ways. Prior to joining ORIGO Education, Sara served as a classroom teacher of mathematics and science in the elementary and middle grades, a mathematics teacher educator at the University of Kentucky, director of the Kentucky Center for Middle School Academic Achievement, and director of mathematics and science at ETA hand2mind. She has authored numerous articles in professional journals and is a co-author of the *Mathematize It!* series of books. She is also a contributing author to *Visible Learning for Mathematics*, as well as co-authoring the Grade 3–5 and Grade 6–8 volumes of the *Teaching Mathematics in the Visible Learning Classroom* series. Sara earned her BA in natural sciences from the Johns Hopkins University, her MSt in general linguistics and comparative philology from the University of Oxford (UK), and her PhD in educational psychology from the University of Virginia. She lives in Kent, Ohio.

 **Kimberly Rimbey** serves as the chief learning officer at KP® Mathematics and also as the mathematics director for the Buckeye (AZ) Elementary School District. A lifelong teacher and learner, her heart's work centers on equipping teachers and helping them fall in love with teaching and learning over and over again. Kim's interests include high-quality professional learning models, building conceptual understanding through multiple representations and meaningful discourse, and building pedagogical content knowledge that goes beyond the theoretical and into the classroom. Always a teacher at heart, Kim has served as the executive director of curriculum and instruction for Buckeye Elementary School District, chief learning officer for the Rodel Foundation of Arizona, and the mathematics program area coordinator for the Paradise Valley (AZ) Unified School District. That said, everything Kim has done in her career is based on what she learned during her 18 years as a mathematics coach and elementary classroom teacher. Having started her teaching career in a kindergarten classroom, she frequently says that everything she needed to know

about teaching she learned in kindergarten. Kim is National Board Certified in Early Adolescence/Mathematics, and she is a recipient of the Presidential Award for Excellence in Mathematics Teaching. Kim is the co-inventor of KP® Ten-Frame Tiles and has authored and co-authored several publications, including the *Math Academy* series for the Actuarial Foundation, *Math Power: Simple Solutions for Mastering Math* for the Rodel Foundation of Arizona, and, most recently, *The Amazing Ten Frame Series* for KP Mathematics. Kim earned her BA in elementary education and mathematics from Grand Canyon University, her MEd degrees in early childhood education and educational leadership from Arizona State University and Northern Arizona University, and her PhD in curriculum and instruction from Arizona State University. She lives in Phoenix, Arizona.

PREFACE

Welcome! This is a math book. And it's all about representing math in ways that make it more relevant, more meaningful, and more accessible to your students. This book intends to help you help your students by using math tools, primarily math manipulatives, in ways that make teaching and learning both profound and productive. Whether you're a classroom teacher, an instructional coach, a paraprofessional, a parent, or a caregiver, this book is for you!

As you engage in this journey of discovering how to make math meaningful for the students with whom you work, you'll be glad to know that this is not the kind of book that typically gets read from cover to cover. So here's a brief look at how it's put together so you can navigate it in a way that supports your work and saves you time.

First, we recommend you skim through the opening chapter, just to see what is in there. It introduces you to some fantastic classroom strategies that will be woven into each chapter of the book. Plus, it provides background on the use of multiple representations, especially manipulatives, as well as some insightful information about using online manipulatives in ways that enhance learning.

Second, you might want to take a peek at the final chapter, given that, along with the opening, it bookends the content and provides tips and answers to many of the family and caregiver questions you're likely to hear from time to time.

And finally, you'll likely spend most of your time perusing the content chapters, with each chapter focused on a different manipulative. Each of those chapters begins with an introduction to the featured manipulative, followed by a set of activities intended to illuminate the range of usefulness for each tool. Keep in mind that this book intends to get you started—it is by no means a comprehensive guide for each manipulative. Rather, its purpose is to get your creative juices flowing.

Each chapter opens with an overview of the manipulative or group of manipulatives discussed:

- Photos and a description of the tools within this category
- A list of mathematical ideas the tools can support
- Key ideas and things to consider
- Information about homemade and virtual options for the tools

At the end of the chapter, there is space for your reflection. How do you currently use these tools? What new ideas have inspired you? In between, each activity generally follows the same structure:

Materials and Organization includes everything you'll need to gather and think about ahead of time. Note that several of the activities feature virtual manipulatives and others physical tools. Please do not feel limited by the selection for that activity. The use of physical and virtual manipulatives is interchangeable throughout.

Mathematical Purpose centers on the math students will encounter through this activity.

Grade-Level Band indicates the grade levels that the activity generally addresses. The darker the color, the more relevant it is to that grade. Once again, do not let yourself feel limited by these indicators—they are just suggestions.

Activity Resources are available for some, but not all, lessons. Most of these are downloadable activity sheets and recording sheets you'll use during the lesson. And some of them include QR codes for you to access a brief demonstration video.

Manipulative Illustrated lets you know what we used for the illustrations in a particular activity. Sometimes the statement is more general, such as Cuisenaire® Rods, and other times it's specific to the company that sells that manipulative or the online app used for that activity.

Steps are provided for each activity, including guiding questions and illustrated examples. You will want to pay particularly close attention to the strategies used to connect concrete representations to other representations, which is explained more under "Featured Connection."

Why This Manipulative? focuses on the specific features of the selected tool and why its unique characteristics make it useful for illustrating the math concept.

Developing Understanding provides insights for you, the teacher, and guides you to think about ways in which you will develop student understanding throughout the activity.

Featured Connection provides further explanation for how to connect the concrete representations to other modes of mathematical representation including visual, symbolic, verbal, and contextual. Once again, we offer suggestions to get you started, with a focus on the six instructional strategies introduced in the opening chapter. (See—you'll be glad you took a look at the opening chapter first!)

So that's it—your short and simple guide for navigating this book. Now it's time to dive in and join in the journey toward making manipulatives meaningful in your classroom!

ACKNOWLEDGMENTS

First and foremost, we thank the teachers and students with whom we have worked over the years. Your teaching, your questions, your engagement, and your risk-taking have helped both of us learn about teaching mathematics with hands-on resources. The activities and ideas here are better because of our work with each of you.

Books are never written in isolation. We are grateful to the team at Corwin for their excellent guidance and expertise. There's a magic in moving from manuscript to book that reminds us of their talents and never ceases to amaze. We also appreciate the input of reviewers and friends who have answered our questions and provided suggestions as we have worked.

~

Kim, thank you for coming on this journey with me. Our collaboration has made this work stronger. I appreciate all I have learned from my colleagues in the mathematics education world—at ETA hand2mind, at ORIGO Education, and at NCSM. I also thank the community at edWeb.net for their feedback and enthusiasm across many years of webinars around hands-on mathematics instruction. I'm grateful to Bill for his constant love, support, and patience.

—Sara

Sara, you are an inspiration to the math education world and to me. This project brought with it an amazing journey, and I'm so grateful we got to travel this road together. To my friends, colleagues, and mentors who have impacted my heart's work—thank you. Your gracious support, patience, and passion for all things teaching and learning continue to shape me into the educator I am today. To Steve—thank you for believing in me after all these years.

—Kim

PUBLISHER'S ACKNOWLEDGMENTS

Corwin gratefully acknowledges the contributions of the following reviewers:

Elizabeth Marquez
Retired Assessment Specialist and Teacher
Princeton University Prize for Excellence in Teaching Recipient
New Jersey Teacher of the Year Selection Committee Member
Presidential Awards in Mathematics, Science, and Computer Science Teaching
National Selection Committee Member
Milltown, New Jersey

Maria Mitchell
Teacher
Purchasing Manager QEP Books
Plano, Texas

Melynee Naegele
Teacher
Claremore Public Schools
Claremore, Oklahoma

Venessa Powell
Mathematics Assessment Officer
Ministry of Education, Jamaica

Georgina Rivera
Elementary STEM Supervisor Affiliation
Bristol Public Schools and NCSM Professional Learning Director
West Hartford, Connecticut

Introduction: We Know Manipulatives Matter, but . . .

The benefits of making mathematics visible for learners permeate math education courses in most pre-service programs. During our math methods classes, so many of us engaged in new ways of teaching and learning math that did not at all resemble the classrooms in which we learned basic fundamentals. However, the journey from college courses to seasoned teacher often includes many twists and turns, and the realities of classroom teaching sometimes get in the way of where we thought we were heading.

Such was the case for this particular group of teachers. During their weekly professional learning community (PLC) discussions, they talked about the importance of teaching elementary and middle school math in ways that made sense to children. These well-seasoned teachers were highly effective in so many ways. They spoke about the value of classroom discourse, context-driven vocabulary development, and the concrete-pictorial-abstract approach for teaching mathematics to young learners.

Regarding the latter, specifically using manipulatives, they also talked about the many things that got in their way. "Time is always the enemy," one teacher said, "and I find it difficult to find the time to let students explore hands-on ideas when I have so much content to cover before state testing."

"That's so true!" replied her teammate. "And sometimes my kids just want to play with the manipulatives instead of using them as tools to help them learn."

This conversation went on for quite some time, with the final agreement being that they would try to find ways to incorporate more hands-on and visual strategies in their upcoming math unit. They all agreed it would be beneficial. However, the realities of their situation got the better of them, again, and little change occurred.

Flash forward to the end of the school year. The entire group was a bit disheartened by their lack of progress with the goal for hands-on, minds-on teaching. As a result, and with buy-in from just about everyone, the instructional coach agreed to inventory the school's math tools over the summer. All teachers brought their manipulatives to the learning lab where the coach was to spend the next three weeks counting and cataloguing all of the tools that were at the school. Everyone dug deep into their cupboards and emptied their shelves of anything that was on the list.

To their surprise, the room was overflowing with tools they didn't even know they had. Some were still in the shrink-wrapped packages in which they'd been delivered five or more years ago. "How did this happen?" one teacher exclaimed, realizing that they had re-purchased class sets of manipulatives that had been hidden away in closets for far too long.

When the teachers returned in the fall, they were greeted by their faculty leadership team's plan. Over the course of the next semester, they were going to spend time during their weekly PLC gatherings diving into the many uses of these tools and how to use them effectively. They were determined to make sure that this lesson didn't go to waste. Each grade level would take ownership of how they would use these tools, and cross-grade teams would talk about how they could build on what had happened in previous years. It wasn't always a smooth path, but over the course of the year, the conversations they engaged in and the strategies they investigated transformed not only the students' experiences, but the ways in which the teachers, themselves, thought about mathematics.

This book, in part, resembles the kinds of discoveries these teachers made during that year as they searched for new and innovative as well as tried-and-true ways for using multiple representations to support the learning of and to communicate ideas about mathematics.

WHAT ARE MANIPULATIVES?

Mathematics, especially when presented as symbols, can be very abstract. This abstraction is both the power and the challenge of mathematics. The abstraction means mathematics applies to a great many situations. It also makes it difficult for students, especially those learning new ideas and those still reasoning in concrete ways, to make sense of the math. Understanding mathematics deeply requires that teachers support students to make sense of these abstract symbols as a pathway to grasping what mathematics can do and how it works. This is where mathematical manipulatives come in.

Broadly defined, **manipulatives** are physical objects teachers and students can use to discover, illustrate, and model mathematical concepts. Manipulatives are critical to this sense-making process because they make mathematics tangible. They allow students to see, to touch, and to build their conceptual understanding of math. We know this is important for young learners, and it is equally important for students in the middle grades as concepts get increasingly complex.

Within this book, we focus on manipulatives that are mathematically concrete, meaning they are physical objects that represent mathematical values and concepts in ways that lead to greater understanding. We are sharing activities and ideas for using tools such as counters, base-ten materials, and various fraction models. We are not addressing measurement tools such as rulers or protractors. We are also not including objects such as coins or spinners. We made this decision so we could focus on manipulatives that are most powerful for teaching a broad range of mathematical ideas.

WHY ARE MANIPULATIVES IMPORTANT FOR STUDENTS?

Students benefit from and are motivated by using physical tools and representations like manipulatives for cognitive, social, and language development reasons. This has been supported by a number of developmental theorists. Piaget's (1971) stages of intellectual development, for example, reinforce the idea that the thought, language, and action of children is different from that of adults and that children learn best from concrete activities. Social interaction is also critical to Piaget's discussion of emerging intellect, allowing students to clarify their own understanding and recognize the thoughts of others. Engagement with manipulatives also supports language development as (1) students describe to themselves, to each other, and to teachers the representations they build and (2) students use manipulatives as supports for their verbal explanations.

Building from Piaget, Jerome Bruner (1960) proposes that students develop understanding rather than merely receiving information from adults. Manipulatives support social engagement with learning when students negotiate and work together using these shared materials. Learning readiness, Bruner suggests, comes from a mix of direct experience, visual representations, and work with abstract symbols. He also suggests that children are more driven to learn when they engage in activities that interest them. The active engagement of hands-on learning can be very motivating.

Lev Vygotsky's (1934/2012) concept of the zone of proximal development also brings the idea of social engagement to the center as students accomplish much learning through interacting with adults to bring form and structure to their thinking. Zoltán Pál Dienes is another researcher, specifically in mathematics education, whose work supports developing mathematical understanding through direct experiences. Dienes (1971) proposes a three-stage process beginning with unstructured play around mathematical ideas. Students move from this open-ended exploration to more structured experiences designed to highlight the mathematics and bring forward the third stage of the formal mathematics concept.

In more recent years, much of this research has come together as the CPA (concrete-pictorial-abstract) approach. While you may sometimes see the word *representational* or *semi-concrete* used rather than *pictorial* or the word *symbolic* used instead of *abstract*, the general idea of moving between and among concrete, visual, and abstract representations builds from the theorists whose work we have just discussed. This idea was developed further by Richard Lesh on the **translation model** in which students connect multiple representations.

Connecting Multiple Representations

The CPA model is often discussed as a linear structure when its real power is in connections, as illustrated by an emphasis on translation between **representations**. The idea of translating between and among representations (Lesh et al., 1987) is an important instance of deep learning (Hattie et al., 2017). Students build conceptual understanding when they can connect or translate from one representation to another. The strength of using these multiple representations lies not in using them in isolation or as a linear progression. Rather, the power comes from students treating them as interconnected, intertwining representations of mathematical thinking (Karp et al., 2021).

There are five basic representations we use for mathematics, as shown in Figure I.1; each of these can be translated to the other representations as well as within the same category.

Figure I.1 Translation Model

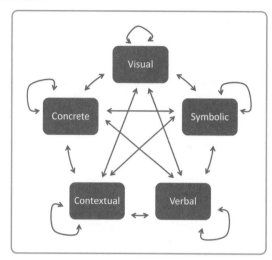

Source: Lesh, Post, & Behr (1987).

Concrete

Concrete representations are those created with physical or tangible objects. These might be formal manipulatives, real-world objects, or common real-world objects repurposed with a mathematical focus. Whether primary children are literally taking books off a bookshelf or students in the middle grades are representing an equation with algebra tiles, both are using concrete representations, the heart of this book. Students connect this representation with itself when they create a second representation using a different manipulative or using the same manipulative in a different way.

Figure I.2 Photograph of a Concrete Representation of Fraction Addition

Visual

Visual representations include a wide range of possibilities. Virtual manipulatives are largely visual, although they can be moved in some ways similar to the actions students can take with concrete objects. Visual representations, also called pictorial or semi-concrete, exist on a continuum more than any other category of representation. This spans from more literal sketches to more mathematical charts and diagrams. We use the term *sketch* to represent visuals showing what a manipulative work surface looks like (see Figure I.3). We use the term *diagram* to represent more formal mathematical visuals such as tables, charts, or graphs. While students certainly might take photographs or screenshots of their work, grabbing these visuals does not prompt the same degree of thinking and active engagement with the mathematics and tools as creating a visual on their own (Wills, 2021). Visuals are connected to themselves when redrawn to be more abstract (e.g., moving from a sketch to a diagram) or to present the ideas differently.

Figure I.3 Visual Representation of Fraction Addition

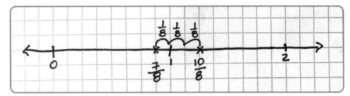

Symbolic

Symbolic representations are the most abstract; they use the formal symbols and notations of mathematics as representations (see Figure I.4). These representations are often efficient and, because they are so abstract, can represent the same mathematical idea as it occurs in many different contexts. Symbolic representations can be connected with each other when we create equivalent expressions or write functions in ways that highlight different features.

Figure I.4 Symbolic Representation of Fraction Addition

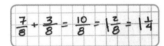

Verbal

Verbal representations are the language we use to communicate our work (see Figure I.5). This language can be oral and/or written. It includes the descriptions we make of manipulatives (e.g., two rods or three red counters and two yellow counters) as well as our ability to read symbolic notation (e.g., knowing that $n \times n$ in the context of area is read "n by n" rather than as a string of three letters, n x n). Verbal representations connect with each other when we move from oral to written or when we refine the language and structure of a verbal representation. This might be accomplished by simply asking students to refine or add on to one another's oral or written explanations.

Figure I.5 Verbal Representation of Fraction Addition

"Seven one-eighth-sized pieces and three more one-eighth-sized pieces is the same as ten one-eighth-sized pieces. Another name for this quantity is one and one-fourth."

Contextual

Contextual representations show the application of mathematics in various contexts (see Figure I.6). For example, the abstract expression 2 + 3 can describe a great many real-world contexts, and students must be able to connect these contexts with the other representations of mathematics they see. Contextual representations connect to each other when we take a general idea (e.g., producing something as an example of **active addition**) and apply it in a number of contexts—we bake cookies, the factory manufactures cars, we create artwork, and so on.

Figure I.6 Contextual Representation of Fraction Addition

Cori had $\frac{7}{8}$ of a pound of freshly picked wild strawberries. She went to another field and picked another $\frac{3}{8}$ of a pound. How many pounds of wild strawberries did she have?

Figure I.7 Multiple Representations of Fraction Addition

Concrete	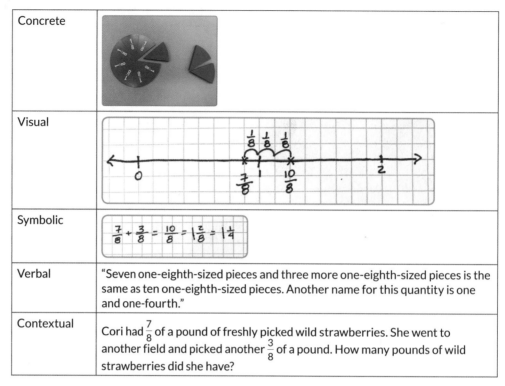
Visual	
Symbolic	$\frac{7}{8} + \frac{3}{8} = \frac{10}{8} = 1\frac{2}{8} = 1\frac{1}{4}$
Verbal	"Seven one-eighth-sized pieces and three more one-eighth-sized pieces is the same as ten one-eighth-sized pieces. Another name for this quantity is one and one-fourth."
Contextual	Cori had $\frac{7}{8}$ of a pound of freshly picked wild strawberries. She went to another field and picked another $\frac{3}{8}$ of a pound. How many pounds of wild strawberries did she have?

Introducing Manipulatives With Notice and Wonder

Before students can use a new manipulative to represent or support their mathematical thinking, they must first explore and understand the tool (Karp et al., 2021), responding to questions like these:

- *What parts and attributes does the tool have?*
- *How do the parts fit together?*
- *Where do I see mathematics in the tool?*

We suggest that you use a *Notice and Wonder Thinking Routine* (Fetter, 2011) when you introduce a new manipulative to your students. Allow 5–15 minutes for the routine before using the new manipulative for a more formal math lesson.

1. Distribute the manipulatives to students.

2. Allow 2–5 minutes of open exploration guided by the questions "What do you notice?" and "What do you wonder?"

3. Invite students to share their noticings and wonderings with the class, creating a collective list. Facilitate connections when one student's noticing might respond to another student's wondering. If necessary, focus the discussion by asking about the "mathy things" students notice and wonder.

4. Invite students to share what mathematics they see in the manipulative. What kinds of problems could this help solve? How does this relate to math they already know? This discussion could take place in small groups or as a whole class. Gather a class list of mathematical potentials, ideally in a place where students can continue to reference it.

5. Close the discussion by connecting student observations and questions to the mathematics focus for the day's lesson.

Strategies for Making Connections

In this book, we share a number of strategies, described in this section, for supporting students to translate between and among representations. Each of these strategies is designed to support students in connecting their thinking from one representation to another representation, with an emphasis on physical representations because of our focus on manipulatives. We incorporate these strategies into the activities of this book. You can use them, of course, with other hands-on activities, and you may decide to emphasize a different connection in an activity by choosing a different strategy. These strategies are listed in an increasingly abstract sequence.

Make a Sketch

In this strategy (see Figure I.8), students sketch a picture or drawing to represent their work with manipulatives (see Figure I.9). This sketch could represent their actions with the

Figure I.8 Translations Highlighted in the Make a Sketch Strategy

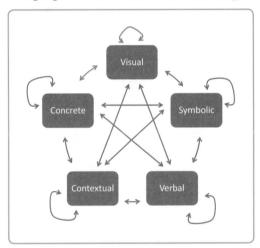

Source: Lesh, Post, & Behr (1987).

Figure I.9 Example of Make a Sketch Strategy

manipulatives (e.g., bundling a group of ten straws) or show a relationship they see (e.g., using Cuisenaire® Rods to illustrate a ratio). Students first represent the mathematics using manipulatives and then create a sketch to represent their work. Actions are illustrated by signals like arrows or circling groups of objects to indicate the ways they moved the materials. Relationships can be shown by how the materials are organized in the sketch. Students might even connect one visual to another as they refine their sketch in this strategy. This translation from physical to visual representations supports students continuing to use these thinking strategies even when they do not have access to physical manipulatives.

Caption Your Picture

In this strategy (see Figure I.10), students have sketched a picture or drawing to represent their work and compose a caption for the picture (see Figure I.11). Depending on age and language proficiency, the caption can be written or oral. The language of captioning suggests that this is not a long description but that it should address the major mathematical ideas in the picture. This supports students translating from a pictorial representation to a verbal representation. Students might use contextual features in their description. They are also likely to refine their language as they create a caption, connecting the verbal feature to itself.

Figure I.10 Translations Highlighted in the Caption Your Picture Strategy

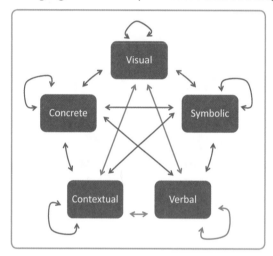

Source: Lesh, Post, & Behr (1987).

Figure I.11 Example of Caption Your Picture

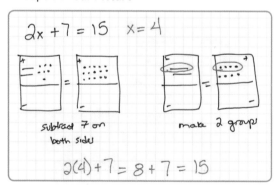

Name Your Model

This strategy (see Figure I.12) supports students in creating an equation or abstract representation for their physical model (see Figure I.13). This "name" is symbolic and is briefer than a caption, encouraging students to use more efficient representations rather than a longer description. In this case, the representations support the following problem:

Figure I.12 Translations Highlighted in the Name Your Model Strategy

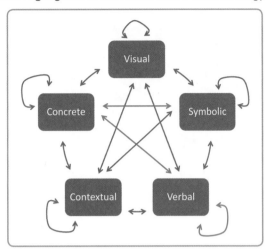

Source: Lesh, Post, & Behr (1987).

Juan received 4 book awards from the library. Each award included a $3 gift card to spend in the school book sale. How much money does Juan have to spend at the book sale?

The students are naming the model when they represent $3 in each section of the bar.

Figure I.13 Example of Name Your Model Strategy

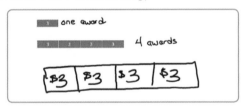

Create a Diagram

In this strategy (see Figure I.14), students move from physical representations to formal mathematical images such as charts, diagrams, or tables of values (see Figure I.15). In this example, students are recording the coordinates of a triangle as it is translated in the coordinate plane.

Figure I.14 Translations Highlighted in the Create a Diagram Strategy

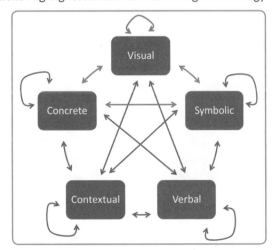

Source: Lesh, Post, & Behr (1987).

Figure I.15 Example of Create a Diagram Strategy

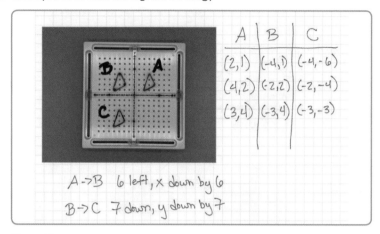

Build the Equation

In this strategy (see Figure I.16), students move from abstract representations to physical representations as they use manipulatives to build a model of a given or derived equation (see Figure I.17).

Figure I.16 Translation Highlighted in the Build the Equation Strategy

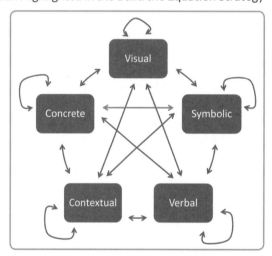

Source: Lesh, Post, & Behr (1987).

Figure I.17 Example of Build the Equation Strategy

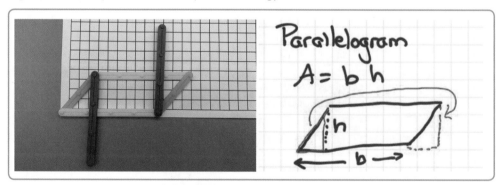

Write a Word Problem

In this strategy (see Figure I.18), students move from a concrete, pictorial, or abstract representation to a contextual representation. Given a number sentence, sketch, diagram, or manipulative model, students contextualize the mathematics by identifying a situation or a word problem that corresponds with the given mathematics (see Figure I.19).

Figure I.18 Translations Highlighted in the Write a Word Problem Strategy

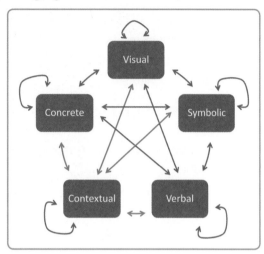

Source: Lesh, Post, & Behr (1987).

Figure I.19 Example of Write a Word Problem Strategy

$$\frac{1}{2} \div 2 = \frac{1}{4}$$

This number sentence could be used to solve a problem like this: *There was half of a pizza left over. The two brothers shared it for lunch. How much of the whole pizza did each brother have to eat?*

How Manipulatives Aid in Access and Equity in Mathematics Learning

Manipulatives are a powerful tool for helping each and every learner reach their full potential in mathematics. Multiple representations of mathematics serve as multiple points of entry to the mathematical ideas. Students who are unclear about the meaning of a mathematical idea might understand more clearly when they build or see a physical model. For example, it is easy to describe numerator and denominator as the top and bottom numbers in a fraction. However, that is not their mathematical meaning. By tearing a set of paper fraction strips or exploring various fraction manipulatives, students understand the distinction between unit fractions (the equally sized parts of the whole represented by the denominator) and the count of those unit fractions (represented by the numerator).

Students who cannot yet explain their thinking in words might be able to create a physical model or visual and then describe it. If teacher and student do not share a common language, this physical or visual model serves as a bridge for their thinking.

By translating between representations, students can build their understanding from areas of greater strength or confidence to representations that may be a greater stretch. Abstract mathematical symbols are just that—abstract. For many students, they are visual squiggles on the page, absent of meaning. By helping students connect an abstract representation to concrete objects, visual images, and contexts, that abstract symbol gains meaning. Marshall et al. (2010) suggest three important instructional principles for developing competence with representation:

- Engaging in explicit dialogue about specific connections between representations
- Discussing connections between representations in both directions
- Selecting representations in a purposeful manner

Furthermore, Karp et al. (2021) share the following principles for successfully using concrete objects to support student learning:

- Consistent use of concrete materials so students are better able to connect them with the concepts they embody
- Avoidance of concrete models that have distracting features, such as using play money for place-value-based operations
- Explicit connection to the relationship between the concrete objects and the math concepts being represented

Implementing these instructional principles using the strategies in this book helps to ensure that each and every student has access to rich mathematics understanding through a variety of representations.

ATTRIBUTES OF MANIPULATIVES

Manipulatives vary greatly in their attributes of color, size, and shape, and it's important to understand why that is, because in some cases, an attribute carries significant meaning that will factor into your choices of what manipulatives to use for what purpose.

Color

For some manipulatives, color is a critical attribute. For example, every pattern-block hexagon is yellow. The Cuisenaire® Rod that's 10 units long is always orange (see Figure I.20). Two-color counters typically have a red side and a not-red side (often yellow

Figure I.20 Cuisenaire® Rods With Consistent Color Sequence

or white). Square tiles or bear counters are made in a variety of colors, and we use them, at times, without regard to color. Color is a familiar attribute, one of the first children learn, and there is confidence, for teacher and student alike, in saying "take the pink piece" and knowing everyone will have the same item and the right item.

On the other hand, students sometimes ascribe meaning to color where they shouldn't, considering yellowness a defining attribute of a hexagon, for example.

Size and Shape

There is also great variation in size and shape. Some manipulatives come in a larger-scale form designed for use by young children whose fine motor skills are still developing. Fraction tools represent a variety of wholes, varying in both shape and size. They are partitioned in different ways as fractional pieces are created, making it essential to understand how the set is designed to know how each fractional part relates to the whole. We talk about many manipulatives as two-dimensional when, in fact, they are all three-dimensional objects, including paper manipulatives, and we generally ignore the height or thickness of the piece.

Each chapter in this book opens with an overview of the category of manipulatives included. We discuss specific instances of color, size, or shape and how they might support developing mathematics or even, potentially, lead to a misconception, as in the example of yellow hexagons.

Beyond color, size, and shape, there are two attributes worthy of particular attention: whether manipulatives are **pre-grouped or groupable** and whether they are **proportional**.

Pre-grouped vs. Groupable Manipulatives

Think about the rod in a set of base-ten blocks, typically a $1 \times 1 \times 10$ cm shape. This piece is already pre-grouped (see Figure I.21); it represents one group of ten (or a set of ten individual unit cubes), and it cannot be decomposed (deconstructed) into those smaller pieces. The flat ($1 \times 10 \times 10$ cm) is also pre-grouped. It represents one group of one hundred

Figure I.21 Pre-grouped Base-Ten Materials

(or ten groups of ten or one hundred individual unit cubes) as a single piece. The same is true for the large cube ($10 \times 10 \times 10$ cm), representing one group of one thousand (or ten groups of one hundred or one hundred groups of ten or one thousand individual unit cubes) as a single piece.

Other manipulatives are groupable; the pieces are not connected in predetermined groups but can be grouped at will. Most counters fall into this category. A single square tile, a single pebble, or a single toy car can be grouped with other (like) counters, but the materials themselves do not provide premade groups.

Manipulatives that connect (linking cubes are a common example) or that can be grouped into holders (such as KP® Ten-Frame Tiles) are an intermediate place for this attribute. The fact that the pieces connect means students can create a group like they would see in a pre-grouped manipulative. There are, for example, some base-ten materials that appear initially as single units and can then be grouped and covered to create a group of ten, a group of one hundred, and so on (see Figure I.22).

Figure I.22 Groupable Base-Ten Materials

There is often an extra button on one end or dimples on some sides that mean the assembled group does not look exactly like a pre-grouped tool. This is fine, but be on the lookout for students who might be confused by this detail.

Proportionality

Proportional manipulatives are in scale with each other. Fraction manipulatives are proportional tools; the whole is 8 times the size (typically length or area) of a one-eighth piece (see Figure I.23). Pattern blocks are also proportional. The pieces are built from the same unit side length and specific angle measures in order to fit together nicely. Most counters, on the other hand, are not proportional. There is not a clear scale factor relationship between a single bear counter and a group of ten bear counters as there is between a unit cube and a rod in a set of base-ten blocks.

While not included in this book, coins are a good example of the problems that can occur when manipulatives are not proportional. For example, there is nothing about the structure of a U.S. coin that indicates its mathematical value: A dime is worth ten cents or one-tenth of

Figure I.23 Proportional Fraction Towers

a dollar, which has more value than a penny (one cent) or a nickel (five cents), yet it is lighter in weight, thinner in height, and smaller in diameter than the other coins. It still has greater value. For students, this can be very confusing.

Proportional manipulatives are powerful tools for building number sense because they give students a clear sense of the relationship between one quantity and another, building on a common unit. How much more is 1,000 times larger? It's precisely the difference between the unit cube and the large cube in a set of base-ten blocks. Generally defined as a single undivided whole, a unit is the foundation of many key ideas. The unit piece in a base-ten set is the smallest cube. The unit whole is the quantity representing one whole when working with fractions.

Manipulatives can help make these ideas visible for students because the physical and visual patterns and structure are easy to identify.

The opening manipulative description in each chapter will include notes about grouping and proportionality because they are essential attributes for making good instructional decisions about using manipulatives.

Virtual Manipulatives

In today's classrooms, virtual manipulatives have come to have a more prominent place in instruction. Virtual manipulatives extend the powerful tangible resources into a digital age, providing students with the convenience of having manipulable images at their fingertips.

When we consider virtual manipulatives, there are two common benefits and one concern. One benefit is that they provide an endless supply of any given piece. While a physical set of fraction tiles typically contains four one-fourth pieces, students working with virtual tools have an endless supply to use in their modeling. A second benefit is that some virtual manipulatives also provide options for grouping and un-grouping rather than remaining fixed as a grouped or un-grouped tool. In this way, a rod valued as one group of ten can be virtually decomposed into ten single-unit cubes, an action that requires trading when working with physical base-ten blocks. The concern lies in the notion of maintaining proportionality. Because proportionality is so important with many manipulatives, it is important that virtual materials are true to the proportionality of their physical counterparts and that the images cannot be resized. Students can easily lose the proportional understanding of tools if they unintentionally (or deliberately) resize an object.

The concern of virtual manipulatives is that accessing them is an equity challenge. Despite the fact that they can actually increase equity for all learners to access mathematical ideas, that only matters if the students can get their hands on them. This is true of both physical and virtual manipulatives. Schools typically do not have sufficient quantities of physical manipulatives to send a supply home with each student, although die-cut alternatives or common household objects (e.g., dry beans as counters) may suffice. When working with virtual manipulatives, technology can be a limiting feature. While virtual manipulatives may be offered in more rural settings or when students are learning remotely or online, we must ask whether every student has a device and sufficient internet access to use the virtual tools, especially at home. A student accessing the internet through a phone connection with limited data is in a very different place than a student with a personal touchscreen tablet or computer with unlimited high-speed data.

While "virtual manipulatives do not replace the power of physical objects in the hands of learners" (National Council of Supervisors of Mathematics, 2013, p. 1), there are definite advantages to digital tools, particularly when we look at more sophisticated uses of them. Wills (2021) provides several insights into ways to increase success with the use of virtual manipulatives:

- Find a balance between teacher-selected and student-selected virtual manipulatives. Although the teacher-selected option may save time, the student-selected option will likely lead to a more robust learning opportunity.

- Provide opportunities for students to learn how to use the online manipulatives. Just as with physical objects, provide students with opportunities to notice and wonder about the features and to experiment with the functions of a new online tool.

- Take time to teach students how to create and share screenshots of the results of their work as well as screen shares of the actions of their work.

- Beware of apps that "steal" the thinking by using virtual manipulatives that replicate the "freedoms" afforded by their physical counterparts as closely as possible.

- Explore the best options for each situation. Sometimes physical objects and drawing/sketches are still the best choice to support student explorations and communication due to the ability to show action. Identify common objects students may be able to find at home to use as manipulatives. For example, students may show place value using cereal Os and uncooked spaghetti, LEGO® pieces, paper clips, or beads and string. They may show computation and operations using buttons, beans, beads, or bottle caps. They may build arrays with cheese crackers. They may show fractions with egg cartons, muffin trays, or toys with different attributes.

Despite the benefits and challenges mentioned, the real question is one of purpose. Most typically, we see teachers using virtual manipulatives to substitute or augment physical tools, keeping many tasks at the Substitution or Augmentation levels. If this is all we do with virtual manipulatives, we fail to gain the real benefits of the digital tools. Instead, teachers should look for opportunities to move to the Modification and Redefinition levels to harness the real power of these tools. Figure I.24 provides examples of what these moves might look like when using virtual manipulatives.

Figure I.24 Example SAMR for Virtual Manipulatives

SAMR MODEL		Virtual Manipulatives Examples
Transformation	**Redefinition** Technology allows for the creation of new tasks, previously inconceivable	Using screen casting software, student creates a series of math tutorial videos featuring virtual manipulatives as a way to demonstrate mathematical ideas.
	Modification Technology allows for significant task redesign	Student uses collaboration features to discuss and determine the best way(s) to represent a mathematical idea using virtual manipulatives.
Enhancement	**Augmentation** Technology acts as a direct tool substitute, with functional improvement	Student uses virtual manipulatives to represent a mathematical idea in multiple ways, using screenshots to place the representations side by side.
	Substitution Technology acts as a direct tool substitute with no functional change	Student uses virtual manipulatives to represent a mathematical idea.

CONSIDERATIONS FOR DISTANCE LEARNING

Ideally, instruction will include both concrete and virtual manipulatives. In distance learning situations, a more balanced approach might not be possible. We have chosen to substitute virtual manipulatives for some of the activities in this book so that our representations and discussion include both physical and virtual manipulatives. As a teacher, you should feel free to swap physical and virtual manipulatives where necessary for your teaching situation.

As much as possible, we encourage you to begin instruction with physical manipulatives, incorporating virtual manipulatives where they add to the mathematics (e.g., the endless supply is useful) or where they can modify or redefine the task. This will typically include the use of additional software and/or the use of digital communication tools.

If you are using virtual manipulatives as a substitute for physical ones, please consider the following:

- Do students have the technical skills to find and manipulate the online figures?
- Are students able to visualize the objects in their three-dimensional forms (geometric solids, pattern blocks, etc.)?
- Are there ways to enhance the use of virtual tools using online apps such as Nearpod, Pear Deck, or other online presentation tools?
- Might students benefit from using copy and paste, snipping, taking a screenshot, screen sharing, and other online actions to communicate their thinking?
- How might the virtual manipulatives be used for students to communicate and evaluate their thinking?
- How might students use the online platform to collaborate with teachers and other students?

In the activities in this book, we have used publicly available virtual manipulative toolboxes. It is also possible to create shared workspaces in online documents such as Google™ Slides.

 To access the virtual manipulative toolboxes, visit **resources.corwin.com/ MasteringMathManips/4–8**

PREPARING TO USE MANIPULATIVES EFFECTIVELY

Manipulatives are widely viewed as an important part of high-quality mathematics instruction. Yet there are still real obstacles and valid worries to address and overcome in their successful implementation. Some of the most commonly cited concerns appear as follows.

- *Access:* "Students lack access to materials." Either schools must have sufficient quantities of physical manipulatives, or students must have sufficient digital access (devices and connectivity) for manipulatives to be used thoughtfully.
- *Distraction:* "My students just want to play." There is a perception that time is wasted when students play with the materials.
- *Curricular Coverage:* "I need to cover the curriculum." There is a perception that time spent in the textbook is more productive in moving learning forward and that manipulatives slow down progress and pacing.
- *Assessment:* "How will I assess my students if they used manipulatives during instruction?" Assessing manipulative-based learning seems challenging.
- *Classroom Management:* "Managing all these materials seems overwhelming." It takes time to organize materials and to teach a manipulative lesson, and students may be more likely to misbehave when "toys" are available.
- *Professional Preparation:* "I honestly don't even know where to begin." Not all of us yet knows enough about teaching with manipulatives to plan effectively.
- *Helping All Learners Develop Deep Understanding:* "I have students in so many different places with their math learning. How do I differentiate with these tools so they meet the needs of *all* my students?"

Each activity in this book provides guidance in how to overcome these obstacles so that the power of learning with manipulatives can be fully realized without sacrificing time, learning progress, or classroom management. For general purposes, explore the following tips to consider how to begin to incorporate manipulatives into instruction.

Access

This can be a problem beyond your control. We encourage you to consider die-cut or homemade alternatives for manipulatives as a way of expanding your collection of physical materials. A great many virtual manipulatives are also available, many at no cost. See the website supporting this book for our list of virtual resources. Devices and bandwidth are still real challenges.

 To access the virtual manipulative toolboxes, visit **resources.corwin.com/ MasteringMathManips/4–8**

Distraction

Toys vs. Tools Discussion

A common objection to using manipulatives in the class centers on the notion that students will play with these tools rather than using them to support learning. Therefore, some teachers opt to withhold opportunities for hands-on learning rather than addressing this issue head-on. One way for you to talk with your students about this issue is to compare and contrast the notion of learning tools vs. toys. Manipulatives, although they may remind students of toys such as building blocks and LEGO® pieces, are intended to support learning rather than to be used in whimsical ways.

A helpful comparison is to compare a LEGO® set with a set of construction tools. While toys provide an open-ended forum for play, learning tools tend to have a more narrow and defined use. When students begin to use manipulatives in ways that are inappropriate, a simple reminder that they are to be used as tools rather than as toys will usually suffice to get students back on track.

Curricular Coverage

Mathematics Lesson Framework

Many teachers find it useful to use a mathematics lesson framework to help shape their lessons. One such framework includes four components:

- Launch
- Develop conceptual understanding
- Practice and application
- Wrap-up

With a lesson framework such as this, one can see that there is room for fitting manipulatives into the structure of the day, sometimes even replacing the content presented in a student textbook. For example, you may launch the lesson by engaging the students in a number routine and then shift into using manipulatives to develop conceptual understanding, perhaps deviating from the textbook's lesson in order to create a hands-on opportunity. Then your students may use those same manipulatives to support their work during the practice and application portion of the lesson.

Going Slow to Go Fast

One must acknowledge that using manipulatives and other hands-on strategies may require additional time compared to a more algorithmic approach to learning. Therefore, a helpful mindset you may adopt is that laying the foundation takes time, and once it is laid, the practice goes much quicker. By taking the time to build conceptual understanding using manipulative tools, your students better understand the mathematics concepts at hand, and the time it takes to connect to visual and symbolic representations often goes relatively quickly. Some call this "going slow to go fast." You may find yourself slowing down a bit in the initial stages, but once understanding is achieved, the later stages often glean faster results.

Assessment

A common adage regarding assessment states, "You should teach the way you'll be tested." With many of our state-mandated standardized assessments, our students are expected to exhibit their learning by answering a handful of questions using only paper-and-pencil methods (along with mental math strategies). Unfortunately, this drives many teaching professionals to conclude that every quiz, every check for understanding, every unit test, and every benchmark assessment should use that same structure.

Of course, the paper-and-pencil-only design is sometimes appropriate—it is an efficient way to assess what students do and do not know at one given point in time. But by no means must every assessment take on that same organization.

The following is a list of several ways one might use manipulatives as part of the assessment process.

- Checklist assessments
- Photos and videos
- Sketching actions
- Checks for understanding
- Diagnostic assessments
- Benchmark assessments

Classroom Management

Classroom Setup and Management

- *Tables vs. desks:* Given the choice, tables provide a more cohesive structure to facilitate student interactions while using a variety of tools to demonstrate their math thinking. A group math tool kit may be located in a tub placed in the center of the table. Individual tool kits may be distributed for students to keep in their desks. This brings with it the individual ownership and accessibility to a variety of tools.

- *Long-term storage:* Not all tools are needed for every unit of study. For example, geometric solids and geoboards have a limited time frame in which they lend themselves to representing the learning at hand. Therefore, finding a just-right location for them to be stored is desirable. Students should still have easy access to them throughout the year. Consider placing them on a shelf in the classroom rather than in a closet behind closed doors in order to maintain accessibility for when they may be used creatively.

- *Traffic patterns:* When distributing and storing manipulatives, consider how students will collect and clean up their materials on a daily basis. This includes attending to traffic patterns that facilitate easy pickup and cleanup of mathematics tool kits, table tubs, and so on.

- *Cleaning up with strategic preparation in mind:* Setting up manipulatives for the next time they are to be used can be a huge timesaver for both you and your students. One of the easiest ways for you to prepare the materials ahead of time is to build in such structures when students are cleaning up during a previous lesson. For example, require that students remove all rubber bands from the geoboards, placing them in their corresponding containers. Or ask students to organize their base-ten blocks or algebra tiles in such a way that they are ready to be used the next time students get them out. This also provides an opportunity to take inventory, with students counting the pieces to be sure everything is included before putting their tools away for the day.

Karp et al. (2021) also mention the following practices you may consider:

- Never avoid using representations due to time constraints—using manipulatives during instruction will enhance learning and help in the long run. Remediation and intervention will take much more time for those students who don't get it the first time.

- Take time to teach students how to use the manipulative as well as how to put it away.

- Provide exploration time when new manipulatives are introduced.

- Keep baskets of manipulatives on the table so students can select appropriate tools when they need them. Remember that a major goal is that *students* select appropriate tools strategically for their learning and communication needs.

- Explicitly teach students how to draw visual representations. Provide helpful hints on how to most efficiently create sketches and drawings for base-ten materials, fraction representations, bar models, diagrams, and so on. Also emphasize that this is not art class—students need not draw fingernails and shoe ties on their mathematical sketches. In fact, in most cases, students can simply draw circles or Xs to represent the objects to which they are referring.

Professional Preparation

Planning: Connecting Activities to the Core Program

The activities in this book stand alone and do not represent a coherent, sequenced unit of study. To get the most from these activities, you will want to be mindful of your core program, thinking about how the activity at hand might lend itself to richer ways of representing the mathematics covered in the curriculum.

For example, Activity 1.6 illustrates base-ten multiplication with an emphasis on the distributive property and area models. Consider where this idea best fits and how to integrate these ideas for representation when it is time for this unit of study.

Planning: Providing Opportunities for Students to Select Appropriate Tools

You may notice that in many cases, different representations may be appropriate for the same concept. We encourage you to consider providing options from which students may select rather than dictating which tool to use each day. This affords students the opportunity to "use appropriate tools strategically." Students should become sufficiently familiar with each tool so as to make sound decisions about which tools will support their thinking.

For example, when working on proportional relationships, students might use Cuisenaire® Rods, counters, coordinate pegboards, or a variety of pictorial ways to support and represent their thinking. They should have ample opportunity to choose a tool that works best for them without being limited by what their teacher or other students choose to use.

This requires that they engage in discussions about the advantages and disadvantages of each tool along the way. One way to provide this foundation is to introduce one manipulative at a time at the beginning of the year. Students discuss and explore that single manipulative as well as use it in the learning process. Then it is added to a tool kit for future use. This practice continues with new manipulatives on a regular basis until students have a rich tool kit of appropriate resources.

Free vs. Guided Exploration

When first introducing various manipulatives to students, you will want to consider whether free exploration or guided exploration is most appropriate. Free exploration is more open-ended, facilitating highly creative uses for the materials. This may lead to new ways of using the tools, although it may lead to students going too far with them, such as using linking cubes to create toy weapons.

Guided exploration, on the other hand, typically begins with a question that guides students through their explorations, pointing them toward discoveries that are more math-oriented. Earlier in this chapter, we described a *Notice and Wonder Thinking Routine* (Fetter, 2011) to use when you introduce students to manipulatives. Asking students what they notice and wonder about a new tool provides a foundational expectation that they are looking for mathematical applications for using the new tool. Each chapter opens with suggestions about key ideas for this routine with the specific manipulative discussed.

Helping All Learners Develop Deep Understanding

Universal Design for Learning (Center for Applied Special Technology, 2018; National Council of Teachers of Mathematics, 2020) suggests that students be provided with multiple modes of engagement, of representation, and of action and expression. We must use a variety of strategies to invite students into learning mathematics and to support students while learning mathematics. Because students learn in many different ways, building hands-on learning experiences into core instruction provides all students with access to supportive thinking structures. Manipulatives help students *develop, communicate, refine,* and *dive deeper* into their thinking. They are a key aspect of providing adequate support to each and every mathematics learner.

First, when students are *developing* their mathematical thinking on a concept, using visual and concrete objects assists them in the learning process. In a sense, the physical models "partner" with the students' thinking, helping them maneuver through mathematical processes and ideas and reinforcing their agency in mathematics. As students' understanding emerges, manipulatives may be especially useful in demonstrating the strengths they bring to the table given the hands-on and visual nature of these tools.

Second, when students use manipulatives to *communicate* their thinking, much thinking has already taken place, and the students may be well on their way to finding the solution. In this case, they are transferring their thinking into the physical world, using the manipulatives as representations of their internal processes. This is especially useful as students develop their language skills, because manipulatives allow learners to communicate their thinking in both verbal and nonverbal ways. It's also important to note that different students may use different manipulatives to communicate their thinking … and that's a good thing! Making multiple representations a routine part of classroom instruction also increases access and agency for students. When everyone has a wider range of representations to use in communicating important mathematical ideas, classroom authority is shared among teachers and learners.

Third, students in a variety of settings may find the use of manipulatives helpful in *refining* their thinking and *diving deeper* into foundational mathematical ideas by extending their thinking about a particular concept. Since the pace of developing deep understanding can differ from one student to the next, teachers should resist the temptation to cover more content at the expense of digging deeper. Using multiple representations and translating between and among them focuses students on clarifying their thinking and consciously communicating ideas that they intuit but do not always fully understand.

MANAGING YOUR MANIPULATIVES

Ensuring that all classrooms have the tools needed for student success is a high priority for teachers and leaders alike. That said, how does one know which tools are the "right" tools and on what to spend precious resources? Let's explore guidance on how to select and manage your manipulatives, including taking inventory, prioritizing purchases, and packing and storing manipulatives.

Taking Inventory

Taking an inventory of the tools that teachers and students already have is a necessary first step. And equally important is taking inventory of how those tools have been used and will be used in the future. This is how you'll decide what else you need to buy, borrow, find, or create.

As you take inventory of the math tools that are in your classroom or school, the amount of each manipulative you have at your disposal will be important. Figure I.25 provides a general rule of thumb for how many of each manipulative is ideal for a single student working alone, a small group of students, or a full class. Note that there is no set rule for how many are necessary—we are simply providing a general guideline here. This can serve as a starting point for your thinking about whether you have enough of a given tool or wish to purchase more.

Figure I.25 Example Suggested Classroom Inventory

Manipulative	Grades K–2	Grades 3–5	Grades 6–8
Algebra Tiles			Per student: 1 set
AngLegs®		1 set per pair of students	1 set per pair of students
Base-Ten Blocks	Per student: 1 flat, 12 rods, and 30 units	Per student: 1 flat, 12 rods, and 30 units, *plus* 10 large cubes for the class	
Color Tiles	Per student: 20 Small group: 100 Whole class: 500	Per student: 100 Small group: 150 Whole class: 1,000	Per student: 100 Small group: 150 Whole class: 1,000
Coordinate Boards		1 per student	1 per student
Cuisenaire® Rods	1 set per student	1 set per student	1 set per student
Fraction Towers Fraction Circles Fraction Tiles/Bars Fraction Squares		1 set per student	1 set per student
Geoboards	1 per student	1 per student	1 per student
Geometric Solids	Per student: 1 set Small group: 1 set Whole class: 1 set per 4 students	Per student: 1 set Small group: 1 set Whole class: 1 set per 4 students	Per student: 1 set Small group: 1 set Whole class: 1 set per 4 students
Linking Cubes	Per student: 20 Small group: 100 Whole class: 500	Per student: 100 Small group: 150 Whole class: 1,000	
Two-Color Counters	Per student: 20 Small group: 100 Whole class: 500	Per student: 20 Small group: 100 Whole class: 500	Per student: 20 Small group: 100 Whole class: 500
Unit Cubes		Per student: 24 Small group: 100 Whole class: 500	Per student: 24 Small group: 100 Whole class: 500

*Note: try to keep the number of pattern blocks proportional by size: for every 1 hexagon, students may need 2 trapezoids, 3 blue rhombi, and 6 triangles. Because squares and tan rhombi are less widely used, the number included in each bag is not as important.

**If students are working in groups, it is helpful for each group member to have a different color.

 To download a copy of this resource, visit **resources.corwin.com/ MasteringMathManips/4–8**

Prioritizing Purchases

You may find yourself in the position of having to choose which manipulatives to purchase. When this is the case, you may need to prioritize your purchases. Here are a few guidelines to assist you. Answering these questions may help you in the prioritization process:

- Major vs. supporting content: Does this manipulative support major content for your grade level, or is it supporting content?

- Versatility and frequency: Does this manipulative have utility across multiple standards and concepts that will be taught throughout the year, or is it limited to a small set of standards and only needed for a couple of weeks?

- Accessibility: Do you have access to this manipulative by borrowing from another classroom or checking it out from a resource library?

- Replaceability: Are there alternatives for this manipulative?

- "On-the-cheap" options: Can you make it yourself? Can you purchase it at a secondhand shop or a teacher outlet? Can you find a lower-cost option? Might you find it at a "retiring teacher garage sale" or an online clearance sale? Can you substitute with everyday objects (e.g., small erasers as counters)?

Storing and Packing Manipulatives

Here is a general rule of thumb: When manipulatives come in sets, find a way to keep them in sets. For example, if your Cuisenaire® blocks come in trays, keep them in the trays and place them in sealable bags. Place sets of fraction tiles (or circles or squares) in sealable quart bags. Drop the x-y coordinate pegboard, along with the corresponding pegs, axes, and bands, into a sealable gallon bag. This will make them easy to sort, to use, and to inventory. This also helps you transport the sets as well as to redistribute across classrooms, when necessary.

It's important to communicate these ideas to parents and caregivers. Please see the closing chapter for tips and strategies for supporting them in their journey toward using manipulatives to support their children's learning.

FREQUENTLY ASKED QUESTIONS

And finally, we know that questions come up frequently, especially as you dive into this important work. This section is our attempt to address some of the questions we frequently encounter regarding the use of manipulatives in the classroom.

Management

Q: What do I do if my students are playing with the manipulatives rather than using them as thinking tools?

A: Prevention is always your best tool for this. When introducing manipulatives to your class, clearly outline the expectations, even to the point of rehearsing appropriate use. Some teachers create anchor charts that describe what appropriate use of manipulatives looks like and sounds like. Review these expectations frequently, as needed. Remind students that manipulatives are tools for thinking and learning, not toys.

Q: What if I don't have enough manipulatives for every student to have a full set?

A: The simplest way to handle this is to have students share manipulatives when health and safety conditions allow for this. Ask students to work in pairs, triads, or groups of four. While one student manipulates the tools, others can be representing the same problem(s) on paper, using different representations. Other approaches may include rotating students through stations or small groups, or making additional sets of manipulatives on a paper cutter or die-cut machine. Homemade options are mentioned at the beginning of each chapter in this book.

Q: Is it better for students to work alone or in small groups when working with manipulatives?

A: This depends on your math goal as well as your management style. Giving students independent work time, especially at the beginning of a learning episode, provides them the opportunity to engage in the thinking and discovery opportunities necessary for grappling with the topic at hand. That said, shifting into pairs and/or small groups after a period is also advisable since learning is primarily a social endeavor. Teaching students ways of engaging in meaningful and accountable discourse, a skill useful in all content areas, can help ensure that students maximize the benefits of collaborative work.

Q: My students may feel they are too old for this. What should I do if they see these tools as babyish?

A: Your students will take their cues from you. Manipulative use is completely appropriate from preK through college, and the way in which you, the teacher, introduce these tools for each learning episode can impact students' perceptions. Remind students that manipulatives are tools, not toys, and that they support both thinking and communication. Be sure to integrate the use of manipulatives into your teaching moves, modeling appropriate use and engaging in "think-alouds" to demonstrate how the manipulatives impact thinking and learning. Occasionally engage students in conversations about the many tools they have at their disposal to represent mathematics in various ways—concrete, pictorial, verbal, symbolic, and contextual.

Rationale

Q: Which manipulatives are most important to have on hand?

A: This depends on your math goals. The manipulatives shared in this book certainly do hone in on the most prominent and basic tools you should have at your disposal. If you are limited on the number of manipulatives available, here is a list of questions to ask yourself:

- What are my math goals for the year?
- Based on the trajectory of concepts and skills I'll be teaching this year, which tools will have the most utility (e.g., which manipulatives can be used for multiple concepts)?
- Does each manipulative have a completely distinct use? (For example, unit tiles have a clear and distinct purpose in grade levels where area is emphasized; however, they do not have the same level of utility in early grades, where they are simply used as counters.)

Q: How can I help families access and support the use of manipulatives at home?

A: Accessibility is often an issue when looking for ways to encourage manipulative use at home. Ideally, sending home a "mathematician's tool kit" with various manipulatives would provide students the access they need. This kit may include either commercial manipulatives or alternatives such as those discussed at the beginning of each chapter in this book (e.g., fun foam versions cut on a paper cutter or die-cut machine). You may also send home a list of things that can be gathered and used at home, such as beans and pasta as counters or paper and scissors for making fraction pieces. To encourage adult support, you may offer live or virtual mini-workshops for adults to give them tips on how to use specific tools to help their children. This has the added benefit of subtly frontloading math content they may or may not need to learn for themselves.

Q: What do I do if my principal sees manipulatives-based learning as playing with toys rather than doing math?

A: Communication is key for this one! Be sure that your lesson planning documents include manipulatives in the materials list and that your objectives clearly connect to the use of the manipulatives you intend to use. Include a diagram of the Lesh model for mathematical representations with your lesson plans, and share it with your principal during pre-observation conferences or in conversations about math instruction. Point out the many ways to represent math thinking and how the physical tools play an important role. Perhaps the best preparation for addressing this head-on is to ensure your management is tight (see the earlier Q&As) and that when your principals or supervisors walk in, they witness students using the tools productively and with ease. You may also include photos and video evidence (see the following section) in post-observation conferences to further provide evidence of the value manipulatives offer.

Testing and Accountability

Q: How do I collect evidence of student thinking and learning while using manipulatives?

A: Photos and videos provide a fantastic opportunity to demonstrate and archive students' learning using manipulatives. Whether in a face-to-face or virtual setting, while students are working, snap photos of their work and save to online portfolios. Furthermore, brief video clips of students explaining their thinking using manipulatives and other tools can show growth in understanding over time. In addition, ask students to record their use of manipulatives on paper along with reflections on which tools they used and how those tools supported their thinking and learning.

Q: My students can't use manipulatives when taking state tests. Wouldn't letting them use manipulatives in class make them less likely to succeed on these important exams?

A: The goal of manipulatives use is to support student thinking, eventually laying a foundation for internalizing mathematical ideas. If students use manipulatives enough, they will eventually develop a mental image of the tools. And if they can picture the manipulatives in their heads, they can sketch them on paper. And if they are adept at sketching, they can use the scratch paper provided during testing as a tool to support their thinking during test taking. Therefore, using manipulatives to the point of internalization will support and enhance students' thinking during test taking.

Virtual Manipulatives

Q: My school has 1:1 tech devices. Can I replace all the physical manipulatives with virtual manipulatives? My school doesn't have the budget for physical manipulatives. Are virtual manipulatives an adequate alternative?

A: Virtual manipulatives, as mentioned throughout this book, offer some features not inherent in their physical counterparts. These include an endless supply of pieces and a natural way for sharing work with peers and teachers over distance. That said, it's important to realize that students do not cognitively process the same way with two-dimensional figures as they do with three-dimensional objects. Although tech devices do allow students to replicate the manipulations on screen, providing an enhanced two-dimensional experience, the truth is that they still fall into the visual category of representation, not the physical. Ideally, students will have access to both physical and virtual manipulatives, capitalizing on the benefits of both and allowing them to connect representations, a major theme in this book.

LET'S GO!

It's time to dig deep into the closet and dust off the manipulatives! We hope this book inspires you to use these powerful tools regularly to develop deep mathematical understanding. Let's get started.

Notes

_____

_____

_____

_____

_____

_____

_____

_____

_____

_____

CHAPTER 1
Base-Ten Blocks

UNDERSTANDING BASE-TEN BLOCKS

Base-ten blocks are designed to model the base-ten place value system. These are proportional manipulatives (meaning the scale between the pieces is precise), and they are pre-grouped (meaning each piece beyond the unit represents a collection of pieces that comes already grouped; students do not actively group them). The typical set of base-ten blocks includes four shapes—a small unit cube, a rod, a flat, and a large cube—and the pieces are typically etched to show the underlying components. Base-ten blocks are used in single-color (all the shapes are the same color) or multicolor sets. If using a multicolor set, be careful your students see value rather than color. Some sets are designed so the pieces interlock and you can construct larger pieces from smaller ones.

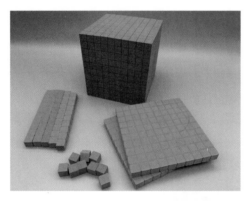 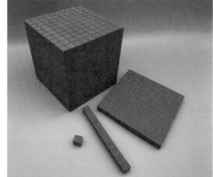

Base-ten materials are particularly effective in teaching these topics:

- Place value, both whole numbers and decimals
- Comparing and ordering numbers
- Whole number operations
- Decimal operations

Introducing Base-Ten Blocks to Students

Encourage learners to explore the blocks using the *Notice and Wonder Thinking Routine* (described in the introductory chapter) before starting to teach with them. Students may notice that the pieces are etched to show the smaller components. They may notice they can build the larger pieces from smaller pieces if they have sufficient supply. They may wonder why there are two pieces in a cube shape, one small and one large. Use this opportunity as an informal assessment of your students' place-value understanding.

Key Ideas With Base-Ten Blocks

- Work with base-ten blocks is particularly important because it sets the stage for work with algebra tools in middle school. The use of these parallel tools and structures helps students see the connections between arithmetic and algebra.

- It feels artificial in the primary grades to separate the names of the pieces (*unit*, *rod*, *flat*, and *cube*) from their values (1, 10, 100, and 1,000) when the pieces are almost always used with the unit (small cube) as 1 (the whole). When students work with decimals, this separation pays off because it is easier to transition to using any piece as the whole. When the flat or the (large) cube is considered the whole, the smaller pieces represent tenths, hundredths, or even thousandths.

- The lessons included here around multiplication and division focus on building an understanding of the algorithms from a conceptual foundation. They build from the **distributive property** as well as the inverse relationship between multiplication and division. Work on multiplying algebraic expressions in Chapter 5 of this book builds from this foundation.

Things to Consider About Base-Ten Blocks

- Base-ten blocks help build number sense, in part, because they are proportional. Students develop a sense of scale as they realize the large cube is 1,000 times the volume of the small unit cube.

- Base-ten blocks are flexible because the four pieces show a relationship of 10 times larger or smaller across the pieces. Each of the pieces can have any value, including either whole numbers or decimal fractions. For example, if the flat is assigned a value of 1, then the rods represent tenths, and the unit cubes represent hundredths.

- It is helpful to separate the name of the piece from its value. In primary classrooms, this typically means calling the small cube the "unit" and giving it a value of 1. Rods (or longs) have a value of 10 in this system, flats are 100, and the (large) cube has a value of 1,000. In this way, the value of each piece can be changed as students explore place value in other ranges. This idea is explored in the decimal lessons in this chapter.

Alternatives to Commercial Base-Ten Blocks

Early learners often use a groupable manipulative before base-ten blocks are introduced. Ten linking cubes can be attached as a rod 10 units long, or 10 coffee stirring sticks can be bundled with a small rubber band. Ten beans can be glued to a craft stick. In these ways, young learners see the transition from 10 ones to 1 ten.

As students move from working with ones and tens, the proportional nature of base-ten blocks is important to developing good number sense. Typical commercial base-ten sets are built on a centimeter unit cube. This means centimeter grid paper is a good alternative for units (a 1×1 square), rods (a 1×10 rectangle), and flats (a 10×10 square). Because these pieces do not have volume, it is difficult to represent a cube ($10 \times 10 \times 10$) with grid paper.

A typical paper milk carton ($\frac{1}{2}$-gallon or 2-liter size) is approximately a 10×10 cm base and can be cut off 10 cm high to easily create more large cubes.

Working With Virtual Base-Ten Blocks

Virtual base-ten blocks can have a number of functional advantages. First, as with most virtual tools, there is an endless supply. Second, some virtual base-ten tools can be grouped or broken apart as students work with them. A rod dragged from the tens column to the ones column might automatically appear as 10 units. Ten units grouped together with the select tool might automatically appear as a rod. Third, students can explore the creation of larger units. What happens if you stack 10 large cubes one atop the other? What is the value of this "super-rod"? The shapes of the pieces (unit, cube, rod, flat) repeat in each period of the place-value system, helping students see how the system grows as they work with larger values.

Notes

_____

_____

_____

_____

_____

_____

_____

_____

_____

Notes

Materials

- Base-ten blocks, one set per student
- Large cubes, one per pair

Organization (physical)

- **Getting Started:** Distribute a bag of materials to each student.
- **Winding Down:** Count and rebag the materials before collecting.

Mathematical Purpose

Students learn to represent and compare numbers in expanded form, using base-ten materials to create proportional physical models.

Manipulatives Illustrated

- Foam and Plastic Base-Ten Blocks
- Didax Virtual Place Value Disks: https://www.didax.com/apps/place-value/

Steps

1. Ask students to represent the number 426 using base-ten blocks. Recognize that there are many ways to represent numbers using base-ten blocks because students can use any combination of blocks that sums to 426. For example, they could use 26 units or 1 rod and 16 units, as well as 2 rods and 6 units, to represent the 26 portion of the number. It is easiest to compare values when they are represented in the most efficient way, using the smallest number of blocks. This representation is accurate, although not the most efficient.

2. Ask students to represent the number 354 efficiently using base-ten blocks. To encourage an efficient representation, ask questions such as these:

   - *Have you used the same piece (unit, rod, flat, or cube) for more than one place-value position?*

   - *Could you make any of these values with a smaller number of blocks?*

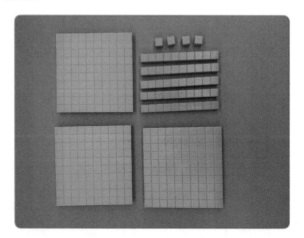

3. Ask students to compare the two values (426 and 354) and use the blocks to describe how they know which value is greater and which is less. Listen first for language comparing each place value: "This value has more/less/the same number of ones/tens/hundreds as that value."

4. Listen next for language comparing the values overall and beginning that comparison with the largest place value: "This one has 4 hundreds while the other has 3 hundreds. The one with 4 hundreds must be greater."

5. Repeat this practice with a variety of number pairs. It is interesting to choose values such as 101 and 98; some students mistake the greater number of pieces required to build 98 for a greater value. If this happens, ask students to stack the two models on top of one another. Students can then see that 98, while comprising a great many individual pieces, is less than 101.

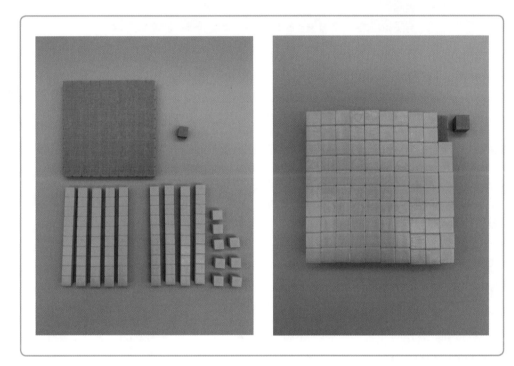

6. Depending on the range of values students are comparing and the class supply of large cubes, it may be helpful to transition from physical base-ten blocks to virtual base-ten blocks to work with larger values.

Why This Manipulative?

As students develop their skill comparing numbers, it is critical to use proportional manipulatives like base-ten blocks. This provides a good sense of magnitude. Using a nonproportional tool like place-value disks means that students cannot physically compare blocks as suggested in Step 5. This means that, while the place-value disks are concrete in a technical sense, they are difficult for students to use if they have not already mastered the abstract ideas of place value.

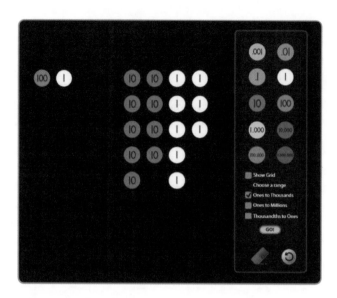

Developing Understanding

The focus of this activity is on understanding place value as it relates to comparing quantities. When students compare all place values, they demonstrate emerging understanding of place value and comparison. They recognize the principles but are not yet efficient. The proportional size of the blocks supports students visually as they transition from reasoning about the physical size of the block collection to the place values represented in abstract notation. In a nonproportional representation, such as the place-value disks pictured, students do not have the option of stacking the two quantities to make a direct comparison.

Featured Connection

Use the Make a Sketch strategy to help students create base-ten representations when physical blocks are not available. While these images will not be proportional in the same way as the physical blocks, they help students create mental images of the blocks, which supports their reasoning. The image here shows typical sketches for each of the four blocks. Students can create more accurate (and proportional) images using grid paper and coloring squares.

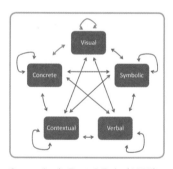

Source: Lesh, Post, & Behr (1987).

Notes

Materials

- Virtual or concrete base-ten blocks, one set per group
- At least 10 large cubes for the class

Organization (virtual)

- **Getting Started:** Ensure students can access and use the virtual tool. Review annotation tools, the process for taking screenshots, and other important supports.
- **Winding Down:** Use screenshots to save student work.

Mathematical Purpose

In this activity, students explore visually what it means that each place-value column is 10 times the value of the one to its right.

Manipulative Illustrated

- Digital Base-Ten Blocks from Mathsbot: https://mathsbot.com/manipulatives/blocks

Steps

Model the following pairs of blocks:

- 10 ones and 1 ten
- 10 tens and 1 hundred
- 10 hundreds and 1 thousand

1. Ask students to share what they notice and wonder about the shapes of the blocks. Ask questions such as these:

   - *Did you use the same pieces to build each value in the pair?*
   - *Tell me about how you built each value. Does each one in the pair represent the same value?*
   - *Could you build these two values so they are the same shape?*
   - *Guide students to notice that small cubes are assembled into a rod (or long). Rods are assembled into a flat, and flats are stacked to make a larger cube.*

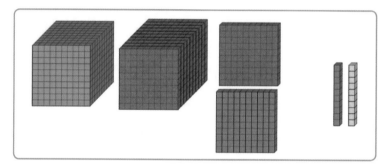

2. Ask students what shape a base-ten piece representing 10 thousands would take, and have them explain the reasoning behind their answer. Following the pattern, 10,000 would be represented by a "super-rod" comprising 10 large cubes. The picture of virtual base-ten blocks includes the main base-ten unit, a rod, and the large cube for scale reference. What would represent 100,000? What would represent 1 million?

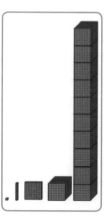

3. Create a chart like the one presented here showing the shapes of the pieces in their place-value positions. For some students, seeing this relationship helps them see the periods in place value for larger numbers and helps them understand the magnitude of the values.

1 million	100,000	10,000	1,000	100	10	1
Super-cube	Super-flat	Super-rod	Cube	Flat	Rod	Unit (small cube)

Why This Manipulative?

One of the limits of physical base-ten blocks is the quantity of large pieces. The blocks become impractical for representing even larger four-digit values. Still, the proportional nature of base-ten blocks, as well as their underlying structure, makes it helpful for students to consider larger values. This activity takes advantage of the endless supply provided by virtual manipulatives and the proportional nature of base-ten blocks to help students understand the magnitude of large numbers. As students move toward the study of decimals, they can imagine partitioning the unit (small cube) into mini-flats where each represents $\frac{1}{10}$ of the unit. Activity 1.3 explores this idea further.

Developing Understanding

An important part of mathematics is seeing structure. This lesson uses the structure designed into base-ten blocks to reveal the structure inherent in the organization of our base-ten place-value system. Increasing by a factor of 10 for each place-value column means numbers increase in magnitude more quickly than an extra digit suggests. One billion is a lot more than 100 million—a greater difference than the difference between 1 million and 100,000. Proportional place-value tools support understanding this scale.

Featured Connection

Use the Create a Diagram strategy to encourage students to include base-ten block images in place-value diagrams such as the chart in Step 3. How will your students use their learning from this activity to represent large values? How does this help students understand the magnitude of numbers?

To make contextual connections to the physical or virtual representations and sketches, identify large values from news stories relevant to your students and incorporate base-ten representations of the values to help students make sense of the quantities in the story.

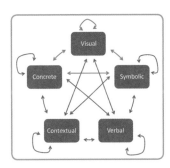

Source: Lesh, Post, & Behr (1987).

Materials

- Base-ten blocks, one set per student

Organization (physical)

- **Getting Started:** Distribute a bag of materials to each student.
- **Winding Down:** Count and rebag the materials before collecting.

Mathematical Purpose

In this activity, students change which piece has a value of 1 to explore decimal fractions. This activity is a key reason for identifying the base-ten blocks by a descriptive name rather than a whole number value.

Manipulative Illustrated

- Base-Ten Blocks (including "mini-flats" sold by several manufacturers to represent $\frac{1}{10}$ of the unit [small cube])

Steps

1. Tell students that today's lesson assigns a value of 1 to the flat in the base-ten blocks. Ask students to reason about the value of other pieces based on this assertion using questions like these:

   - *How many flats are equivalent to a large cube? If the flat has a value of 1, what is the value of the large cube?*

   - *How many rods are equivalent to a flat? If the flat has a value of 1, what is the value of each rod?*

   - *How many units are equivalent to a rod? If the rod has a value of $\frac{1}{10}$ (0.1), what is the value of a unit? Does your answer make sense when you consider that 100 units are also equivalent to a flat?*

2. Ask students to represent the following values with the blocks: 1 whole, 2 tenths, and 3 hundredths. Look for students to have the correct quantity of the appropriate pieces each time.

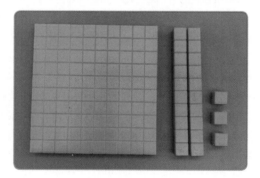

3. Ask students to represent additional values with the blocks, practicing as necessary. The flat continues to have a value of 1. Make sure that values including a zero (such as 1.04) are included so students recognize when a particular block is *not* part of a model.

4. Once students are comfortable representing decimals, ask them to compare decimals. This should follow a similar process to the work done in Activity 1.1. The blocks have different values (they have shifted position on the place-value chart), but the underlying structure remains the same.

Why This Manipulative?

Using the same blocks for decimal values less than 1 emphasizes the underlying structure of the base-ten place-value system. This helps students understand that decimals are an integrated part of the number system they know and that there are connections to fractions through values such as $\frac{1}{10}$. The pattern of shapes (rod, flat, and cube) continues to cycle, even though the place-value labels might change depending on which piece is identified as having a value of 1.

Developing Understanding

This lesson can be extended in two ways. First, use the large cube to represent one whole, allowing the small cube to represent $\frac{1}{1,000}$ or 0.001. Ask students to represent and compare values using the large cube as the whole. It is helpful to include some of the same values you used in the activity as written so students can see how the image of a value changes depending on which block represents the whole.

Second, using their knowledge of the structure of base-ten blocks (from Activity 1.2), students can imagine the size and shape of the piece $\frac{1}{10}$ the size of the small cube (a tiny flat) and $\frac{1}{10}$ the size of that tiny flat (a tiny rod). Seeing how quickly the pieces become quite small or quite large, beginning with a 1 cm cube as the anchor helps students understand the power of each place value as 10 times larger or smaller than the one beside it.

Featured Connection

Use the Name Your Model strategy to help students connect their concrete representations with the abstract notation of comparison. Students may need to sketch the pieces as an intermediate step in their thinking. It is helpful to label the flat with its value as a reference point for the diagram.

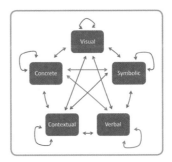

Source: Lesh, Post, & Behr (1987).

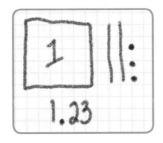

Another variation of this strategy is to represent the same value with different pieces as the whole. Challenge your students to figure out which block represents 1 in each model and defend their choices. The accompanying images show 1.23 represented in two additional ways. Which piece has a value of 1 in each representation? You can see the "mini-flats" in the image where the rod has a value of 1.

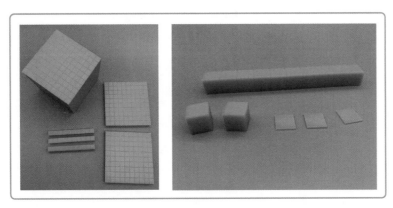

Materials

- Base-ten blocks, one set per student

Organization (physical)

- **Getting Started:** Distribute a bag of materials to each student.
- **Winding Down:** Count and rebag the materials before collecting.

Mathematical Purpose

In this activity, students use base-ten blocks to support adding decimal fractions. This process mirrors the strategy students used to add whole numbers with base-ten blocks, including the need for regrouping at times. By showing the consistent structure, students see decimal fractions as more closely related to whole numbers.

Manipulative Illustrated

- Base-Ten Blocks

Steps

1. Students have used base-ten blocks to add whole numbers in the primary grades (see Activity 5.7 in the K–3 volume of this set). This activity extends this thinking to decimal addition.

2. Using the flat as one whole, ask students to represent 1.42 and 2.56. Then ask questions like these:

   - *What is the sum of these two values? How do you know?*
   - *How do the base-ten blocks help you know what parts to add together?*
   - *How do you know what parts to add together without the blocks?*

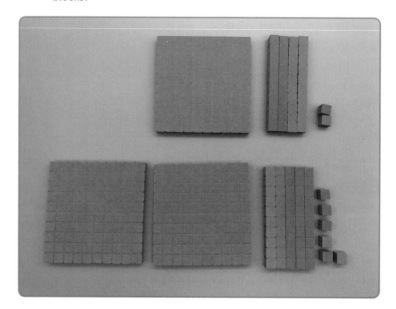

3. Ask students to use the same strategy to add 1.65 and 1.27. Watch to see how they handle the regrouping in the hundredths place, supporting them to make a trade of 1 tenth for 10 hundredths as needed using questions like this:

   - *What is the value of your blocks?*
   - *Can you represent the same value using a smaller number of blocks?*

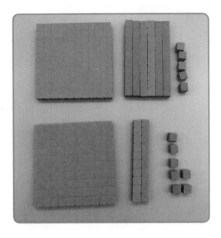

Why This Manipulative?

There is essentially no difference between adding with whole numbers and adding with decimals except where the number is positioned on the place-value chart. By using the same materials and approaches students used for early work with whole numbers, they are supported to see decimals as an extension of the place-value system.

Developing Understanding

It is important for the teacher to illustrate the connections between decimal addition and whole-number addition. The approach illustrated here relies on working with a single shape of base-ten blocks at any time. This connects to the traditional algorithm through the idea of working with a single place-value column at a time. You may notice students working with the place-value positions "out of order," from left to right, for example. There is no mathematical reason requiring students to work from right to left. It can be more efficient, and it's certainly easier to avoid missing a column when working sequentially, but many people do mental math from left to right. Notice your own process next time; it might surprise you.

Featured Connection

Use the Build the Equation strategy to help students connect their physical representations with the abstract notation traditionally used for decimal operations. As students work, help them connect the elements of their physical model to the notation used for recording decimal addition. Aligning the place-value columns (using the decimal point as a marker) makes working with one shape (one place-value position) at a time easy. The notation of regrouping illustrates the idea of having 12 hundredths rather than 1 tenth and 2 hundredths.

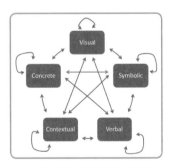

Source: Lesh, Post, & Behr (1987).

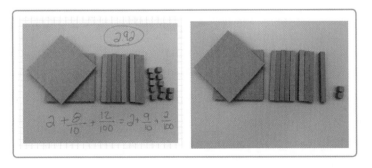

Materials

- Virtual or concrete base-ten blocks, one set per student

Organization (virtual)

- **Getting Started:** Ensure students can access and use the virtual tool. Review annotation tools, the process for taking screenshots, and other important supports.

- **Winding Down:** Use screenshots to save student work.

Mathematical Purpose

In this activity, students use base-ten blocks to support subtracting decimal fractions, with and without regrouping. This process mirrors the strategy students used to add whole numbers with base-ten blocks, including the need for regrouping at times. By showing the consistent structure, students see decimal fractions as more closely related to whole numbers.

Activity 1.5 Resources

- *Subtracting Decimal Fractions* Activity Video

online resources

To access resource visit resources.corwin.com/ MasteringMath Manips/4–8

Manipulative Illustrated

- Virtual Base-Ten Blocks at Mathigon: https://mathigon.org/ polypad

Steps

1. Students have used base-ten blocks to subtract whole numbers in the primary grades (see Activity 5.8 in the K–3 volume of this set). This lesson extends this thinking to decimal subtraction.

2. Write the subtraction expression 2.84 – 1.52 for students and ask them to use base-ten blocks to model this problem. Students can build the first value and then physically remove the second value, acting out the take-from approach to subtraction. The accompanying image shows the result of this process with the removed parts crossed out in a pile at the bottom right. Support students' thinking with questions like these:

   - *Do you have to build both numbers in order to take one away? Why or why not?*

   - *Does it matter which block you use to represent the whole?*

   - *Use mathematical language to tell me what you are doing. How do your actions match the problem you are solving?*

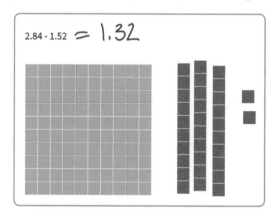

2.84 - 1.52 ≈ 1.32

3. When students are ready, introduce a subtraction problem requiring regrouping, 1.26 – 0.43. Support students to see that they can trade the flat (1 whole) for 10 tenths, creating a model of 12 tenths subtract 4 tenths and finding a difference of 0.83, as shown in the video. Support students to build connections to the notation and thinking used for subtracting whole numbers, building on the continuity of the place-value system in both directions from the decimal point. If necessary, ask students to return to using the unit (small cube) as the whole and model subtracting 126 – 43. The physical actions are the same; the different definition of the whole changes the values.

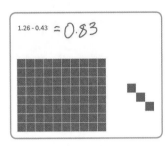

Why This Manipulative?

There is essentially no difference between subtracting whole numbers and subtracting decimals except where the number is positioned on the place-value chart. By using the same materials and approaches students used for early work with whole numbers, they are supported to see decimals as an extension of the place-value system.

Developing Understanding

It is important for the teacher to illustrate the connections between decimal subtraction and whole-number subtraction. The approach illustrated here relies on working with a single shape of base-ten blocks at any time. This connects to the traditional algorithm through the idea of working with a single place-value column at a time.

Recognize that students might use either the large cube or the flat to represent 1 whole in these problems; either one is appropriate. Encourage students who chose different wholes to discuss their work and see that, while the shape of each piece is different, their actual process for subtracting is the same.

Featured Connection

Use the Caption Your Picture strategy to help students connect their physical representations with the abstract notation traditionally used for decimal operations. As students work, help them connect the elements of their physical model to the notation used for recording decimal addition and subtraction. Aligning the place-value columns (using the decimal point as a marker) makes working with one shape (one place-value position) at a time easy. The notation of regrouping illustrates the idea of having 12 tenths rather than 1 whole and 2 tenths.

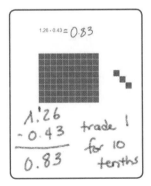

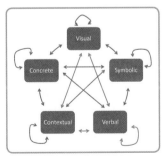

Source: Lesh, Post, & Behr (1987).

Materials

- Base-ten blocks, one set per student
- Multiplication mat

Organization (physical)

- **Getting Started:** Distribute a bag of materials to each student.
- **Winding Down:** Count and rebag the materials before collecting.

Mathematical Purpose

Students use the distributive property to model multiplying a one-digit factor by a three- or four-digit factor. This both emphasizes the distributive property and lays the foundation for multi-digit multiplication with **partial products**.

Activity 1.6 Resources

- Multiplication Mat

 To view and download resource, please visit resources.corwin.com/ MasteringMathManips/ 4–8

Manipulative Illustrated

- Foam Base-Ten Blocks and Multiplication Frame from hand2mind

Steps

1. Ask students to think about the product of 3 and 24 using questions such as these:

   - *Can you multiply 3 and 24 mentally?*
   - *What strategy might you use to find this product?*
   - *How could you partition 24 into chunks you can manage with mental math?*

2. Have students build the **factors** with base-ten blocks. Position the blocks on the multiplication mat as shown in the photo, as if they are the dimensions of a rectangle. The legs of the frame or mat are oriented as in the first **quadrant** of the coordinate plane (left and below the space for the product).

3. Ask students how they might figure out the area of the rectangle defined by the base-ten blocks. Encourage students to talk with a partner and brainstorm strategies. Support their thinking using questions like these:

   - *Could you use the blocks to help you figure out the area by counting? Are there different options for doing this?*
   - *Do you have to find the entire area at once? Why or why not?*
   - *Are there parts of the area you can figure out in your head? How can you mark those in your work?*

4. Encourage students to begin by multiplying 3×10. They can fill this section of the rectangle using three rods to represent the first partial product.

5. Work through the remaining two partial products, another 3×10 and 3×4. Discuss the representation with students using questions such as these:

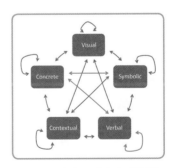

- *How does the model help you see the product of 3 and 24? What is the product?*

- *Could you have partitioned 24 another way?*

6. Support students to try additional examples for one-digit by two-digit multiplication. Encourage students to partition the factors in different ways as they work to develop flexible thinking. Discuss these problems using questions such as these:

- *How did you choose to partition the factors?*

- *What mental math facts and strategies helped you find these products?*

- *Did you have to regroup in your work? Tell me about how you did that.*

Why This Manipulative?

Area is part of the work of multiplication. This use of base-ten blocks builds on this conceptual foundation for area, alongside the distributive property, to show students how and why a typical multiplication algorithm works. Students extend their learning from using square tiles for multiplication basic facts into place-value understanding with base-ten blocks for multi-digit multiplication. This will further extend to **polynomial** multiplication in algebra class.

Developing Understanding

The focus of this lesson is on place value, the distributive property, and the idea of multiplication as area. Once students are confident of basic facts, the structure provided by the base-ten blocks (and, ultimately, **open arrays** with partial products in the next activity) provides confidence that students have worked completely through the process. Even if students struggle to remember the steps of the algorithm, they can consider the physical area model in their minds (or a sketch) and work successfully through the process.

Using base-ten blocks, students could count the area using single blocks. Support students who start here to work toward more efficient strategies, as they will be essential when students transfer this learning to algebra (see Activity 5.10).

Featured Connection

Students can use the Name Your Model strategy to move from sketching pictures of base-ten blocks to using an open array representation. As shown in the accompanying photo, the distributive property is highlighted in this model. This representation can easily be connected to the partial products algorithm developed in Activity 1.7. The base-ten model becomes impractical as whole-number values grow beyond the teens; the open array and partial products strategies are effective for any larger whole-number values.

Source: Lesh, Post, & Behr (1987).

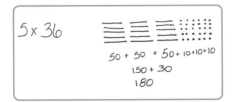

Materials

- Virtual or concrete base-ten blocks, one set per student
- Multiplication mat

Organization (virtual)

- **Getting Started:** Ensure students can access and use the virtual tool. Review annotation tools, the process for taking screenshots, and other important supports.
- **Winding Down:** Use screenshots to save student work.

Mathematical Purpose

Students build from the area model through open arrays to partial products for two-digit multiplication. This progression highlights the role of the distributive property in understanding why the multiplication algorithm works.

Activity 1.7 Resources

- Multiplication Mat
- *Multiplying Two-Digit Numbers* Activity Video

 To access resources visit resources.corwin.com/ MasteringMathManips/ 4–8

Manipulative Illustrated

- Math Learning Center Number Pieces app: https://apps.math learningcenter.org/number-pieces/

Steps

1. Ask students to model 12 and 14 using base-ten blocks. Position the blocks on the multiplication mat as shown in the photo, as if they are the dimensions of a rectangle.

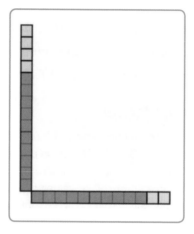

2. Ask students how they might figure out the area of the rectangle defined by the base-ten blocks. Encourage students to talk with a partner and brainstorm strategies. Support their thinking using questions like these:

   - *Could you use the blocks to help you figure out the area by counting? Are there different options for doing this?*
   - *Do you have to find the entire area at once? Why or why not?*
   - *Are there parts of the area you can figure out in your head? How can you mark those in your work?*

3. Encourage students to begin by multiplying 10×10. They can use a flat to fill in the appropriate area on the multiplication mat. This is the first of four rectangular area sections (partial products) students must figure out.

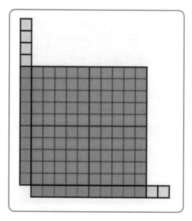

4. Work through the next three sections of partial products, 10×2, 4×10, and 2×4. Ask students to total the blocks within the rectangle to find the product of 12 and 14 or 168. Support students to work through additional examples of teen number products until they are comfortable building these models.

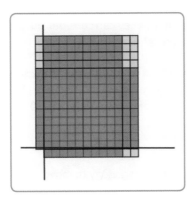

5. Have students use the Sketch a Picture strategy to record their work for these problems. As students understand the process, show them how to represent factors of 20 or greater, such as this example of 22×11. While the strategy becomes less efficient, expanding to these greater factors helps ensure students understand the model.

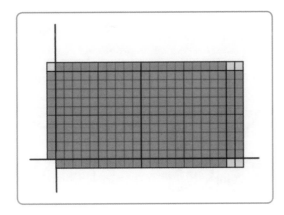

Why This Manipulative?

Area is part of the work of multiplication. This use of base-ten blocks builds on this conceptual foundation for area, alongside the distributive property, to show students how and why a typical multiplication algorithm works. Students extend their learning from using square tiles for multiplication basic facts into place-value understanding with base-ten blocks for multi-digit multiplication. This will further extend to polynomial multiplication in algebra class.

Some students include the factors within the product when reading the solution from an area model like this. The pictures show lines drawn to separate the factors and products. This is also the function of the mats and tracks shown with the physical base-ten blocks or the lines on the multiplication work mat.

Developing Understanding

The focus of this lesson is on place value, the distributive property, and the idea of multiplication as area. Once students are confident of basic facts, the structure provided by the base-ten blocks (and, ultimately, open arrays with partial products) provides confidence that students have worked completely through the process. Even if students struggle to remember the steps of the algorithm, they can consider the physical area model in their minds (or a sketch) and work successfully through the process.

Using base-ten blocks, students could count the area using single blocks. Support students who start here to work toward more efficient strategies, as they will be essential when students transfer this learning to algebra (see Activity 5.10).

Featured Connection

Students can use the Create a Diagram strategy to move from sketching pictures of base-ten blocks to using an open array representation. This representation can easily be connected to the partial products algorithm as shown in the video. The base-ten model becomes impractical as whole-number values grow beyond the teens; the open array and partial products strategies are effective for any larger whole-number values.

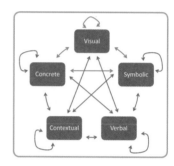

Source: Lesh, Post, & Behr (1987).

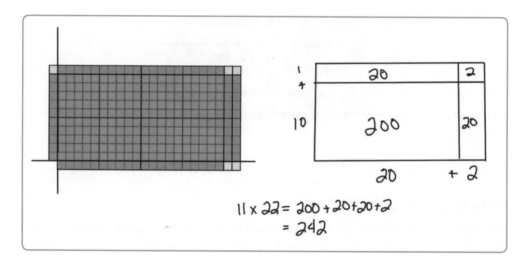

Notes

_____

_____

_____

_____

Notes

Materials

- Base-ten blocks, one set per student

Organization (physical)

- **Getting Started:** Distribute a bag of materials to each student.
- **Winding Down:** Count and rebag the materials before collecting.

Mathematical Purpose

In this activity, students look at division as missing factor multiplication. They use what they know of multiplication with base-ten blocks to find the missing factor using a **partial quotients** approach.

Activity 1.8 Resources

- Multiplication Mat

 To access resource visit resources.corwin.com/ MasteringMathManips/ 4–8

Manipulative Illustrated

- Base-Ten Blocks and Area Modeler (EAI Education)

Steps

1. Share the division expression 168 ÷ 12 with students and ask how they might model it with base-ten blocks. Provide time for students to model, discuss, and share their thinking. Support students to consider division as a case of multiplication where one factor is unknown using questions like this:

   - *If another way to write this expression is as 12 × _____ = 168, how could you model that with base-ten blocks?*

2. Using the multiplication mat, have students model 12 as one factor and pile the 168 blocks of the product in the middle of the mat. Note how this is a messy variation of the multiplication work students completed in Activity 1.6. The product is not organized, but it is still represented in the total area.

3. Use a partial quotients strategy to figure out the other factor in a question like this:

   - *How many 12s are in 168? I'm not sure, but I know there are at least 10 because 10 × 12 = 120. [Record a 10 as part of the second factor and build 120 as a partial product.]*

   Students might not be confident that there are at least 10 twelves in 168. If so, begin with the quantity they are confident about.

4. Continue the work with questions like this:

   » *How much of 168 remains unfactored?* There are 48 blocks remaining and $12 \times 4 = 48$ so the remainder of the unknown factor must be 4. $10 + 4 = 14$, so $12 \times 14 = 168$ or $168 \div 12 = 14$.

5. Practice this strategy with $143 \div 13$, allowing students to partition the partial product in any way they wish. As students develop understanding of this approach, encourage them to work toward efficient partitions, including multiples of 10 and 5. Note that the regrouped pieces are "parked" at the corner of the mat so students can track the exchanges more easily.

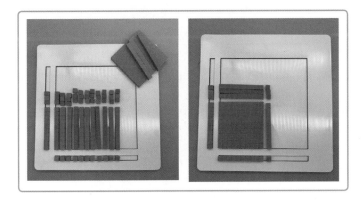

Why This Manipulative?

This activity is the flip side of the prior two-digit multiplication lesson (Activity 1.7). Division is the inverse operation to multiplication. This activity uses the power of the area model and the proportionality of base-ten blocks to model the reasoning of long division for students by having them build from what they know. This strategy can be extended forward to use for factoring in algebra.

Developing Understanding

The power of partial quotients is that students can use any factors that are reasonable for them in terms of mental math. They may partition the quotient into more (and smaller) pieces, but following the process will get them to a correct solution. The challenge then becomes developing efficiency. Students can do the math and make sense of it, the essential knowledge, and build efficiency as they develop confidence in and experience with the process.

When choosing problems, begin with problems that divide evenly and consider the number of trades required. It is generally easier to begin with problems requiring fewer trades.

Featured Connection

Use the Build the Equation strategy to help students record their thinking about partial products division. Students will fill in each section of the drawing as they identify a portion of the quotient. This can be recorded as the partial quotients algorithm shown in the accompanying photo.

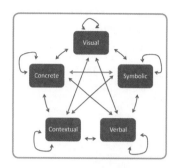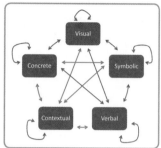

Source: Lesh, Post, & Behr (1987).

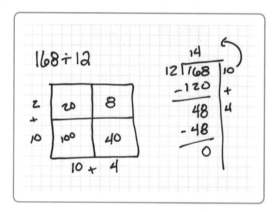

Students can also Write a Word Problem to help them think about this computation in context.

Notes

_____

_____

_____

_____

_____

_____

_____

_____

_____

CLOSING REFLECTION: BASE-TEN BLOCKS

How do I use base-ten blocks in my classroom now? What concepts do I use them to teach?

_____

_____

_____

_____

_____

What new ways have I found to use base-ten blocks to better support student understanding?

_____

_____

_____

_____

_____

What are my goals to make base-ten blocks a more regular part of my instruction?

_____

_____

_____

_____

_____

CHAPTER 2
Fraction Manipulatives

UNDERSTANDING FRACTION MANIPULATIVES

Commercial fraction manipulatives are available in a variety of shapes—the traditional circles, squares, oblongs, and three-dimensional square prisms that link together. They may be called circles, towers, tiles, bars, or squares. These are proportional manipulatives (meaning the scale between the pieces is precise), and they are un-grouped (meaning each unit fraction piece is separate). Many commercial suppliers have a standard color sequence for the pieces so the corresponding values (e.g., halves) are always the same color in all tools from that supplier.

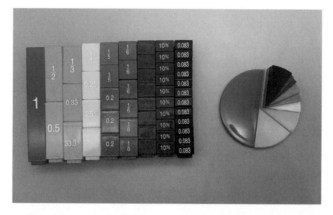

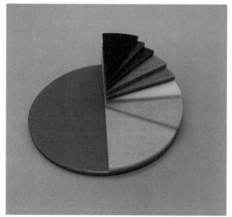

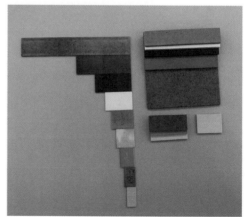

Fraction tools are particularly helpful for teaching these key ideas:

- Understanding unit fractions
- Comparing and ordering fractions
- Fraction operations
- **Angles** as wedges (using the central angle of fraction circles)

Introducing Fraction Manipulatives to Students

Your students may have worked with these tools in the primary grades to introduce the idea of partitioning shapes, to understand unit fractions, and to compare fractional values. You may introduce different shapes for the whole—a more linear fraction bar or tower rather than a circle, for example. If you use the *Notice and Wonder Thinking Routine* (described in the introductory chapter), students may make observations about the number of pieces and the labeling of those pieces (e.g., there are three $\frac{1}{3}$ pieces, or each $\frac{1}{4}$ piece is labeled with 25%) or about how the pieces fit together (e.g., all three of the lined-up $\frac{1}{3}$ pieces are the same length as all eight of the lined-up $\frac{1}{8}$ pieces). They may notice that the more same-sized pieces it takes to make a whole, the smaller those pieces get. Use this exploration as an informal assessment of your students' fraction understanding. What key ideas have they brought to your class? What key ideas do you need to establish or strengthen?

Key Ideas With Fraction Manipulatives

- Use a variety of shapes as your **unit whole** when representing fractions. This encourages students to think flexibly about the relationship between the various fractional values.

- Be careful about simplifying fractions, including improper fractions, too quickly. Not only do many standards delay or skip this skill, but simplifying a fraction can hide the underlying mathematics from students.

- Deliberately help your students know how precisely to represent fractions. When building physical models, precision is helpful. Diagrams or sketches can be labeled; this means freehand sketches can be approximations of the actual values.

- It is helpful to have students model a series of fraction computations in order to see the pattern or structure in the computation. Choose your examples deliberately so that the structure you want to highlight is evident.

- It can be helpful for students to develop multiple strategies or algorithms for fraction computation. They can move from one to another depending on the specific values and computation.

- There are two basic shell questions for a naked number division problem in the form $a \div b$. It can be helpful for students to state a fraction division problem verbally by translating into one of these forms:
  - » How many b are in a?
  - » What happens when I share a among b people?

Things to Consider About Fraction Manipulatives

- Depending on where you purchase fraction manipulatives, you may notice color-coding across sets or shapes with each value (whole, half, third, etc.) always the same color. This can be helpful to the teacher ("take your pink pieces") but runs the risk that students will over-associate the color with the value and think that pink is always a half.

- To work with mixed numbers, you will need more than one set per group if there's only one whole within a single set. Die-cut alternatives can be helpful here.

- Using a variety of fraction tools is helpful for students because it provides them with a wide range of references for the whole. If students only see circular examples (pizza, pie, or fraction circles) in class, they may struggle when they encounter fractions where the whole is not a circle. Rectangular models (fraction bars, tiles, or towers) are becoming more common because they link nicely to the number line.

- Fraction squares can be challenging to use because they are cut in different ways depending on the unit fraction. For fraction circles, the wedges always get smaller. For fraction bars, the sections get smaller. For fraction squares, there are slices that get smaller to start (commonly up through fifths—see the accompanying image), and then sixths are thirds cut in half rather than a slimmer slice. The same is true for eighths and tenths with twelfths often presented as thirds of a fourth. While this partitioning is accurate from an area perspective, it makes the tool more difficult to use.

- Fraction manipulatives can be labeled or unlabeled. Some sets may have decimal or percentage labeling options as well. There is greater flexibility in unlabeled sets, or at least having a blank side on your fraction manipulatives, because you can change the value of the unit whole.

Alternatives to Commercial Fraction Manipulatives

Cutting strips to fold or tear your own set of fraction tiles from construction paper is an excellent activity for building understanding of unit fractions. This appears in Activity 2.1 in this chapter. As students work with fraction computation, they benefit from the precision of commercial or die-cut alternatives. There are commercial dies available for a variety of fraction shapes. It is also possible to create your own sets of more precise fraction pieces on graph paper for some groups of denominators (halves, thirds, fourths, and sixths work well on a 1 × 12 rectangle, for example).

Other commercial manipulatives can also be used to represent fractional relationships. Base-ten blocks are excellent for representing tenths or hundredths when making the connection to decimals, while pattern blocks represent halves, thirds, and sixths nicely when the yellow hexagon is used as the whole. By using an add-on set available from some manufacturers or by defining the whole as a shape other than one single hexagon, fourths and eighths are also possible. Pattern-block fraction tasks are also included in the K–3 volume of this series (see Chapter 6). Tangrams provide a good example of fourths, eighths, and sixteenths, with half of a complete seven-piece set easy to identify as the two large triangles. Cuisenaire® Rods provide interesting fraction opportunities when each different color is identified as the whole and students are asked to identify the fractional name of each of the other rods in relation to the stated whole (see Activity 3.4 in the next chapter).

Working With Virtual Fraction Tools

Virtual fraction tools continue the benefit of an endless supply of all the pieces, particularly as students are counting by unit fractions when they learn to add and subtract. When using virtual fraction tools, be careful that the pieces cannot be scaled so the fractions fall out of relationship with the whole. It is helpful for pieces to snap together (wedge-to-wedge for circles and end-to-end for more linear models) so that students can easily find a whole. Consider how the whole is represented and how easily students can see equivalent values (e.g., that $\frac{1}{2}$ is the same length or area as $\frac{2}{4}$ and $\frac{4}{8}$).

Notes

Materials

- One set of construction paper strips per student (one colored strip for each unit fraction and one for the whole)

- One zip-top bag per student

Organization (physical)

- **Getting Started:** This activity is easiest if the strips are cut to 2" × 24" from 18" × 24" construction paper. Black is good for the whole as it is difficult to write on. Stack the colors of paper and cut in sets if possible. If using smaller paper strips, it is more difficult to create smaller unit fractions. Have extra strips on hand, especially for colors in the thirds and fifths families.

- **Winding Down:** At the end of the activity, have students put their fraction bar set in a plastic bag for safekeeping.

Mathematical Purpose

In this activity, students fold and tear paper strips to create unit fraction sets. This builds understanding of the relationship between the size of the piece and the number of partitions of the whole. Students can also use the set to support other fraction work, noting that the set will not be as precise as a commercial set of fraction materials.

Manipulative Illustrated

- Fraction bars or tiles, created by students

Steps

1. Distribute a set of paper strips to each student. If you want the class to use the same color for each unit fraction, tell the students this from the beginning. It is helpful in this case to make a written key (on the board or a shared screen) available to students while they work.

2. Ask the students to take the black strip and label it "one whole." Ask the students to take a second color strip and think about how they could represent one half, supporting their thinking with questions like these:

   - *What does one half mean? How many pieces will you partition the entire strip into?*

   - *Is there more than one way to identify half of the strip? How many different ways can you identify?*

3. Tell students that for this activity, the strips will be partitioned like a **bar model**, folding and tearing parallel to the shorter side. It is important to tear the partitions rather than cut with scissors so that the orientation remains correct when the pieces approach a square. Construction paper will tear nicely if folded firmly before tearing.

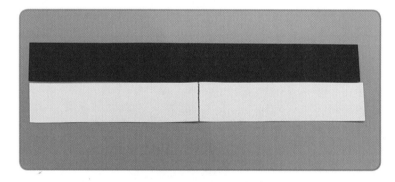

4. Continue to partition strips into additional unit fractions. It can be helpful to work in batches of related denominators. One strategy is to create halves, fourths, and eighths first. Then fold thirds and use those to create sixths and twelfths. Fold fifths and create tenths from them. For folding thirds and fifths, teach students to make a fan or zigzag fold, adjusting the segments to be as even in length as possible before pressing the folds into the paper and tearing.

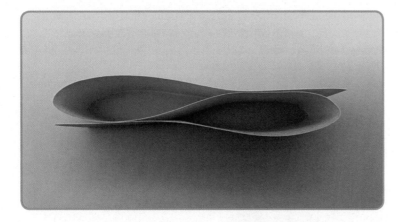

Support students' thinking with questions like these:

- *How might you create thirds without using a ruler?*

- *Why is it important to make the sections as even as possible?*

- *Why are we creating thirds and sixths [halves, fourths, and eighths; fifths and tenths] together? How do these numbers relate to each other in ways that make folding easier?*

- *What do you notice is happening to the size of each piece as you create more pieces from a given whole strip?*

5. Encourage students to label one side of each unit fraction piece so the values can be readily determined without reassembling the whole.

6. These paper fraction bar sets can be used to represent fractions, to compare fractions, and to create equivalent fractions. When comparing fractions, note that visual comparisons of fractions that are almost equal might not be accurate, depending on the error in the student's work. Sets of equivalent fractions might not be exactly equal for the same reason.

Why This Manipulative?

The active construction of a manipulative set helps students understand the pieces in the set. Students see that the whole is the same each time because they began with a set of **congruent** paper strips. They actively experience the fact that it takes much more folding and tearing to make a set of twelfths than to make a set of halves. There are more pieces from the unit whole, and each piece of value $\frac{1}{12}$ is smaller. Even in these photographs, you can see the error creeping in as the pieces do not fit back together tightly or are not torn evenly. While students will benefit in future lessons from the precision of commercial fraction bars or tiles, there is great learning in constructing a set for themselves.

Developing Understanding

This activity helps students ground their sense of unit fractions in concrete experiences. There is great pride in doing mathematics with tools students have made themselves because students have ownership over the entire process. Students will recognize that the pieces might not fit together exactly, as shown in the accompanying photo, and can transition smoothly from these personal fraction bar sets to more precise commercial tools.

Students can use these fraction pieces to mark fractions on a number line or for activities comparing and ordering fractions. Be careful with tasks where precision is important because there is error in these handmade tools.

Featured Connection

Students use the Name Your Model strategy when they label each piece of their newly constructed fraction bar set. As shown in the picture, the fraction pieces can be labeled in different ways, depending on the language focus of the lesson.

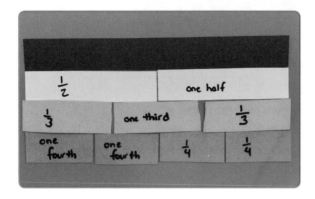
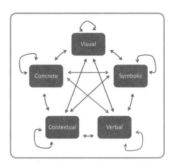

Source: Lesh, Post, & Behr (1987).

Notes

_____

_____

_____

_____

_____

_____

_____

_____

_____

_____

Notes

Materials

- Virtual or concrete fraction circles (one set per student, stored in a resealable bag)

Organization (virtual)

- **Getting Started:** Ensure students can access and use the virtual tool. Review annotation tools, the process for taking screenshots, and other important supports.

- **Winding Down:** Use screenshots to save student work.

Mathematical Purpose

In this activity, students compare fractions using three strategies—common **denominators**, common **numerators**, and a benchmark fraction.

Manipulative Illustrated

- Math Learning Center Fraction Tools app: https://apps.mathlearningcenter.org/fractions/

Note: The fraction tools app allows fill in a range of colors. This is different from working with physical pieces.

Steps

1. Write these fractions on the board: $\frac{7}{8}, \frac{3}{8}, \frac{4}{8}$. Tell students that these are all fractions of the same whole and ask them which has the greatest value and which has the least value. Discuss their reasoning using questions like these:

   - *Why do you think _____ is the fraction with the greatest value? How did you figure that out?*

   - *Why do you think _____ is the fraction with the least value? How did you figure that out?*

   - *What do all these fractions have in common?*

   - *How are these fractions different?*

   - *Would your answer change if we wrote $\frac{4}{8}$ as $\frac{1}{2}$ or $\frac{2}{4}$?*

2. As students discuss the fractions, encourage them to build representations using the fraction circles. This is particularly helpful for the questions about similarities and differences. They might build models that look like this.

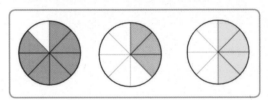

3. Repeat this discussion using the fractions $\frac{3}{5}, \frac{3}{2}$, and $\frac{3}{4}$. In this case, you might consider rewriting $\frac{3}{2}$ as $1\frac{1}{2}$ during the discussion. Encourage students to realize that the value of a fraction does not change even when we write an equivalent form. Some forms are easier for comparison or computation than others. In the image that follows, you see both a rectangle and an extra label identify the $\frac{3}{2}$ as a single item for comparison.

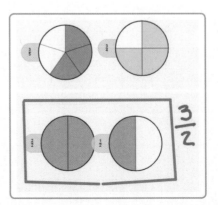

4. In both of these discussions, students are comparing either the quantity of same-size pieces (the first example where eighths is a common denominator) or the size of pieces when we have the same quantity of unit fractions (the second example where 3 is a common numerator).

5. The third basic strategy for comparing fractions is using a benchmark. Ask students to build and compare $\frac{5}{6}$, $\frac{7}{8}$, and $\frac{11}{12}$.

   Discuss their thinking using these questions to guide the discussion:

   • *What do you notice about the fraction pieces you used to build each value?*

   • *Can you use the missing part to help you compare quantities?*

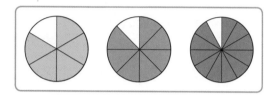

6. Using 1 as a benchmark, students can see that each fraction is one unit fraction away from the whole. $\frac{1}{12}$ is the smallest unit fraction of the group, so $\frac{11}{12}$ is closest to 1 or the greatest value in the group. $\frac{1}{6}$ is the largest unit fraction of the group, so $\frac{5}{6}$ is furthest from 1 or the smallest value in the group.

7. Benchmarks can also be used when two fractions are clearly on either side of the benchmark. Ask students to build and compare $\frac{3}{5}$ and $\frac{4}{10}$.

   Discuss their thinking using these questions as a guide:

   • *What do you notice about these fractions?*

   • *Is there a fraction you know that can help you compare them?*

   • *How can you be sure that one is greater than $\frac{1}{2}$ and the other is less than $\frac{1}{2}$?*

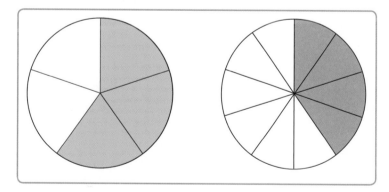

Why This Manipulative?

Fraction circles are particularly helpful for the benchmark fraction strategies. Benchmarks such as $\frac{1}{2}$ or 1 whole are easily seen with fraction circles no matter which pieces are in use.

When working with quantities greater than one, be sure students have a way to clearly identify the entire quantity, even if it is more than one circle of fraction pieces.

Developing Understanding

As students understand how to reason about fraction comparisons, they become strategic in their use of various representations. For any given fraction pair, it might be easier to find a common numerator than a common denominator (e.g., $\frac{2}{7}$ and $\frac{4}{5}$). When you explicitly teach students to compare fractions using reasoning—same-size pieces (how many do I have?) or same quantity of pieces (what size are they?)—students develop a sense of fractions as numbers along with better reasoning skills.

Featured Connection

Students can use the Caption Your Picture strategy to annotate and explain their reasoning about comparison problems like these. They can write both symbolic representations $\left(\frac{7}{8} > \frac{4}{8} > \frac{3}{8}\right)$ and explanations like this: "All the pieces are the same size. $\frac{7}{8}$ has the most pieces, so it is the biggest. $\frac{3}{8}$ has the fewest pieces, so it is the smallest."

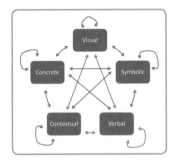

Source: Lesh, Post, & Behr (1987).

Notes

_____

_____

_____

_____

_____

_____

_____

_____

_____

_____

_____

Notes

Materials

- Fraction circles (one set per student, stored in a resealable bag)

Organization (physical)

- **Getting Started:** Students work in pairs; each pair has two bags of fraction circles. Have each student take out the $\frac{1}{8}$ pieces at the beginning and count that there are eight.

- **Winding Down:** At the end of the activity, have students count to be sure each student puts eight $\frac{1}{8}$ pieces back in their bag when they take the model apart.

Mathematical Purpose

In this activity, students use fraction circle pieces to model adding fractions with like denominators and a sum greater than one. The model emphasizes the importance of the numerator as the count (how many pieces) and the denominator as the size of the piece (the unit of measure).

Activity 2.3 Resources

- *Adding Fractions With Like Denominators* Activity Video

online resources ↖

To access resource visit resources.corwin.com/ MasteringMathManips/ 4–8

Steps

1. Pose the following problem for students:

> Cori had $\frac{7}{8}$ of a pound of freshly picked strawberries. She went to another field and picked another $\frac{3}{8}$ of a pound. How many pounds of strawberries did she have?

2. Talk with students about the problem, supporting their thinking with questions like these:

   - *What is happening in this problem? When have you solved a problem like this before?*

   - *Restate the problem using "some" or a whole number for the quantities. How does that help you understand what is happening? What operation will you use to solve this problem?*

   Support students to recognize that this problem is similar to a problem from first grade that might ask about picking 7 pounds of apples one day and another 3 pounds of apples the next day. Confirm that students must add $\frac{7}{8}$ and $\frac{3}{8}$ to solve the problem.

3. Have each student model one of the addends using a personal set of fraction circle pieces. In this case, one student will build $\frac{7}{8}$, and one will build $\frac{3}{8}$.

When we add whole numbers, we typically start with the larger addend because it is more efficient; we will do the same thing here. Start with $\frac{7}{8}$ and count on $\frac{3}{8}$ more. Listen to this in the video. Adding the first $\frac{1}{8}$ piece completes the whole (circle), and there are still two more $\frac{1}{8}$ pieces to go. You might say "seven one-eighth pieces and one more one-eighth piece makes eight one-eighth pieces or one whole" to represent this part of the work.

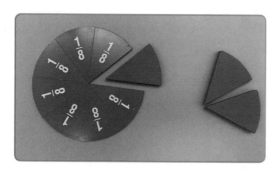

4. The next two $\frac{1}{8}$ pieces show the beginning of a second whole. This tells us that the answer is between 1 and 2 and we can read the answer as ten-eighths, because we have ten $\frac{1}{8}$ pieces, or one and two-eighths, because we can see one whole and two more $\frac{1}{8}$ pieces. Spend some time on the $1\frac{2}{8}$ solution to emphasize that we are adding eighths and regrouping for each whole. In this case, the whole is eight-eighths.

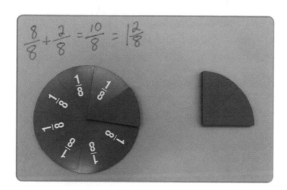

Why This Manipulative?

Students develop two important understandings from this work. First, we want them to see that we are counting up $\frac{1}{8}$ pieces (or $\frac{1}{8}$-sized pieces—decide what is most clear for your students) and that when we fill one whole, we start on the next. Students might connect this to working with place value: Once we have ten ones, that's one ten, and we start counting the next group of ten ones. With fractions, eight eighths makes one whole, and we start counting the next one whole. The fraction circle model makes this very visible for students.

It is perhaps less obvious that we are simply adding 7 and 3 in this problem; the denominator of 8 simply tells us what size piece to use. To emphasize this second understanding, hold the $\frac{1}{8}$ pieces in your hand and deal them out, counting seven and then counting on three more to ten: "eight, nine, ten." Then the ten pieces can be arranged in one full whole (circle) and the two more starting a second whole (circle).

Developing Understanding

Students will need to solve multiple problems like this to understand what is happening with the manipulatives in this addition process. Use language, as modeled earlier, to help them see that the denominator tells what size piece to use and the numerator tells how many to add.

1. Have students solve several problems in the "basic facts" range (sum is between 1 and 2) in order to reinforce the connection to arithmetic.

2. Ask questions such as these:
   - *What part of the fraction tells you what size piece to use?*
   - *What part of the fraction tells you how many pieces to use?*

This same model supports students subtracting fractions with like denominators. You might begin with problems like $\frac{11}{12} - \frac{5}{12}$. Then move to problems written as fractions greater than one such as $\frac{12}{8} - \frac{5}{8}$ and finally to mixed-number problems like $1\frac{3}{5} - \frac{4}{5}$. In the last situation, students will need to remember to think about and build the 1 as five $\frac{1}{5}$ pieces. Emphasize that students can also use a strategy similar to bridging 10 in problems like the last example. $1\frac{3}{5} - \frac{3}{5} = 1$, and then there's one more $\frac{1}{5}$ piece to subtract from the 1. This is similar to the strategy of thinking about 13 − 5 in 39 two steps: "I know 13 − 3 is 10, and then I need to subtract 2 more. 10 − 2 is 8, so 13 − 5 must be 8."

Featured Connection

Use the Create a Diagram strategy to connect this physical representation to a pictorial representation in the form of a number line. Give the students a number line marked in eighths and ask them to represent their manipulative solution on the number line. One partner can re-create the manipulative action, while the other records on the number line.

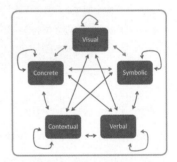

Source: Lesh, Post, & Behr (1987).

Starting with 7 one-eighth pieces means beginning at $\frac{7}{8}$ on the number line. Adding 3 more eighths means taking 3 steps, each one-eighth in size, to advance to $\frac{10}{8}$ or $1\frac{2}{8}$ or $1\frac{1}{4}$. This reinforces the idea that the denominator is the unit of measure (the size of the step in this case) and that the numerator indicates how many steps to take.

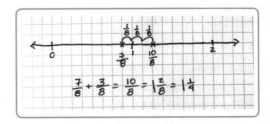

Notes

Materials

- Fraction bars (one set per student, stored in a resealable bag)

Organization (physical)

- **Getting Started:** Students work in pairs; each pair has two bags of fraction bars. Have all students check that their sets are complete at the beginning of the activity.

- **Winding Down:** At the end of the activity, have students count to be sure they put the full set back in their bag when they take the model apart.

Mathematical Purpose

In this activity, students use fraction bars to model adding fractions with unlike denominators and a sum greater than one. The model emphasizes the importance of the numerator as the count (how many pieces) and the denominator as the size of the piece (the unit of measure).

Manipulative Illustrated

- Fraction bars (Didax)

Steps

1. This lesson finds the sum of $\frac{1}{2}$ and $\frac{2}{3}$. Begin by asking each student in the pair to represent one of the two addends.

2. Align the fraction bar pieces together as in a train and ask the students if they have been added. The two groups have been combined; this is addition in one sense. The problem is that we still do not know what to call this combined train.

Support their thinking with questions like these:

- *If I combine counters like this (a train of three linking cubes in one color with a train of four cubes in a different color), have I added them? How do I name the sum?*

- *What happens if I just have the two $\frac{1}{3}$ pieces? How can I name the sum?*

- *What is different about this train of fraction bars?*

This discussion helps students understand the need for a common denominator. We need to build each addend from the same unit fraction in order to add effectively.

3. Ask students to use their other fraction bar pieces to find a unit fraction that can be used to build exactly these bars. Students should build the new model directly below the given problem. Use questions like these to support their thinking:

- *What fraction bar pieces can you use to make a train exactly this long using copies of only one unit fraction?*

- *How can you know if you have made a good choice before you lay out all the unit fractions? [It will fill the $\frac{1}{2}$ with a whole number of pieces.]*

- *Can the denominators of the fractions we know ($\frac{1}{2}$ and $\frac{1}{3}$) help you predict what unit fractions to try?*

4. Some students may choose sixths, and others may choose twelfths. Either one is appropriate because each serves the purpose of a common unit. As the image shows, we can still see both addends, $\frac{1}{2}$ as $\frac{3}{6}$ or $\frac{6}{12}$ and $\frac{2}{3}$ as $\frac{4}{6}$ or $\frac{8}{12}$.

5. With the towers joined, we can now read the sum as $\frac{7}{6}$ or $\frac{14}{12}$. Students might also recognize that this is more than one whole and reframe the sum as $1\frac{1}{6}$ or $1\frac{2}{12}$.

Why This Manipulative?

Fraction towers or bars can serve as a smooth transition to the number line for representing fraction operations. The length model is also easy to align when demonstrating equivalence and more straightforward to use than fraction circles. Creating equivalent fractions requires precision with the pieces, making this activity more appropriate for commercial or die-cut manipulatives than student-created fraction sets.

Developing Understanding

Students should see this lesson as an extension of the previous lesson. In order to name a sum (or compute a difference), fractions must be named in terms of the same unit fraction. When adding or subtracting fractions, first we must name the fractions in terms of the same unit, and then we can find the answer.

To give students practice subtracting fractions with regrouping, with or without finding a common denominator, turn this addition task into related subtraction tasks. Students could solve $1\frac{1}{6} - \frac{1}{2}$ or $1\frac{1}{6} - \frac{2}{3}$. Encourage students to find a common denominator and then count down, bridging whole values by renaming them in fractional terms.

Featured Connection

Use the Make a Sketch strategy to connect concrete and pictorial representations.

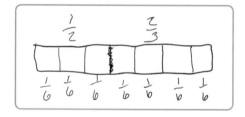

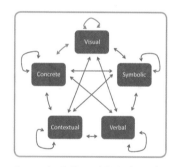

Source: Lesh, Post, & Behr (1987).

As students move from concrete to visual representations, they must learn to sketch the meaningful attributes of the physical objects they use. In the case of fraction manipulatives, this means being accurate enough to understand the diagram without obsessing over precisely equal spacing. In the case of this task, encourage students to sketch (even by tracing) the basic problem $\frac{1}{2} + \frac{2}{3}$ built from the fraction towers. Then, ask them to freehand sketch the equivalent fractions they built. If they used sixths, for example, they'll need to divide the $\frac{1}{2}$ piece into three roughly equal sections. Each of the $\frac{1}{3}$ pieces would be divided roughly in half to show sixths. If you wish, it is now a direct link to translate from this sketch of the objects to a number line as shown in the previous lesson.

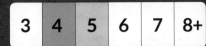
Materials

- Virtual or concrete fraction towers or bars (one set per student, stored in a resealable bag)

Organization (virtual)

- **Getting Started:** Ensure students can access and use the virtual tool. Review annotation tools, the process for taking screenshots, and other important supports.

- **Winding Down:** Use screenshots to save student work.

Mathematical Purpose

In this activity, students use fraction tower pieces to model multiplying a fraction by a whole number in situations where the whole number is the multiplier or the number of groups.

Activity 2.5 Resources

- *Multiplying a Fraction and a Whole Number* Activity Video

online resources ⌖ To access resource visit resources.corwin.com/ MasteringMathManips/ 4–8

Manipulative Illustrated

- Mathies Fraction Strips app (Apple and Google Play Stores): https://mathies.ca/apps.php#gsc.tab=0

Steps

> Robert is helping his grandfather make 3 batches of biscuits for a family party. Each batch of biscuits requires $\frac{1}{2}$ cup of shortening. How much shortening must Robert measure to make this triple batch?

1. Talk with students about the problem, supporting their thinking with questions like these:

   - *What is happening in this problem? When have you solved a problem like this before?*

   - *Restate the problem using "some" or a whole number for the quantities. How does that help you understand what is happening? What operation will you use to solve this problem?*

   Guide the students to understand that this is an **equal groups multiplication** problem with 3 groups (batches) of $\frac{1}{2}$ cup each. Ask each pair to identify the fraction tower piece that represents the $\frac{1}{2}$ cup of shortening in each batch.

2. Ask students to build a representation of 3 batches of biscuits and tell the operation they would use to find the total shortening in this triple batch of biscuits.

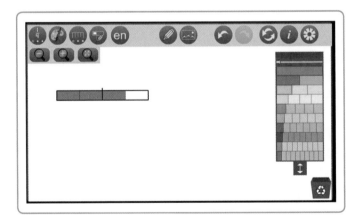

3. Discuss how each equation matches the model (3 copies of $\frac{1}{2}$ for $3 \times \frac{1}{2}$ or combining 3 groups of $\frac{1}{2}$ for $\frac{1}{2} + \frac{1}{2} + \frac{1}{2}$) using questions like these to support students' thinking:

   - *Where do you see the 3 groups [3 batches of biscuits] in the model?*

- *Where do you see the $\frac{1}{2}$ cup of shortening per batch in the model?*
- *How does this model represent an addition sentence? How does it represent a multiplication sentence?*

Notice that the denominator remains the same as a unit of measure (all pieces are the same color) and that we multiply the number of groups by the numerator to see how many copies we have.

4. To test this idea, you might tell the students that each batch of biscuits also requires $\frac{3}{4}$ cup of milk. How can we model the milk needed for 3 batches?

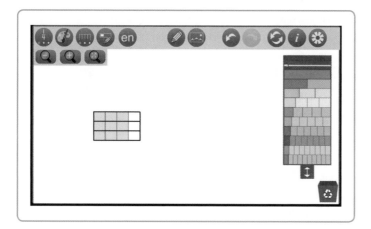

Using questions parallel to those in Step 3, discuss this second model. How can the $\frac{1}{4}$ pieces in the model be moved around to more clearly show the total amount of milk required? The video talks through this discussion.

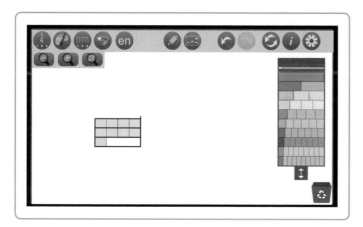

Why This Manipulative?

We are building an "equal groups" understanding of fraction multiplication through this activity, which looks at computing a whole number of copies (the multiplier) of fraction-sized groups (the measure) (Moore et al., 2020). The activity can be completed with any fraction manipulative as long as there are sufficient pieces for the product. Linear models (such as towers or tiles) help students make the connection to number line representations of the same computation.

Developing Understanding

This model is easiest to understand in a situation like 3 batches of biscuits with $\frac{1}{2}$ cup shortening in each batch because the manipulative representation (3 copies of the $\frac{1}{2}$ piece) matches the problem context. For students who struggle to understand the situation, present the same problem with whole numbers (each batch uses 2 cups of flour). This can help students recognize the equal groups situation and see that multiplication is the appropriate operation. The student would then substitute the value for this task ($\frac{1}{2}$ cup) for the whole-number placeholder.

Because this is an equal groups situation, the idea of repeated addition is a reasonable solution strategy. Three halves are easy to add, so it's an efficient strategy as well. You may wish to ask students who used repeated addition what they would do if the numbers were less friendly (e.g., $7 \times 1\frac{3}{5}$) to encourage the move to multiplication. This is also important because repeated addition does not model all multiplication situations. The area situation and model will be used for a fraction-by-fraction multiplication situation in the next example.

Featured Connection

Use the Build the Equation strategy to connect concrete and abstract representations. Fraction towers or tiles are particularly helpful for connecting with a number line representation as the linear nature of the tool makes the "walk" down the number line visible. We have discussed that in earlier fraction activities. Here we are focusing on connecting the concrete with the abstract by naming the parts of the model. Using this strategy, students use their physical model and the basic structure of equal groups multiplication (multiplier × measure = product) to record the model they built. In this case, there are 3 groups (or copies) of the $\frac{1}{2}$ cup of flour. We can record that using addition or multiplication.

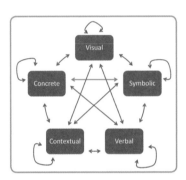

Source: Lesh, Post, & Behr (1987).

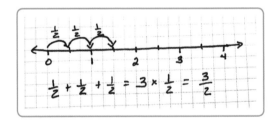

Notes

_____

_____

_____

_____

Notes

_____

_____

_____

_____

_____

_____

_____

_____

_____

_____

_____

_____

_____

_____

_____

_____

_____

_____

_____

_____

_____

_____

_____

MULTIPLYING A FRACTION BY A FRACTION

Materials

- Fraction squares, one set per pair
- Two colors of pen or pencil for tracing
- Plain paper for tracing

Organization (physical)

- **Getting Started:** Have students check that all the fraction square pieces are complete by counting or assembling the squares.
- **Winding Down:** Count or assemble the squares as they are returned to the bag.

Mathematical Purpose

In this activity, students will use an area model to understand fraction-by-fraction multiplication.

Activity 2.6 Resources

- *Multiplying a Fraction by a Fraction* Activity Video

online resources → To access resource visit resources.corwin.com/ MasteringMathManips/ 4–8

Manipulative Illustrated

- Fraction squares

Steps

$$\frac{1}{2} \times \frac{2}{3} =$$

1. Have students trace the square "whole" on their paper.

2. Review the idea of area as the space covered by a shape. In this problem, we're making a rectangle that is $\frac{1}{2}$ unit on one side and $\frac{2}{3}$ unit on the other side.

   Use the fraction square pieces to partition the two sides of the unit square into halves on one dimension and thirds on the other dimension. Draw dotted lines between the marks so you can see halves and thirds in the figure.

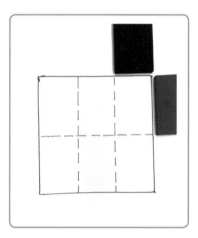

3. Mark the dimensions of the rectangle in the problem on the diagram. Outline the full diagram.

4. Discuss the area of the smaller rectangle you've drawn, guiding students' thinking with questions like these:

   - *What do you notice about the area of the small rectangle?*
   - *What are the dimensions of the small rectangle? Is each small rectangle the same dimensions and area?*
   - *How many of the small rectangles represent the product of $\frac{1}{2}$ and $\frac{2}{3}$? How do you know?*

5. Based on the previous discussion, guide students to see that each small rectangle has an area of $\frac{1}{6}$; the unit whole square is partitioned into six equal pieces.

6. If each small rectangle has an area of $\frac{1}{6}$, the area of the rectangle under discussion is $\frac{2}{6}$.

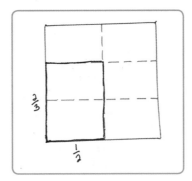

7. Record the equation as $\frac{1}{2} \times \frac{2}{3} = \frac{2}{6}$.

Why This Manipulative?

Fraction squares make it easy to draw the unit square and partition it into fractional pieces. Because they are an area model themselves, students can overlay the pieces on the diagram to see that the area of the solution is the area where the pieces representing the factors overlap. This is evident in the video.

The model also works with a factor (or factors) greater than one. There will be multiple whole unit squares, so each side length is appropriate. For example, multiplying $1\frac{1}{2} \times \frac{2}{3}$ would require two stacked unit squares, so the vertical side length (following the pattern of the images in this lesson) is $1\frac{1}{2}$ and the horizontal length remains $\frac{2}{3}$. It may help students to write the problem as $\frac{3}{2} \times \frac{2}{3}$, and they will find $\frac{6}{6}$ as the area.

Developing Understanding

This representation helps students reinforce the connection between multiplication and area. The area model also helps students understand that the unit of the product, in an area problem, is different from the units of the factors. When we find a "part of a part" in this context, we have a new unit of measure. In this case, each factor represents a length of the side of the unit whole square. In the product, the area is expressed in sixths of the square. It is important *not* to simplify the product so that students can see the relationship.

Students should have multiple experiences with multiplying fractions using fraction squares as described here so they come to understand the pattern of what happens, especially with the denominator of the product. If students are ready, this work can move to grid paper without the fraction squares, allowing a wider range of denominators.

Featured Connection

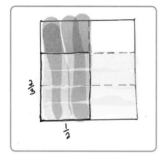

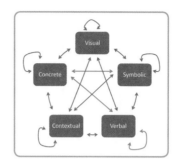

Source: Lesh, Post, & Behr (1987).

Use the Name Your Model strategy to connect the pictorial and abstract representations.

$$\frac{1}{2} \times \frac{2}{3} = \frac{1 \times 2}{2 \times 3} = \frac{2}{6}$$

Guide students to identify each element of the equation in the diagram pictured. The two factors appear as the dimensions of the green rectangle, the area with double-shading.

When the numerators are multiplied, we are counting the number of pieces in the resulting area. For this problem, $1 \times 2 = 2$ pieces in the final area.

When the denominators are multiplied, we see the number of unit area pieces into which the larger unit whole is partitioned. In this problem, 2 (halves in a whole) $\times$ 3 (thirds in a whole) means the unit whole square is partitioned into sixths, six smaller rectangles.

The product in this problem is the area of the green rectangle and includes two of those $\frac{1}{6}$ square unit rectangles.

Notes

_____

_____

_____

_____

_____

_____

_____

_____

_____

Notes

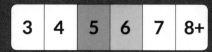

ACTIVITY
2.7

DIVIDING A WHOLE NUMBER BY A UNIT FRACTION

| 3 | 4 | 5 | 6 | 7 | 8+ |

Materials

- Fraction circles (one set per pair of students)

Organization (physical)

- **Getting Started:** Have students check that all the fraction circle pieces are complete by counting or assembling the circles.

- **Winding Down:** Count or assemble the circles as they are returned to the bag.

Mathematical Purpose

In this activity, students model dividing a whole number by a unit fraction, asking the question, "How many unit fraction pieces are in this whole?"

Manipulative Illustrated

- Fraction circles (hand2mind)

Steps

> How many $\frac{1}{4}$-pound servings are there in 1 pound of granola? How can you use your fraction circles to model this situation?

1. Share the task with the class. Give each pair 2–3 minutes to create a model for the situation, then ask students to explain their models to the class or have a brief gallery walk.

2. Discuss students' thinking using questions like these:

    - *What piece did you select to represent one serving of granola? Why?*

    - *What piece represents a full pound of granola? How do these two pieces relate to each other?*

    - *If the yellow quarter-circle wedge represents one serving, how many servings are in the full pound, represented by the red circle?*

    - *If the serving size is a unit fraction, how can you predict how many servings there will be in one whole portion?*

3. Once students connect this question to the pattern of four fourths in a whole, ask how many $\frac{1}{8}$-pound servings there would be. How many $\frac{1}{3}$-pound servings? How many $\frac{1}{17}$-pound servings? This encourages students to extend the pattern.

4. Teachers can extend students' thinking by changing the number of whole pounds. How many $\frac{1}{4}$-pound servings are there in 3 pounds? How many $\frac{1}{2}$-pound servings are there in 4 pounds?

5. Teachers can also extend students' thinking by dividing by a fraction other than a unit fraction. If there are eight $\frac{1}{8}$-pound servings in a pound, how many $\frac{2}{8}$-pound servings would there be? It is important *not* to simplify fractions so students can see the

connections easily. In this case, the eight $\frac{1}{8}$-pound pieces are grouped in twos to reflect the serving size of $\frac{2}{8}$-pound.

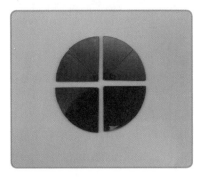

Why This Manipulative?

This activity emphasizes the connection of six sixths or eight eighths in a whole, so the clearly visible circle as the unit whole is helpful. When students work too early with more linear models—fraction towers, bars, or number lines—they can miscount the number of unit fractions in a single whole.

Developing Understanding

In this activity, students return to and connect two fundamental ideas. First, one type of division emphasizes repeated subtraction or "How many of these are in those?" This was true for whole numbers (8 ÷ 2 can be interpreted as "How many twos are in eight?") and remains true for fractions. The second fundamental idea is that a unit fraction is defined as the number of pieces when a whole is partitioned evenly. There are always four fourths in one whole, eight fourths in two wholes, and so forth. By connecting these key ideas, students develop a mental model for dividing any whole number by a fraction.

Featured Connection

Use the Caption Your Picture strategy to connect physical and verbal representations. Students should be able to connect their equation and their concrete model using language.

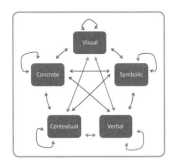

Source: Lesh, Post, & Behr (1987).

One divided by one-fourth is another way of asking how many yellow one-fourth pieces are in one red whole circle.

One divided by two-eighths is another way of asking how many pairs of blue one-eighth pieces are in one red whole circle. If there are eight eighths, there must be four groups of two-eighths.

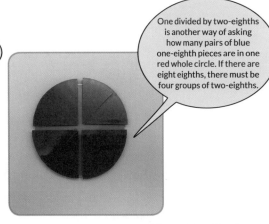

DIVIDING A FRACTION BY A WHOLE NUMBER

| 3 | 4 | 5 | 6 | 7 | 8+ |

Materials

- Fraction towers (one set per pair of students)

Organization (physical)

- **Getting Started:** Have students check that all the fraction towers are complete by counting or assembling the towers.

- **Winding Down:** Count or assemble the towers as they are returned to the bag.

Mathematical Purpose

In this activity, students model dividing a fraction by a whole number, asking the question, "What happens if I share this fraction among this many people?"

Manipulative Illustrated

- Fraction equivalency towers (hand2mind)

Steps

1. Ask students to build $\frac{2}{3}$ using their fraction tower pieces. Ask them to model what happens when this quantity $\left(\frac{2}{3}\right)$ is divided by 2, using these questions to guide the discussion:

   - *What can it mean to divide something by two? What situations can you think of where a quantity would be divided by two?*

   - *What makes dividing by two easy in this specific example?*

2. Considering a new example, ask students to show $\frac{1}{2}$ using a single fraction tower piece. What happens when this piece is divided by 2? Guide the discussion using questions like these:

   - *Remember what it means to divide by two. What's a situation where you might need to divide one-half into two parts? Can the item you're sharing be partitioned easily? [For example, cereal can be shared more easily than an apple—no cutting!]*

   - *We cannot cut the fraction tower in half. How can we represent one-half so it is easy to share in two parts?*

3. Students may know that half of $\frac{1}{2}$ is $\frac{1}{4}$. If they move directly to the answer, redirect the conversation to how this is modeled using the fraction towers. This helps them understand the process so students can figure it out for facts they do not know from memory.

4. Students may reference cutting the $\frac{1}{2}$ piece to split it into two equal shares. Since the pieces cannot be cut, what is another way to handle this? Encourage students to build an equivalent tower that can be separated into two equal groups.

$$\frac{1}{2} \div 2 = \frac{1}{4}$$

5. Notice how students build their towers. Three $\frac{1}{6}$ pieces is equivalent to $\frac{1}{2}$ but cannot be easily divided into two portions. Two $\frac{1}{4}$ pieces or four $\frac{1}{8}$ pieces will work.

6. Continue to develop this idea by modeling additional examples of fractions divided by whole numbers. Encourage students to find patterns in their answers.

Why This Manipulative?

This activity emphasizes division as partitioning a quantity into equal groups. Because fraction towers connect together, it is easy to see the "before and after" of the work and to explore the various ways terms can be built to make it easy (or not) to form the groups.

Developing Understanding

Students should see connections to their work with whole numbers in this activity. Sharing two $\frac{1}{3}$ pieces between two groups is mathematically equivalent to sharing two apples between two people—each person gets one. If there is only one apple, it can be cut to share fairly. Since the fraction tower pieces cannot be cut, students must create an equivalent fraction to share fairly.

Students with strong number sense about fractions will quickly be able to solve these problems mentally. Practice with a variety of fractions and number of groups to help students understand the pattern. As with much early fraction work, it is important *not* to simplify so students can see what is happening in the computation. Students are developing their understanding of the relationship between multiplication and division—dividing by two is the same as multiplying by one-half. Students might also notice that, if the divisor is written in fractional form ($\frac{2}{1}$), it also works to divide across.

Featured Connection

$$\frac{1}{2} \div 2 = \frac{1}{4}$$

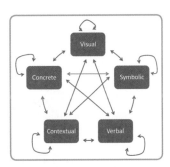

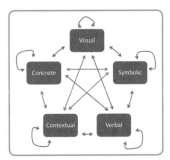

Source: Lesh, Post, & Behr (1987).

Use the Build the Equation strategy to connect the physical and abstract representations.

Students should be able to explain the connection between their physical representation and the equation or algorithm they choose to use to record their work. In the upper equation, the student is thinking about dividing by two as giving half to each person. This is reflected in the multiplication expression. In the lower equation, the student is thinking about partitioning the two $\frac{1}{4}$ pieces into two groups. Dividing across the numerators shows two pieces shared into two groups, while dividing across the denominators shows the size of the piece does not change.

Students can also Write a Word Problem to identify a context in which they might divide a fraction by a whole number. While not always the case, it is often helpful to think about sharing situations for problems like this.

Materials

- Virtual or concrete fraction towers or bars (one set per student, stored in a resealable bag)

Organization (virtual)

- **Getting Started:** Ensure students can access and use the virtual tool. Review annotation tools, the process for taking screenshots, and other important supports.
- **Winding Down:** Use screenshots to save student work.

Mathematical Purpose

In this activity, students use fraction towers to model fraction-by-fraction division in a situation where there is a remainder. Activity 3.5 illustrates fraction division without a remainder using Cuisenaire® Rods. These tools are interchangeable for this idea, and both activities can be completed with either tool.

Manipulative Illustrated

- Toy Theater Fraction Strips (labeled): https://toytheater.com/fraction-strips/
- Toy Theater Fraction Bars (unlabeled): https://toytheater.com/fraction-bars/

Steps

> One serving of granola cereal is $\frac{3}{4}$ of a cup. The box has $1\frac{1}{4}$ cups left. How many servings of cereal are left in the box?

1. Ask students to read and discuss the problem situation, guiding the discussion with questions like these:

   - *What is happening here? Have you solved a problem like this before?*
   - *Replace the quantities with whole-number values or with "some" if students struggle to understand the fraction situation.*
   - *What operation can help you solve this problem? How do you know?*

   Have students identify fraction tower representations for the serving size and cereal in the box.

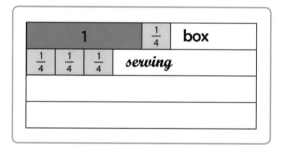

2. Ask students to use their number sense and representation to estimate the quotient. Is this less than one? About one? More than one? A lot more than one? How many $\frac{3}{4}$ are in $1\frac{1}{4}$ is a way to verbalize the division equation $1\frac{1}{4} \div \frac{3}{4}$ and support estimation here.

   Ask students to use their model to justify their estimate. Some students may build a second $\frac{3}{4}$ tower to show that the $1\frac{1}{4}$ is more than one $\frac{3}{4}$ and less than two $\frac{3}{4}$. How much of the second $\frac{3}{4}$ is part of the solution? Support students to see that two of the three $\frac{1}{4}$ pieces are included in the $1\frac{1}{4}$. We might describe this as "1 serving with a remainder of $\frac{2}{4}$."

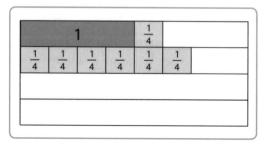

What fraction of a complete serving ($\frac{3}{4}$ cup) are the two remaining $\frac{1}{4}$ pieces? This will allow us to write the solution as a mixed number. To identify this fraction, it helps to turn the fraction tower pieces to the blank side so students focus less on the fact that these were originally $\frac{1}{4}$-cup pieces and can now think about the relationship between the remainder $\left(\frac{2}{4}\right)$ and the divisor $\left(\frac{3}{4}\right)$. Students can see that if the divisor has three sections (thirds), the remainder represents two of those so the remainder is $\frac{2}{3}$. We have $1\frac{2}{3}$ servings of cereal.

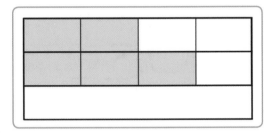

Why This Manipulative?

A formal fraction manipulative makes it easy to see what is happening in the problem situation and easy to represent the remainder as a fraction of the group size. Handmade (cut or torn) manipulatives may not have the precision required to address the remainder as a fraction of the divisor.

This activity can be done with any fraction manipulative. Fraction circles or squares can be more challenging than a linear model like towers or tiles when working with mixed numbers.

Developing Understanding

There are two essential understandings from this experience. The first is that fraction-by-fraction division has the same meaning as whole-number division. It can be read as "How many of these are in that?" The second is that we must define a new unit whole in order to name the remainder as a fraction. The remainder is a fraction of the group we are pulling out, not a fraction of the original whole.

The estimation step in the lesson is essential for helping students reason about fraction division. Because we may be fighting against the idea that division makes things smaller, asking students to look at physical models and reason about the result gives them confidence in their number sense and computation skills.

Featured Connection

Use the Make a Sketch strategy to help students connect physical and pictorial representations. This activity is built from a repeated subtraction or measurement model of division because this model makes it easy for students to see what is happening when we divide fractions. Students will need to generalize this thinking to any division computation, even those that do not represent measurement division situations. Help students connect their experience with whole number division to fraction

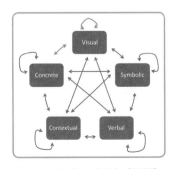

Source: Lesh, Post, & Behr (1987).

division as they work with these examples; this reinforces the connection between the operations even when the number category changes.

A sketch like the one that follows mimics early division experiences using unit fractions rather than counters. Each loop represents one serving of cereal, and we portion out each serving one at a time. We can see the one full serving and the two $\frac{1}{4}$ pieces included in the second serving. Because we know that the full serving is $\frac{3}{4}$ cup, we know that the two pieces are $\frac{2}{3}$ of the serving.

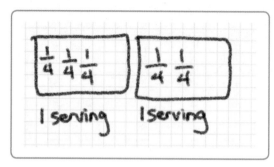

Notes

_____

_____

_____

_____

_____

_____

_____

_____

_____

_____

_____

_____

Notes

Materials

- Fraction towers (one set per student, stored in a resealable bag)

Organization (physical)

- **Getting Started:** Students are working in pairs. For this problem, each pair needs two sets of fraction towers. Students should begin by checking that all the pieces are included in their set.

- **Winding Down:** Have students "build a whole" for each group of fraction tiles they pulled from the bag before repacking their pieces. This will ensure all pieces are available for the next activity.

Mathematical Purpose

In this activity, students explore what is happening when they invert and multiply to divide fractions.

Activity 2.10 Resources

- *What Happens When We Invert and Multiply?* Activity Video

online resources 🔍 To access resource visit resources.corwin.com/ MasteringMathManips/ 4–8]

Manipulative Illustrated

- Fraction equivalency towers (hand2mind)

Steps

1. Begin by asking students to identify the pattern when dividing a whole number by a unit fraction. Students might build models with fraction tower pieces as they complete the following table to start their reflection. The first potential model is pictured below the table.

$1 \div \frac{1}{5} =$	
$2 \div \frac{1}{5} =$	
$3 \div \frac{1}{5} =$	
$4 \div \frac{1}{5} =$	
$5 \div \frac{1}{5} =$	

2. Use questions such as these to guide the discussion:

   - *What pattern do you see in the table you created?*

   - *How can you find how many fifths there are in any whole number?*

   - *How can you find the number of unit fractions (of any size) in any whole number?*

3. Ask students to compare these two fraction division problems.

$$2 \div \frac{1}{5} =$$

$$2 \div \frac{2}{5} =$$

   - *How are these problems alike, and how are they different?*

- *How can you use what you know about the first problem to help you figure out the second problem?*
- *What is the relationship between the number of $\frac{1}{5}$ parts and the number of $\frac{2}{5}$ parts in 2 wholes?*

4. Two ideas are central at this point:
   - *When we multiply by the denominator of a unit fraction, we are figuring out how many unit fractions are in our whole.*
   - *When we have groups of more than one unit fraction (e.g., $\frac{2}{5}$), we can figure out how many groups there are by dividing the number of unit fractions by the size of the denominator. In this example, there are half as many $\frac{2}{5}$ groups in 2 wholes as there are $\frac{1}{5}$ groups.*

5. Now we will use these ideas to understand what happens when we invert and multiply. $2 \div \frac{2}{5} = \frac{2}{1} \times \frac{5}{2}$

When we multiply the numerators after inverting, we are finding the number of $\frac{1}{5}$ pieces in 2 wholes—we are breaking down the starting value into its smallest, unit fraction, pieces.

When we divide by 2 (the new denominator), we are taking those unit fractions and creating groups of $\frac{2}{5}$ pieces. We know there are half as many $\frac{2}{5}$ as $\frac{1}{5}$ pieces in the same total amount.

6. Look at another example. $4 \div \frac{2}{3} = \frac{4}{1} \times \frac{3}{2}$

In this case, we want to know how many $\frac{2}{3}$ are in 4. We can find that out by calculating the number of $\frac{1}{3}$ pieces in 4 (there are $3 \times 4 = 12$) and then dividing that result by 2 because we are taking our $\frac{1}{3}$ pieces in groups of 2.

Why This Manipulative?

Fraction towers are helpful for seeing what happens when you convert a total amount into unit fraction pieces and then form those pieces into groups.

Developing Understanding

This activity is different from the other activities in this book. It serves more as an exploration or demonstration of what happens when we invert and multiply rather than a path for students to figure out the process themselves. It helps students use the process correctly because it provides an image of what is happening as students follow the process. It is important to develop a strong conceptual understanding of division with fractions before working through this activity.

Featured Connection

When students describe what is happening with each step of the calculation, they are using the Caption Your Picture and Build the Equation strategies. The activity walks through the process of building each step of the algorithm, and students caption the picture as they describe what is happening. Listen to a caption in the video of this activity.

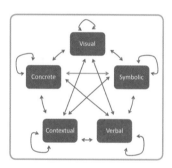 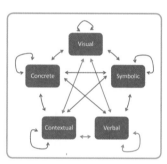

Source: Lesh, Post, & Behr (1987).

Notes

_____

_____

_____

_____

_____

_____

CLOSING REFLECTION: FRACTION MANIPULATIVES

How do I use fraction manipulatives in my classroom now? What concepts do I use them to teach?

_____

_____

_____

_____

_____

What new ways have I found to use fraction manipulatives to better support student understanding?

_____

_____

_____

_____

_____

What are my goals to make fraction manipulatives a more regular part of my instruction?

_____

_____

_____

_____

_____

Chapter 3
Cuisenaire® Rods

UNDERSTANDING CUISENAIRE RODS

Cuisenaire Rods have been a part of mathematics teaching for almost 100 years. They are proportional manipulatives made from a series of rods of increasing length. The white unit cube (1 cm per side) is the smallest piece. The pieces increase in length by 1-cm increments through the tenth (orange) rod, which is 10 cm long with a 1-cm^2 cross section. The color sequence for Cuisenaire Rods is fixed. The rods are available in traditional wood or plastic, with end connectors, and in a jumbo size (based on a 2-cm cube) for young learners.

  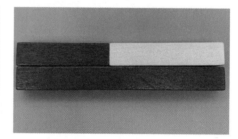

Cuisenaire Rods are particularly effective when teaching these topics:

- Representing and comparing fractions
- **Ratio** and proportional relationships
- Understanding bar models, **tape diagrams**, and double number lines

Introducing Cuisenaire Rods to Students

Encourage learners to explore the rods using the *Notice and Wonder Thinking Routine* (described in the introductory chapter) before starting to teach with them. Students may notice that same-size rods are also the same color. They may build staircases, highlighting the constant difference in length. They may create trains where they explore combinations of rods with the same total length. Encourage students to wonder about the relationships between different-colored rods. These can be additive relationships: What two-rod combinations are the same length as yellow (5) or orange (10)? Or they can be multiplicative relationships: How many copies of red (2) does it take to make orange (10)? These can be good informal assessments of your students' number sense and relational thinking.

Key Ideas With Cuisenaire Rods

- Cuisenaire Rods can be used as length models (as Activity 3.1 does when thinking about fractions) or as quantities (as Activity 3.3 does when exploring ratio and rate).

- The linear structure of Cuisenaire Rods makes them a good tool for connecting physical representations to linear visual representations, including bar models and number lines.

- In addition to the examples included here, Cuisenaire Rods can be used when working with measurement for two- and three-dimensional figures. The white cubes are 1 cm^3, ideal for measuring volume, and the single-centimeter side lengths are reasonable for building and counting or calculating perimeter, area, surface area, and volume.

Things to Consider About Cuisenaire Rods

- Cuisenaire Rods are a very flexible manipulative. Because the rods are unlabeled (other than by color), they can take on many values and show a wide range of relationships.

- Cuisenaire Rods are useful for helping students unitize. As students become confident that the yellow rod is always 5 white rods long, they can see the yellow rod as the quantity 5, rather than 5 copies of a quantity of 1.

- Be cautious about rigidly labeling the white unit cube as always having a value of 1 as this can make it difficult to view the pieces flexibly later. As students learn about the rods, consider asking them the value of various colored rods if the white unit cube has a value of 2 or $\frac{1}{2}$ or another age-appropriate quantity. This is why the rods are not labeled with a number value.

Alternatives to Commercial Cuisenaire Rods

Cuisenaire Rods are built from a 1-cm unit cube. This means centimeter grid paper provides a useful alternative if rods are not available. Students can use the same 10 colors (white, red, light green, purple, yellow, dark green, black, brown, blue, and orange) to color strips of the same length (1–10 cm in order). Students can then cut apart and manipulate the strips. Students who have more experience with the rods might simply sketch the relationships without first working with a physical rod.

Working With Virtual Cuisenaire Rods

Virtual Cuisenaire Rods have the advantage of an endless supply. A snapping feature is useful when making trains so rods are well aligned and lengths can be compared. As with many manipulatives, Cuisenaire Rods are proportional. Teachers should be careful that students do not resize the pieces and change the proportional relationships unintentionally.

Materials

- Cuisenaire Rods, one set per pair of students
- Paper for recording results (centimeter grid paper allows for easy sketches)

Organization (physical)

- **Getting Started:** Distribute one set of rods (in a bag or tray) per pair of students.
- **Winding Down:** Return the rods to their bag or tray.

Mathematical Purpose

In this activity, students explore factors and multiples by creating single-color trains of rods. Students extend the exploration to common factors and multiples by comparing trains.

Manipulative Illustrated

- Cuisenaire Rods (available from multiple sources)

Steps

1. Distribute Cuisenaire Rods and ask students to represent 12 by creating trains of rods, each in a single color. Share the variety of trains created and discuss them using questions such as these:

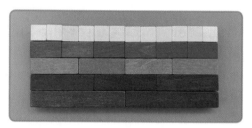

- *How do you know each train represents 12?*
- *What multiplication sentence could you write for each train?*
- *How can you describe your trains using the terms factor and multiple?*
- *What do you notice about the factor pairs for each train?*
- *As one factor increases, what happens to the other factor?*
- *Where the two factors are the same, do the trains look the same?*

2. Ask students to create all the possible trains for additional values. Both 20 and 24 have a large number of possible trains. Choose values such as 8, 10, 15, or 16 for more constrained options. Discuss the trains using similar questions to highlight students' understanding of the idea of factors and multiples.

3. To extend the discussion to common factors, look at the trains for two values at the same time. For example, it is possible to build red trains for both 12 and 16.

This shows that red (2) is a common factor between 12 and 16. Ask students to build all the trains for 12 and 16, discussing them using questions such as these:

- *Are there any colors that appear in both sets of trains? What does that tell you about that factor?*
- *Which is the greatest value that serves as a common factor between these values?*

4. Approached slightly differently, single-color trains can also be used to find common multiples. In this case, students build single-color trains of increasing numbers of cars and look for pairs of trains that are the same length. For example, build a series of red trains to represent the multiples of 2. Build a similar series of light-green trains to represent multiples of 3. The common multiple of 6 is circled. If you align the two parts of this row, you see that two groups of 3 (2 light-green rods) is the same length as three groups of 2 (3 red rods).

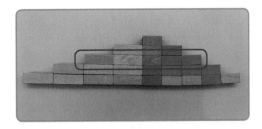

Discuss the models using questions such as these:

- *Write a multiplication sentence for each train. What do you notice about the products?*
- *Are there any trains in both sets that are the same length? Which ones?*
- *What does it mean that these are the same length?*

Why This Manipulative?

The proportional nature of Cuisenaire Rods, combined with the fact that each rod represents a different factor, makes it easy to represent equal groups situations using the rods. The single-color trains represent repeated addition or equal groups multiplication. As long as trains are the same length, they have the same product. Activity 3.2 also uses the rods to represent equal groups situations, with an emphasis on problem solving rather than factors and multiples.

Developing Understanding

In this application, students are representing multiplication using length models. They could also show area if the activity were organized differently, but it's harder to see the constant product.

Featured Connection

Students Caption Your Picture when they write a multiplication sentence for each train and explain how the trains are related. Depending on the specifics of the lesson, these captions are excellent opportunities for vocabulary about properties of operations.

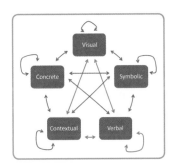

Source: Lesh, Post, & Behr (1987).

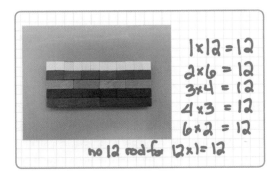

CREATING BAR MODELS FOR EQUAL GROUPS MULTIPLICATION AND DIVISION

Materials

- Virtual or concrete Cuisenaire Rods, one set per pair of students
- Paper for recording results (centimeter grid paper allows for easy sketches)
- Activity sheet (one for each student)

Organization (virtual)

- **Getting Started:** Ensure students can access and use the virtual tool. Review annotation tools, the process for taking screenshots, and other important supports.
- **Winding Down:** Use screenshots to save student work.

Mathematical Purpose

In this activity, students create bar models to represent equal groups multiplication and division situations.

Activity 3.2 Resources

- *Equal Groups Multiplication and Division Problems* Activity Sheet

 To access resource visit resources.corwin.com/ MasteringMathManips/ 4–8

Manipulative Illustrated

- Virtual number bars (Mathigon): https://mathigon.org/polypad

Steps

> Juan received 4 book awards from the library. Each award included a $3 gift card to spend in the school book sale. How much money does Juan have to spend at the book sale?

1. Share the first problem with students. Ask them to discuss the problem in a small group and create a representation for the problem with Cuisenaire Rods. If necessary, support their understanding of the problem situation with questions like these:

   - *Tell me what you know about the problem. What makes sense to you?*

   - *Are there any parts of the problem that don't make sense? Which one(s)?*

   - *How might you use the rods to represent the problem? If the rods don't make sense for you, what other tool might you use? Build that model first, then try again with the rods.*

   - *What question are you trying to answer?*

2. As students share their thinking and representations, listen for their understanding of these important elements:

   - *How many groups are there? Where are these groups in your representation?*

   - *How large is each group? Where can we see this in your representation?*

   - *What is the total amount? Where does this appear in your representation?*

3. Use the Make a Sketch and Name Your Model strategies to support students while they sketch and label a bar model for their solution.

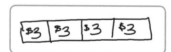

4. Repeat this cycle with the other two problems on the activity sheet. Problems 2 and 3 are also equal groups situations, but are typically described as division situations because students are figuring out the number of groups or the size of each group.

Why This Manipulative?

Visually, Cuisenaire Rods look like bar models. With smaller quantities, such as those in these problems, students can choose bars whose length represents the value in the problem. In this case, you see the red rods (3 units in length) used to represent each award. Because the rods are not marked with their length, this representation could be used for any problem with four equal groups, regardless of group size.

The number bars in this virtual tool function like Cuisenaire Rods, although they do not follow the color sequence. This is particularly important to note when students are moving back and forth between concrete and virtual representations. It can be confusing to have the same color represent different quantities. In Cuisenaire Rods, red has a length of 2 units, and light green represents the piece 3 units long.

Developing Understanding

In equal groups situations, the two factors in the multiplication problem do different jobs. One tells the number of groups while the other tells the size of the group. The product is the total quantity or value. In the first problem, each group is an award of $3. In the second problem, each group is the flowers for one friend, and students are figuring out how many flowers each friend will receive. In the third problem, each group is 4 songs played for one friend, and students are figuring out how many friends can hear 4 songs without repetition. This range of contexts supports students to understand the wide range of situations where equal groups thinking can support their work.

Your students may need additional practice and support with the multiplication version of equal groups (Problem 1) before moving on to the division variations (Problems 2 and 3). You can use this same structure to solve additional equal groups situations, remembering that the rods can have any value students choose.

Featured Connection

This activity uses the Make a Sketch and Name Your Model strategies to support students while they draw and label a bar model for their solution. The images here show the solutions to Problems 2 and 3 on the handout. The bar model is easy to draw when beginning with Cuisenaire Rods because the figure already looks like a bar model. By naming the model, students connect the physical and visual representations with the written equation. Notice that the two division situations have been written both as missing-factor multiplication and as more traditional division equations. Units are included to help students see the role of each factor in the situation.

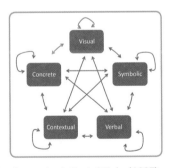 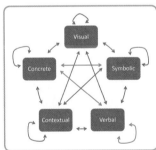

Source: Lesh, Post, & Behr (1987).

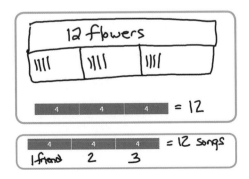

Materials

- Cuisenaire Rods, one set per pair of students
- Activity sheet (one for each student)

Organization (physical)

- **Getting Started:** Distribute one set of rods (in a bag or tray) per pair of students.
- **Winding Down:** Return the rods to their bag or tray.

Mathematical Purpose

In this activity, students use Cuisenaire Rods to model "times as many" situations, building their understanding of **multiplicative comparison**. An **additive comparison** model is also provided so students can see the difference.

Activity 3.3 Resources

- *Comparison Word Problems Activity Sheet*

 To access resource visit resources.corwin.com/MasteringMathManips/4–8

Manipulative Illustrated

- Cuisenaire Rods

Steps

> The zoo has 3 times as many spiders as snakes in its "meet the animals" exhibit. There are 2 snakes in the exhibit. How many spiders are there?

1. Distribute the rods and problem page to the class. Ask students to use the rods to represent the first problem situation. Share the different approaches students used and discuss the ways each representation helps them understand the problem situation. Use these questions to guide the discussion:
   - *Where does each quantity from the problem appear in the model?*
   - *Where is "times as many" visible?*
   - *How does this represent what is happening in the problem?*

2. Allow students time to represent and solve the next two problems on the page.

3. Ask students what they notice and wonder about the three representations they have created. Guide the discussion using these questions:
   - *Where does each value in the **equation** appear in the representations?*
   - *How does "times as many" appear in each model?*
   - *How can you use this thinking to be ready to solve another problem like these?*

4. Ask students to represent the three additive comparison problems at the bottom of the page. Guide a discussion of their work with these questions:
   - *What do you notice and wonder about these three situations?*
   - *What is the same about each problem situation?*

- *What does "two more" look like in each representation?*
- *How are these problems similar to and different from the first problems you solved?*

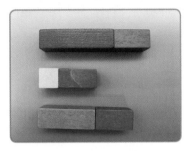

5. Discuss the difference between additive and multiplicative comparison situations, emphasizing that one is about a constant difference (additive comparison) and one is about copies of an initial value (multiplicative comparison).

Why This Manipulative?

Cuisenaire Rods are useful for highlighting this distinction with small whole-number values. The fact that there is a different-color rod for each value means that students can easily see copies of a base value (in multiplicative comparison) or the constant difference of additive comparison. As students begin to work with fractions, they will need to extend these understandings to new values and to understand what less than one copy of something means (when multiplying by a fraction less than one). The experience in this lesson provides a foundation for these discussions.

Developing Understanding

Developing multiplicative reasoning is a critical foundation for middle-grades mathematics. This experience provides a concrete illustration of the difference between additive and multiplicative comparison. Students can extend this understanding in two ways. First, as students work with larger values, the rods can represent any quantity other than their unit length. Second, as students begin to work with fractions, they will need to understand what less than one copy of something means (when multiplying by a fraction less than one). The experience in this activity provides a foundation for these discussions.

Featured Connection

In this lesson, the Build the Equation strategy helps students connect the abstract symbols used to represent multiplicative comparison with the physical and visual representations created. The Cuisenaire Rod lends itself to a bar model, and this lesson is ideal for transitioning to bar models for multiplicative comparison. By adding names to the model, students focus on where in the model the "times as many" element appears. As you work with students on these connections, focus on the units of the factors and knowing the work they do more than the position of either factor in the equation.

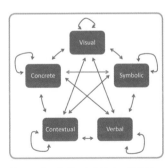

Source: Lesh, Post, & Behr (1987).

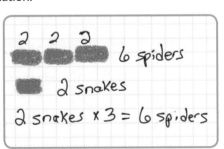

Materials

- Cuisenaire Rods, one set per pair of students
- Paper for recording results (centimeter grid paper allows for easy sketches)

Organization (physical)

- **Getting Started:** Distribute one set of rods (in a bag or tray) per pair of students.
- **Winding Down:** Return the rods to their bag or tray.

Mathematical Purpose

In this activity, students identify fractional values greater and less than one for a variety of fractional relationships. Students learn to extend their fractional reasoning beyond the explicit relationships in fraction manipulatives.

Manipulative Illustrated

- Cuisenaire Rods

Steps

1. Ask students to use the Cuisenaire Rods to model $\frac{1}{2}$. Encourage them to explore and justify that they have found all the possible ways to represent $\frac{1}{2}$ using the rods. Encourage discussion using questions such as these:

   - *Which rod represents the whole, and which rod represents the half in this model? [Point to one to select.]*
   - *How do you know that the half is half of the whole?*
   - *Why does the [pick a color] rod represent half in this model and a whole in that one?*
   - *Can you use any color rod to represent the whole in this task? Why or why not?*

2. Choose one rod to represent the whole. For example, if the purple rod is $\frac{1}{2}$ of the brown rod, the brown rod is the whole. If brown represents 1 whole, what is the fractional value of each other rod? Students have already determined that purple is $\frac{1}{2}$ and will work to find the fractional value of each other rod.

3. As students work, use questions like these to help them explain their thinking:

   - *How do you know this rod has this value?*
   - *Can you predict which rods will be worth more than one and which will be worth less than one?*
   - *Do you see a pattern in the naming of the rods?*

4. Repeat the activity with different rods as the whole. Extend the range of the activity by including combination rods—orange plus another rod. Extending beyond orange would be orange + white, orange + red, orange + light green, orange + purple, and orange + yellow. The first two extensions are shown in the accompanying image.

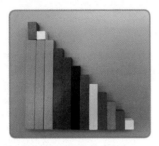

Why This Manipulative?

Cuisenaire Rods are useful for extending fraction thinking beyond formal fraction tools for several reasons. First, they echo the shape of fraction tiles or towers and lend themselves to a number line representation. Second, the size increments between pieces are clear so there is a straightforward structure to the work. Third, the rods will be useful for ratio and proportion thinking, another possible use of fraction notation. By connecting the rods with part-whole fractions, students begin to see the rods as a tool for representing relationships between quantities.

Developing Understanding

It is important for students to see fractions with a variety of tools. Typical fraction manipulatives (like those in Chapter 2) are important for understanding fractions. Activities like this one help students transfer their thinking about fractions to a tool not specifically designed for fractions. They expand thinking to another whole and develop the idea that the fractional value of each piece changes depending on the defined whole. You can follow this same activity structure with pattern blocks and/or tangrams to have a wider range of shapes for the wholes and parts.

Featured Connection

Use the Make a Sketch strategy with centimeter grid paper to create number line representations of each set of fractional relationships. Students use the length of each rod to indicate a position from 0 on the number line and label each point with its assigned fractional value. If students keep a constant denominator (i.e., record $\frac{2}{4}$ for red rather than $\frac{1}{2}$ when the whole is purple), it will be easy to see the pattern of counting by a unit fraction.

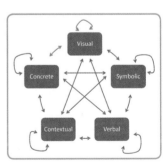

Source: Lesh, Post, & Behr (1987).

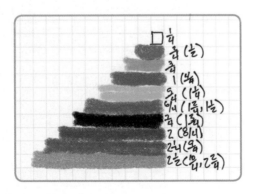

Materials

- Virtual or concrete Cuisenaire Rods

Organization (virtual)

- **Getting Started:** Ensure students can access and use the virtual tool. Review annotation tools, the process for taking screenshots, and other important supports.

- **Winding Down:** Use screenshots to save student work.

Mathematical Purpose

In this activity, students represent fraction division using Cuisenaire Rods. This example does not include a remainder. Activity 2.9 illustrates fraction division with a remainder using fraction tools. These tools are interchangeable for this idea, and both activities can be completed with either tool.

Manipulative Illustrated

- Virtual Cuisenaire Rods: https://app.brainingcamp.com/ manipulatives/cuisenaire-rods

Steps

> The class has $1\frac{1}{2}$ gallons of red paint to use for painting the stairs to their classroom. It takes $\frac{1}{4}$-gallon to paint each step. How many steps can the class paint?

1. Share the problem with the class and discuss the situation using questions such as these:

   - *Tell me what you know about the problem. What makes sense to you?*

   - *Are there any parts of the problem that don't make sense? Which one(s)?*

   - *How might you use the rods to represent the problem? If the rods don't make sense for you, what other tool might you use? Build that model first, then try again with the rods.*

   - *What question are you trying to answer?*

2. If students struggle to understand that this is a division problem where they want to find how many $\frac{1}{4}$-gallon portions there are in the $1\frac{1}{2}$ gallons of paint, share this problem with them.

> The class has 6 gallons of red paint to use for painting the stairs to their classroom. It takes 1 gallon to paint each step. How many steps can the class paint?

Discuss this problem with the class using similar questions and support them to see, first, that this is a division problem (how many 1-gallon portions are there in 6 gallons of paint?) and, second, that this is exactly the same problem as the fraction variation. This means that the equation for the whole-number problem has the same structure as the equation for the fraction problem.

$$6 \div 1 = x$$

$$1\frac{1}{2} \div \frac{1}{4} = x$$

3. Choose a whole from the Cuisenaire Rods to represent these fractions. Given the denominators of 2 and 4, either the purple rod (4 units long) or the brown rod (8 units long) will be most straightforward. Ask students to represent both the $1\frac{1}{2}$ total gallons of paint and the $\frac{1}{4}$-gallon required for each step using the rods.

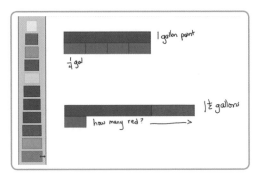

4. Ask students to estimate their answer first—how many red rods ($\frac{1}{4}$-gallon) are in the brown + purple train ($1\frac{1}{2}$ gallons)? Then use the rods to figure out the answer. Support students to describe their thinking in the context of the problem: "There are six $\frac{1}{4}$-gallon portions in $1\frac{1}{2}$ gallons of paint. This means the class has enough paint for six steps."

Why This Manipulative?

Cuisenaire Rods are a flexible tool for representing fractions. Because students can also use the rods to represent whole-number division (how many reds are in one orange rod is the equivalent of 10 ÷ 2), they can see the commonalities of division (how many of these are in that) regardless of value.

Developing Understanding

This activity provides an opportunity to address two challenges with fraction division. First, many students believe division "makes things smaller," so the idea of 6 as the quotient does not make sense. The rods provide a visual starting point for estimation—there are clearly "a bunch" of red rods in the brown + purple train. Second, students may struggle to see that the structure of the problem is the same as it would be with whole numbers. By representing the problem with whole-number values, students are supported to make this connection and use this reasoning for other fraction division situations.

Featured Connection

Use the Write a Word Problem strategy with students after completing this activity. Provide students with a handful of fraction division expressions (or number sentences) and ask them to create a word problem that could be solved by each equation. Students should build a representation of each problem and show where each element of the equation appears in the representation and in the word problem. See the example for the stair painting problem here.

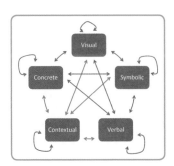

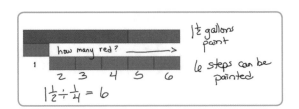

Source: Lesh, Post, & Behr (1987).

Materials

- Cuisenaire Rods, one set per pair of students
- Centimeter grid paper

Organization (physical)

- **Getting Started:** Distribute one set of rods (in a bag or tray) per pair of students.
- **Winding Down:** Return the rods to their bag or tray.

Mathematical Purpose

In this activity, students learn to use Cuisenaire Rods to represent a ratio and then to find equivalent ratios. To model the ratios, students use the Cuisenaire Rods as elements of the model, focusing on the number of rods used rather than the length of each rod.

Manipulative Illustrated

- Cuisenaire Rods

Steps

1. Pose the following problem to students:

> *Devinka is making fresh pasta. The recipe specifies a ratio of 3 eggs for every 2 cups of flour. This amount will serve 4 people. How many eggs and how much flour should Devinka use to make pasta for 12 people? If Devinka has 5 eggs, how much flour should she use to make pasta?*

Ask students to identify rods to represent the eggs and flour, selecting rods so that 3 of the egg rods are the same length as 2 of the flour rods. This makes one batch of pasta a single rectangle of rods. In this case, the left image shows using a red rod to represent each egg and a light-green rod to represent each cup of flour; on the right, the same relationship is shown using purple and dark-green rods.

2. To solve the first problem, students can iterate (or make copies of) the basic ratio relationship. If one copy of the ratio will serve 4 people, how many copies are required to serve 12 people?

Discuss students' thinking using the following questions:

- *How many eggs and how many cups of flour are included in these three copies?*
- *How did you know to make three copies?*

3. Students can use the model they just created to answer the second question. It is straightforward to identify 5 eggs in the model by counting red rods and then to approximate the amount of flour required for the proper ratio.

4. After the questions are answered, create a **double number line** that corresponds to the physical rods on centimeter grid paper to document students' thinking. Students should work through the process with the rods until they can clearly identify each element of the problem in a double-number-line representation. (See the image in "Featured Connection.")

Why This Manipulative?

Cuisenaire Rods are helpful tools for building understanding of bar models and double number lines. Having a rod of each unit length from 1 to 10 makes it fairly easy to find pairs of rods to illustrate a given relationship. By building a copy of the ratio each time, students see the creation of equivalent ratios and can more easily connect this thinking to what they know about equivalent fractions. When a student creates two copies of this 3:2 (eggs:flour) ratio, they are doubling each part and, in fractional form, multiplying by $\frac{2}{2}$ or 1.

Developing Understanding

As students solve this problem, highlight the idea that there are 2 cups of flour for every 3 eggs used in the pasta dough. If you are working with virtual manipulatives that include grouping and copying features, you can group the core pieces of the model and make digital copies to generate equivalent ratios. With physical tools, students will build copies of the model as they iterate.

Featured Connection

Use the Create a Diagram strategy to help students draw a double number line to represent their thinking. When working on centimeter grid paper, the increments are easy to indicate by placing the rods on the grid paper. While Cuisenaire Rod models are clearly best for simple relationships, their power is in helping students see where the quantities in a problem situation appear in the diagram. Once students see the connection, they are on their way to transferring their understanding from the physical model to the visual model.

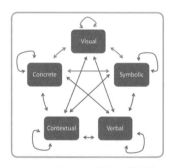

Source: Lesh, Post, & Behr (1987).

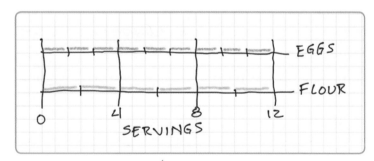

CLOSING REFLECTION: CUISENAIRE RODS

How do I use Cuisenaire Rods in my classroom now? What concepts do I use them to teach?

_____

_____

_____

_____

_____

_____

_____

_____

_____

_____

What new ways have I found to use Cuisenaire Rods to better support student understanding?

_____

_____

_____

_____

_____

_____

_____

_____

_____

_____

_____

_____

What are my goals to make Cuisenaire Rods a more regular part of my instruction?

_____

_____

_____

_____

_____

_____

_____

_____

_____

_____

_____

_____

Chapter 4

Unit Squares and Cubes

UNDERSTANDING UNIT SQUARES AND CUBES

This chapter includes activities with both unit squares (typically small squares) and unit cubes. Unit squares are used in the primary grades in many of the same ways as counters. They are small square units, often 1 inch per side, and this gives them the added advantage of representing **area** easily. In the intermediate and middle grades, unit squares are typically used to explore two-dimensional geometry and measurement. Unit squares are available in a variety of colors and materials, including wood, hard plastic, and foam.

Unit cubes are small cubes (often 1 centimeter or 1 inch per edge) that can be used for three-dimensional geometry and measurement exploration. While some unit cubes are available as linking cubes, the buttons and snaps required to link the cubes can disrupt explorations of **volume**. Unit cubes are available in a variety of colors and materials, including wood, hard plastic, and foam.

Unit squares and cubes are particularly effective for teaching these topics:

- Fractions of a set
- Ratios (part:part and part:whole)
- Representing data
- Descriptive statistics (e.g., mean, median, and mode)
- Area
- Volume

Introducing Unit Squares to Students

Use the *Notice and Wonder Thinking Routine* (described in the introductory chapter) to introduce unit squares or cubes to your students. Students may notice the square shape, the congruent sides, the **right angles**, or the fact that the shapes tessellate. Students may wonder how tall a tower they can build or how to use the squares or cubes to create letters or other familiar shapes.

Key Ideas With Unit Squares and Cubes

- Unit squares and cubes are typically made in a variety of colors. Color can be useful for highlighting aspects of a pattern or bringing emphasis to one part of a representation. At other times, students will need to work without regard to color. It is important to discuss this with students so they understand how to decide when color is important.

- When working with data representations, students will often use digital tools for creating charts or graphs and identifying descriptive statistics. Deliberate practice with hands-on tools and small data sets provides insight into what happens "behind the curtain" of digital tools. Encourage students to create representations by hand (with manipulatives or on grid paper) to see the impact of an outlier on each measure of central tendency. This will help make the output of digital tools make more sense.

- Filling shapes with unit cubes is a different experience than filling containers with liquid or liquid-like material (e.g., water or dry fill like sand). This chapter emphasizes the formulas for volume of shapes easily filled by packing with cubes. Chapter 6 includes activities looking at the volume of less packable shapes such as cylinders, cones, and pyramids.

Things to Consider About Unit Squares and Cubes

- In the United States, most unit squares are squares, 1 inch on each side. If you mix squares or cubes from multiple sources, be sure they have the same side length.

- You can use unit squares to iterate length. It is important to help students recognize that they are using only one side of the square to represent length. The rest of the square functions as a "handle" in this context.

- Unit squares can help students establish a benchmark understanding of 1 square inch of area or 100 square inches of area as they use them repeatedly.

- Unit cubes can be used to represent volume by building solid figures or packing hollow shapes.

Alternatives to Commercial Unit Squares and Cubes

Unit bathroom squares from the hardware store or Habitat for Humanity ReStores make great sturdy substitutes for unit squares. Just be sure all your squares really are the same size. It is also easy to cut unit squares from a die-cut machine or to cut apart 1-inch grid paper to make unit squares.

Cubes can be cut from wood or foam, but this is not an easy way to make a large quantity of unit cubes. Some teachers use sugar cubes, but must be careful to clean up well or risk attracting ants and other bugs.

Working With Virtual Unit Squares

Virtual unit squares have the same functionality as physical unit squares. There is an endless supply and no real risk around resizing the squares as long as all the squares resize the same way.

Virtual unit cubes should have a snapping feature to make it easy to align them. They are often pictured isometrically so that the user can see three **faces** and clearly identify the cube as a three-dimensional object. This can take some getting used to if students are not familiar with this representation.

It is always important to consider how much annotation students can do in the workspace as this is more efficient than annotating a screenshot. It is also helpful if the squares can be grouped and moved together rather than handling them one by one.

Materials

- Unit cubes (enough to fill the boxes)
- Small boxes (sized to fill with the cubes)

Organization (physical)

- **Getting Started:** Distribute the unit cubes and a box or two to each group of students.
- **Winding Down:** Return the unit cubes to their container and stack the boxes for easy storage.

Mathematical Purpose

This activity models volume from the perspective of packing: How many unit cubes will fit into a given box? How much space is within this container? It lays a foundation for calculating volume by building shapes in Activity 4.2.

Manipulative Illustrated

- Plastic centimeter cubes

Steps

1. Distribute small boxes and centimeter cubes to each group of students. Ask students to predict how many cubes will fill their box. Have students write down their estimates and then place five cubes in the box. They can use this information to refine their estimates, including a note about why they made any change they made.

2. Ask students to fill the box with cubes and count how many fill the box with no overlaps and no gaps between cubes. This is most effective if the boxes fit the cubes closely. Look out for students who pour a handful of cubes in the box rather than packing it closely.

3. Because volume is the amount of space something occupies, it is measured in three-dimensional terms. Discuss the idea of a cubic centimeter (or cubic inch, if that is the block size in use) and why this is a measure of volume—it has height, width, and depth. The small cubes are 1 cm on each side or 1 cm³ in volume. The count of cubes is an approximation of the volume of the small box. Depending on how tightly the cubes fit the box, the estimation is closer or further from the actual volume.

4. Discuss the idea of volume with students, using ideas and questions such as these:

   - *Volume is the amount of space something occupies or the capacity of a container. How closely does your cube count match the actual volume or capacity of the box? Where does the error in your estimation come from?*

   - *How would your results be different if you could fill the box with water and then measure the volume of the water? Remember, 1 cubic centimeter is the same as 1 milliliter of water.*

   - *How can you use your estimates to compare the volume of the different boxes we filled?*

Why This Manipulative?

Unit cubes are the basic unit for volume measurement. This activity provides students an opportunity to begin exploring the concept of volume as filling space before they explore the formulae we use for calculating volume for rectangular **prisms**.

Developing Understanding

When students begin their exploration of volume with the formula, they often miss the broader idea of filling space. This principle of filling space is a key idea for both mathematics and science and an essential beginning for reasoning about volume. Students begin with volume of a rectangular prism (explored more fully in Activity 4.2) and will expand these principles to other shapes as they work through measurement in the middle grades.

Featured Connection

Use the Create a Word Problem strategy to encourage students to think about contexts for volume as they relate their concrete experience to everyday life. Invite students to identify situations where they would need to fill boxes (or other containers) to identify relevant contexts for using volume.

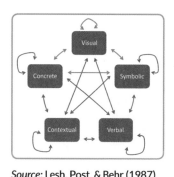

Source: Lesh, Post, & Behr (1987).

Notes

_____

_____

_____

_____

_____

_____

_____

_____

_____

_____

Materials

- Unit cubes, approximately 100 per student or per pair
- Three dice
- Recording sheet (one for each student)

Organization (physical)

- **Getting Started:** Distribute the unit cubes.
- **Winding Down:** Repackage the cubes to return to storage.

Mathematical Purpose

This activity builds understanding of the volume formula as students construct rectangular prisms from unit cubes and use multiplication to count the cubes efficiently. Balanced with the previous activity on volume as packing, students develop a core understanding of what volume is and how it can be calculated.

Activity 4.2 Resources

- *Calculating Volume for Rectangular Prisms* Recording Sheet

 To access resource visit resources.corwin.com/ MasteringMathManips/ 4–8

Manipulative Illustrated

- Foam cubes

Steps

1. Activity 4.1 focused on volume from the perspective of filling containers. While this is a useful key concept for volume, it does not support understanding the basic formula for volume of a rectangular prism. This activity is designed to help students understand the relationship between the concept and the formula.

2. Distribute unit cubes and ask students to build a 3×5 array of cubes. Discuss the models using these questions:

   - *How many cubes are included in the array? How do you know?*

   - *What if students build a structure with 3 rows of this size? How many cubes will be included?*

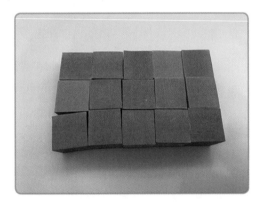

3. Encourage students to use their equal groups thinking to respond to this series of questions. The first structure is an array, but then 3 layers become 3 groups of that size (15 cubes each). Encourage students to include units in their volume conversations as well. One layer is 15 cubes, and 3 layers is 45 cubes. The block with dimensions $3 \times 3 \times 5$ has a volume of 45 cubes or 45 cubic units.

4. Distribute three dice to each student or group of students. Have students roll the dice to determine the dimensions of the next rectangular prism they build. Students should record their dimensions and volume calculations on the recording sheet.

5. After students have built and found the volume for several prisms, ask them to look for patterns in the data they see on their recording sheet. Guide their discussion with questions like these:

    *   *How did you figure out the total number of blocks in a given structure? Share with your classmates to find other strategies you might use.*

    *   *Roll the dice to define a prism. How many cubes will you need for the first layer? How do you know?*

    *   *Is there more than one prism you can build from a single roll? Will all prisms built from a single roll have the same volume?*

    *   *How can you predict the number of cubes you will need to build the entire prism?*

Support students to recognize that the volume of a rectangular prism is the product of the three dimensions or the number of cubes in the first layer times the number of layers.

Why This Manipulative?

Unit cubes are the basic unit for volume measurement. This activity supports students to understand the formula for volume of a rectangular prism.

Developing Understanding

This exercise supports students to begin thinking about multiplication in three dimensions, with three factors. While multiplication can involve three factors, most experiences are with two factors (number of groups × group size or length × width), and moving to three factors in the context of volume is a significant leap for many learners.

It is important to help students see volume not only as the product of the three dimensions but also as the area of the base (the first layer) multiplied by the height (the number of layers). While the first layer of a prism actually has volume, this general principle will help when students learn about the volume of cylinders and non-rectangular prisms.

Featured Connection

This activity uses the Name Your Model strategy to help students connect their physical representations of volume to the more abstract representations of tables and charts.

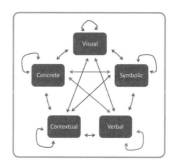

Source: Lesh, Post, & Behr (1987).

Materials

- Square tiles, in at least two colors (e.g., blue and red)

Organization (physical)

- **Getting Started:** Distribute 12 blue tiles and 12 red tiles to each student.
- **Winding Down:** Gather the tiles and return them to their storage containers.

Mathematical Purpose

In this activity, students use square tiles to represent ratios, both part:part and part:whole. Understanding focuses on recognizing each kind of ratio in a given situation.

Manipulative Illustrated

- Foam square tiles

Steps

1. Distribute tiles to students and ask them to build the following groups of tiles: one set with 2 red tiles and 1 blue tile; one set with 6 red tiles and 3 blue tiles; and one set with 4 red tiles and 2 blue tiles. Ask students to notice and wonder about the three collections, focusing on what is the same in each and what is different. Support students to recognize that there are always twice as many red tiles as blue tiles, no matter how large or small the collection is.

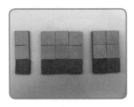

2. Ask students to predict how many red tiles there would be for various numbers of blue tiles in collections larger than they can build. Guide the discussion with the following questions, including more examples as needed:

   - *If there are 10 blue tiles, how many red tiles will there be? How do you know?*

   - *If there are 75 blue tiles, how many red tiles will there be? How do you know?*

   - *What pattern helps you predict the number of red tiles based on the number of blue tiles (or the reverse)?*

   Use the discussion to introduce the notation of a 2:1 ratio of red:blue tiles and to reinforce the meaning that there are always twice as many red tiles as blue tiles or two red tiles for every one blue tile.

3. Re-sort the tiles into their two color piles and ask students to create a collection of tiles where the ratio of red:blue tiles is 3:1. Discuss the models students built, looking at the size of each collection, the number of tiles of each color, and the relationship between the number of tiles of each color. Use these questions to guide the discussion:

   » *How many tiles of each color are in your collection? How does this reflect the ratio given in the task?*

   » *How can you arrange your tiles to show the 3:1 ratio most clearly?*

4. As students develop confidence in building ratios, introduce ratios from their own experience and have students use counters to model these ratios.

Why This Manipulative?

Studying fractions leads to an emphasis on part:whole ratios—that's what fractions are, at least in the elementary grades. This use of counters in a set context to create part:part ratios is designed to broaden student experience and see that we also think about the relationship between parts within a set.

Developing Understanding

This activity models part:part ratios. As students develop understanding of part:part ratios, this can be extended in at least two ways.

1. Introduce part:whole ratios as suggested by your standards. The activity structure is the same, but the ratios will describe the relationship between one part and the total quantity. With counters, this is a set model for fractions. You might ask a question like this for the model built in Step 3:

   • *What is the relationship between the total number of tiles and the number of blue tiles? How does this relationship appear in the 3:1 ratio we started with?*

2. Introduce ratios with more than two parts. For example, create a set of counters with a color ratio of 2:1:1 for red:blue:yellow counters.

If the models are arranged linearly, they can begin to represent tape diagrams.

Featured Connection

Use the Make a Sketch strategy to make the connection between physical models of ratios and tape diagram visual representations.

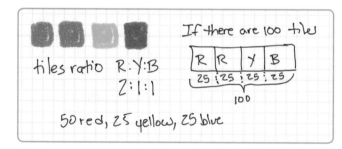

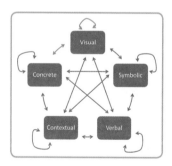

Source: Lesh, Post, & Behr (1987).

Materials

- Virtual or concrete square tiles or unit cubes
- Centimeter grid paper

Organization (virtual)

- **Getting Started:** Ensure students can access and use the virtual tool. Review annotation tools, the process for taking screenshots, and other important supports.
- **Winding Down:** Use screenshots to save student work.

Mathematical Purpose

Building from an understanding of multiplication as area, students create **rectangles** to find the factor pairs of a given number. Students use their results to identify both prime and composite numbers.

Activity 4.4 Resources

- Centimeter grid paper

Manipulative Illustrated

- Virtual Color Tiles from GeoGebra: www.geogebra.org/m/NPDu3rCm#material/adgkzVZs

Steps

1. Ask each student (or pair) to take 12 cubes and make all the rectangles they can with those cubes. Encourage students to organize their list of dimensions to be sure they have all the possible combinations. Provide time and support to be sure all students have found all the possible rectangles. Use questions such as these to help students:

   » *Show me your list of rectangles you have built so far. How do you know each rectangle includes 12 cubes?*

   » *Do you see any patterns in the dimensions of the rectangles you have built? If so, what pattern(s) do you see? If not, how could you arrange your list to make it easier to see any patterns?*

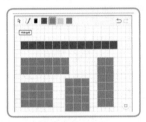

2. As students work through this activity, discuss the questions that arise around the commutative property: Is a 3×4 rectangle the same as a 4×3 rectangle? Support students to think about this question in context using questions like these:

   - *If you are tiling a floor and need to know how many tiles you need, are the two situations the same?*

   - *When might you have a situation with equal groups instead of area? Then are the two multiplication sentences the same? For example, 3 groups of 4 candies each is not the same as 4 groups of 3 candies if there are 4 people to share the candy! In both cases, we need 12 pieces of candy—that part is the same.*

   For this activity, we are focused on the total number, not how they are arranged, so we will consider 3×4 and 4×3 as the same factor pair.

   (Note: only the horizontal 1×12 arrangement appears here because this virtual model does not provide space for a vertical 1×12 rectangle.)

3. Once students understand the task, ask students to build all the rectangles for a wide range of values. Both 24 and 60 are options with many possible factor pairs. This activity can be used to discuss prime or composite numbers and to discuss why we call numbers like 4, 9, 16, 25, and 36 square numbers.

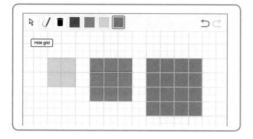

Why This Manipulative?

This activity is equally effective with unit squares or unit cubes. Both tools create area models easily and are available in sufficient quantities for working with larger numbers or creating multiple rectangles for the same number.

Developing Understanding

One way to understand factors is to recognize them as the dimensions of rectangles that can be built from a given number of cubes. This is also an opportunity to develop skills in making organized lists so students are sure they have tracked all the possible combinations. This activity is particularly helpful for distinguishing prime and composite numbers. Prime numbers will create only one rectangle, of dimensions $1 \times n$. Composite numbers will create multiple rectangles with a variety of factor pairs. Square numbers are readily identified as having one pair where both factors are the same; the model in this case is a square shape, hence identifying x^2 as x squared.

Featured Connection

Students can use the Make a Sketch strategy, along with Name Your Model, to connect the physical representations they build to visual and abstract notations. This activity lends itself to sketching on grid paper and writing an expression (or two) to name each model. This is a situation where virtual manipulatives can be particularly helpful if students create all the possible images on one screen and label them.

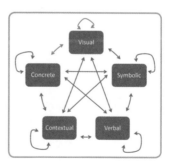 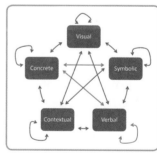

Source: Lesh, Post, & Behr (1987).

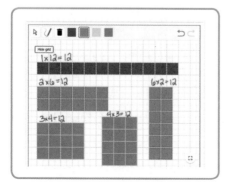 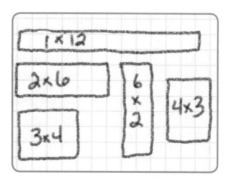

Materials

- Unit cubes
- Adding machine tape (or similar long strips of paper)
- Tape
- Recording sheet (one for each student)

Organization (physical)

- **Getting Started:** Distribute cubes, paper strips, and tape to each group of students.
- **Winding Down:** Return cubes and tape to homes, and discard trash.

Mathematical Purpose

In this activity, students explore the range of rectangles they can create with a constant **perimeter**. A paper strip is used to hold the perimeter constant, and students record the dimensions and the area of each rectangle created. Both this activity and Activity 4.6 build off the same idea as the factor pairs exploration in Activity 4.4. These activities extend that thinking beyond factor pairs to noticing patterns about area and perimeter of rectangles.

Steps

1. Ask students to build a 3 × 4 rectangle with foam cubes and count or calculate the perimeter (14). Tape a piece of adding machine tape firmly around the cubes so its length reflects the perimeter of 14. It is better not to crease the corners since they will be at different places for different models. The paper ring should gently hold the cubes together when the figure is lifted off the table.

2. Have students pop the cubes out and fill the paper ring with other cubes, creating other rectangles with a perimeter of 14. Watch the video to see this process in action. Use the recording sheet to track all the rectangles built with a perimeter of 14.

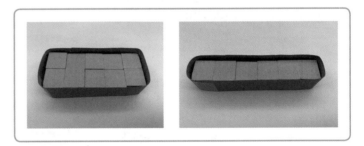

3. Have students choose an even value between 20 and 40. Different students or pairs should select different values. Build a rectangle with that perimeter to create an appropriate length paper band. Build and record all the possible rectangles with that perimeter.

4. Support students to explore their data using questions like these:

   » *What shape gives the maximum area for a given perimeter? How do you know?*

   » *What shape gives the minimum area? Why do you think this?*

   » *Is it possible for a rectangle to have an odd perimeter? Why or why not?*

Why This Manipulative?

Foam cubes of this size are easy to handle and work well with the strips of paper. Flat square tiles can also be used but the strip of paper doesn't hold as well. As with many activities in this chapter, this one builds on the direct connection between unit squares (in this case the upper surface of unit cubes) and area or perimeter.

Developing Understanding

Reinforce with students that area is about the flat tops of the cubes, not the full volume of the cubes. The data exploration questions in Step 4 are designed to help students reason about the relationship between area and perimeter. Depending on how students have organized their information, it may help to have them revise their charts so that the areas are listed in increasing or decreasing order so they can see the pattern.

Featured Connection

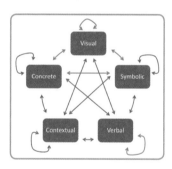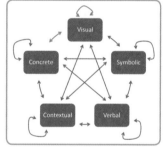

Source: Lesh, Post, & Behr (1987).

Use the Create a Diagram strategy to help students organize their information to see patterns in the values. The recording sheet provides a structure for the chart; students can also use grid paper with the Make a Sketch strategy to see the shapes of the various rectangles more clearly than the dimensions on the chart may communicate.

Perimeter	Length	Width	Area	Sketch
14	3	4	12	
14	2	5	10	
14	1	6	6	

Activity 4.5 Resources

- *Exploring a Constant Perimeter* Recording Sheet
- *Exploring a Constant Perimeter* Activity Video

online resources ⌖ To access resources visit resources.corwin.com/ MasteringMathManips/ 4–8

Manipulative Illustrated

- Foam unit cubes

Materials

- One-inch foam cubes
- Recording sheet (one for each student)

Organization (physical)

- **Getting Started:** Distribute 24 cubes to each student or pair.
- **Winding Down:** Collect the cubes and return them to their home.

Mathematical Purpose

In this activity, students use foam cubes to explore the rectangles that can be made with a constant area. The recording sheet allows them to document the dimensions and perimeter of each shape.

Activity 4.6 Resources

- *Exploring a Constant Area Recording Sheet*

 To access resource visit resources.corwin.com/ MasteringMathManips/ 4–8

Manipulative Illustrated

- Foam unit cubes

Steps

1. Ask students to use their 24 cubes to build a rectangle. Record the dimensions of the rectangle on the recording sheet along with the area and perimeter. The teacher can determine if everyone should build the same rectangle for this initial experience.

2. Talk with the class about the idea of constant area to be sure everyone understands that using 24 cubes will give a constant area (the top of the structure) of 24 square units.

3. Have students create all possible rectangles with an area of 24 square units. Students should use the recording sheet to track information about their models and may wish to sketch their rectangles on grid paper.

4. Support students to explore their data using questions like these:

   - *How do you know you have all possible rectangles with an area of 24 square units?*

   - *What kind of rectangle gives the largest perimeter? Why do you think this happens?*

   - *Which gives the smallest perimeter? Why are these perimeters smaller?*

   - *What are examples of situations in everyday life where this information could be helpful?*

Why This Manipulative?

Foam cubes of this size are easy to handle and work well with the strips of paper. Flat square tiles or plastic cubes can also be used, but the strip of paper doesn't hold as well. As with many activities in this chapter, this one builds on the direct connection between unit squares (in this case the upper surface of unit cubes) and area or perimeter.

Developing Understanding

This exploration is closely related to the constant perimeter exploration in Activity 4.5. This pair of experiences helps students understand the relationship between area and perimeter, a relationship important when maximizing use of fencing or packing contexts.

Featured Connection

Use the Create a Diagram strategy to help students organize their information to see patterns in the values. The recording sheet provides a structure for the chart; students can also use grid paper with the Make a Sketch strategy to see the shapes of the various rectangles more clearly than the dimensions on the chart may communicate.

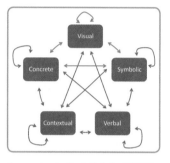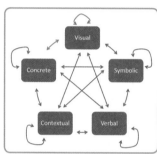

Source: Lesh, Post, & Behr (1987).

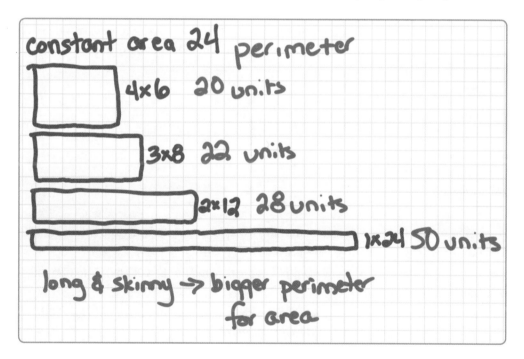

constant area 24 perimeter

4x6 20 units

3x8 22 units

2x12 28 units

1x24 50 units

long & skinny → bigger perimeter for area

Materials

- Virtual or concrete unit squares or cubes in assorted colors
- Activity sheet (one for each student)

Organization (virtual)

- **Getting Started:** Ensure students can access and use the virtual tool. Review annotation tools, the process for taking screenshots, and other important supports.
- **Winding Down:** Use screenshots to save student work.

Mathematical Purpose

In this activity, students extend a pattern and work to predict the next terms in the pattern.

Activity 4.7 Resources

- *Visual Pattern Options* Activity Sheet

 To access resource visit resources.corwin.com/ MasteringMathManips/ 4–8

Manipulative Illustrated

- Virtual Counters from Toy Theater: https://toytheater.com/ color-counters/

Steps

1. Build the first three steps of the plus pattern shown on the activity sheet. Ask students to use the *Notice and Wonder Thinking Routine* to look at the images and record the mathematical ideas they notice and wonder about.

2. Distribute materials and ask students to re-create the first three steps of the pattern. Does this provide additional insight into their *Notice and Wonder* list?

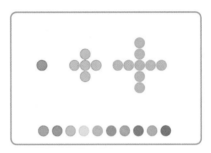

3. Ask students to build the next few terms of the pattern. Challenge them to predict how many pieces they will need for the next term and count that number out before building.

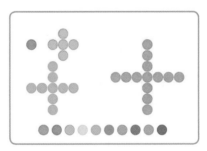

4. Once students have a feel for the pattern, discuss extending the pattern using questions like these:

   - *How many pieces are required for the 10th term? How do you know?*

   - *How many pieces are required for the 25th term? The 100th term? How do you know?*

   - *How can you predict the number of pieces when you can't build the figure? What gives you confidence in your thinking? Can you test your modeling on the figures you can build?*

These experiences challenge students to make predictions for terms they cannot readily build and look for more powerful mathematical descriptions of the patterns they see.

5. Ask students to make a mathematical description of their prediction process. The notation and language used will depend on the age of and learning goals for the students.

Why This Manipulative?

Any counters can be used for this activity. It is important for students to have access to a variety of colors or styles to highlight different features of the pattern that are important to them. The virtual counters used here have a good array of color for highlighting various features of the pattern, but the workspace is tight, so the terms cannot be arranged in a linear sequence.

Developing Understanding

This activity is easily scaled depending on the complexity of the pattern chosen and the expectations teachers set about how students describe their findings. This activity can be relatively informal and descriptive or quite algebraic; this is teacher's choice based on student readiness and standards to be met. The three patterns proposed on the activity sheet provide a range of options for teachers to begin. These patterns can be easily modified (how many arms does the plus have? Is the increase in length the same for each arm?) to adapt the experience to suit students' learning needs.

Notice how students make their prediction for the number of pieces in a given term. Do they predict based on the previous term (each model requires 4 more cubes) or based on the term number (this model needs 4 times the term number plus one more for the middle)? The latter strategy is a more powerful approach because any term can be created without having to create the previous terms.

Featured Connection

Use the Name Your Model strategy to help students use abstract language and notation to describe the patterns they see and the prediction strategy they develop. Challenge students to identify each part of their model name in the physical representations they have created. They can use color in their images to help highlight key components.

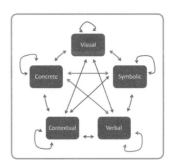

Source: Lesh, Post, & Behr (1987).

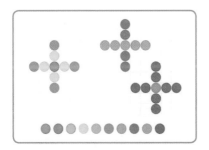

Materials

- Unit cubes, index cards, or sticky notes for labeling data
- Grid paper
- Activity sheet (one for each student)

Organization (physical)

- **Getting Started:** Distribute a bag of cubes to each pair of students.
- **Winding Down:** Rebag and collect the cubes.

Mathematical Purpose

This activity models creating a **line plot** from a data set. Students sketch their line plot to create the more traditional visual form of this graph.

Activity 4.8 Resources

- *Line Plot Measurement Data* Activity Sheet

 To access resource visit resources.corwin.com/ MasteringMathManips/ 4-8

Manipulative Illustrated

- Centimeter cubes

Steps

1. This activity requires a set of data. Ideally, the class will work through this activity with personally relevant data. The sample data set provided in the activity sheet shows the results from rolling a die 25 times.

2. Write and say the phrase *line plot* and ask students what the term means to them. Discuss their thinking, focusing on the idea that this is a plot, a graph of data, and that the data are presented in a linear form, building from a number line.

3. Distribute the data students will use for their line plot. The accompanying images use the data set from the activity sheet. Have students use the blank table to organize the data in numerical order and tally the number of data points at each value.

25 Rolls of a die

2, 5, 6, 4, 1, 4, 3, 6, 1, 5, 1, 6, 4, 6, 3, 3, 2, 3, 2, 2, 5, 5, 6, 6, 3

Value	Frequency	
1	III	3
2	IIII	4
3	IIHI	5
4	II	2
5	IIII	4
6	HTI	6

Ask students to use a sticky note to create a label for each possible data value, even if there are no data points for a value. Students should also count cubes to represent the number of times each value occurs.

4. Put the sticky notes in numerical order across the desk. Align the cubes vertically above the corresponding data point.

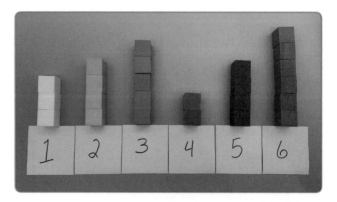

5. Have the students draw a number line on grid paper and represent the data points appropriately along the number line. Discuss the formatting of the sketch using questions and comments like these:

- *What values are important on your base number line? How do you know?*

- *How should these values be spaced? Do we have any gaps in our data set? How can we represent those gaps?*

- *How are we going to show the number of cases at each value? What can we do to make sure our line plot shows the data fairly?*

6. Have students place a mark above the data point to represent each occurrence of that event. This is a line plot.

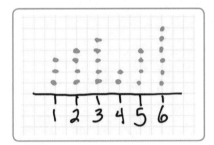

Why This Manipulative?

Any counter is appropriate for this activity. By working with physical materials, students experience the process of creating a line plot in a more tangible way. Because graphing can be a challenging skill for students, this approach is particularly forgiving. If a student makes a mistake with the cubes and labels, it is easy to correct before sketching the result.

Developing Understanding

Students must have a solid understanding of number lines to complete this activity successfully. They must be able to order their data values and track both the values themselves and their frequencies. Providing charts with more structure or marked number lines can support students who are still developing these skills.

Featured Connection

This activity uses the Make a Sketch strategy in Steps 5 and 6 to have students create a visual line plot from their physical model. Because students have built the model with blocks, they can use their physical model to help position the number line on the page so there is room for all the dots. They can check one representation against the other to see that there is the same number of dots as blocks. The connection between concrete and visual gives students confidence in the accuracy of their representation.

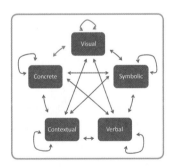

Source: Lesh, Post, & Behr (1987).

MODELING EXPONENTS (SQUARES AND CUBES)

| 3 | 4 | 5 | 6 | 7 | 8+ |

Materials

- Unit cubes

Organization (physical)

- **Getting Started:** Distribute 125 unit cubes per student or per small group.
- **Winding Down:** Return cubes to their home base.

Mathematical Purpose

In this activity, students explore the relationship between multiplication and exponentiation as they look at square and cube numbers. Students also have the opportunity to understand the language of squares and cubes as they examine the visual models created.

Manipulative Illustrated

- Centimeter unit cubes

Steps

1. Ask students to use their cubes to build the first few square numbers (4, 9, 16, etc.). Discuss the connection between multiplication, area, and the term *"square"* numbers using questions like these:

   » *What do you notice about the shapes of these figures?*

   » *How does the square shape relate to the factors of the number?*

   » *Why might we call these numbers "squares" or "perfect squares"?*

   Use both notations to describe the figures: 3×3 and 3^2.

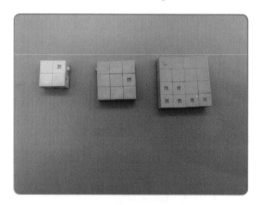

2. Ask students to extend their flat two-dimensional shapes (one row of materials high) to be three-dimensional shapes—as tall as they are long and wide.

3. Ask students to think about the term *cube* and how cubes relate to squares. Encourage them to use their knowledge of geometry and measurement to make the connection between two- and three-dimensional figures. Encourage students to sketch their figures on grid paper and label the images with both multiplication and exponential notation.

4. Discuss their models using questions such as these:

> *How many cubes are required to build this three-dimensional structure?*

> *How might you write an expression to describe your figure? Where is each element of the expression in your physical model?*

> *What do the expressions have in common?*

Why This Manipulative?

Unit cubes, as the name suggests, embody the fundamental relationship between a square and a cube. They are assumed to have a side length of 1, often 1 centimeter or 1 inch. By creating "flat" figures and then extending them to three dimensions of equal size, students are encouraged to see this connection in action. As is typical in many manipulative constructions, we assume an object 1 layer deep is actually flat (two-dimensional) even though, in reality, it has **height** as well.

Developing Understanding

This activity builds connections between physical shapes in two and three dimensions with the multiplication and **exponent** relationships these shapes illustrate. By seeing all three representations together, students build a stronger mental image of the meaning of exponents and the relationship between exponents and multiplication, even back to addition.

Repeated addition is evident in the square shapes: $3 + 3 + 3$ is the same as 3×3 or 3^2. Repeated multiplication extends in the cube shape as that 3×3 square is extended up 3 rows in height: $3 \times 3 \times 3$ or 3^3.

Featured Connection

This activity uses the Caption Your Picture strategy to connect physical, visual, and abstract representations of the mathematics. This supports students to understand the meaning behind the notations and use them with experience and understanding rather than as isolated, sometimes random, symbols.

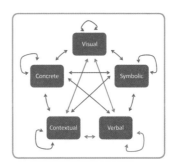

Source: Lesh, Post, & Behr (1987).

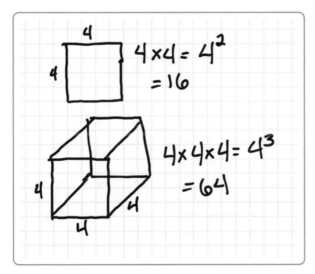

Materials

- Unit squares or cubes
- Activity sheet (one for each student)

Organization (physical)

- **Getting Started:** Distribute a bag of squares or cubes to each group of students.
- **Winding Down:** Rebag and collect the squares or cubes.

Mathematical Purpose

In this activity, students represent a data set and identify the median and mode of the data.

Activity 4.10 Resources

- *Median and Mode Data* Activity Sheet

 To access resource visit resources.corwin.com/ MasteringMathManips/ 4–8

Manipulative Illustrated

- Unit cubes

Steps

1. Ideally, the students will work through this activity with data about themselves. You might ask them how many siblings they have or how much time they spend doing a particular activity each day (activities might include traveling to school, playing games, exercising, practicing a sport or hobby, homework, reading, supervising siblings, and so on). The sample data set shows the number of siblings in a class of 30 students.

2. Share the data with students (either their own data or the sample set) and ask students to create a line plot of the data using unit cubes. See Activity 4.8 for more specific instructions, if needed.

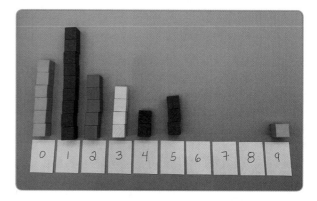

3. Talk with students about summarizing the data. Use questions like these to guide the discussion:

   - *If you had to tell us about the number of siblings each person in our class has, what value would you use, and why?*

   - *What patterns do you see or hear in the suggestions we made?*

   - *Can we talk about the most common number of siblings? What might that tell us?*

   - *Is there a way to find the value "in the middle" of these data? How might you do that?*

   Discuss the options students present and build connections to the three measures of central tendency typically used: **mean**, **median**, and **mode**. Activity 4.11 focuses on mean while this activity emphasizes median and mode. As much as possible, use the students' thinking to develop definitions of median (the value in the middle) and mode (the most common value).

4. Have students identify the mode of their data set. Depending on the data in use, there might be more than one mode, an interesting point for discussion.

5. Ask students to think about how they can identify the median of their data set. Discuss the importance of having written data in order before counting to find the middle position. The data set provided has an even number of values, and the two "middle" data points (items 15 and 16 in the list) are the final entry with value 1 and the first entry with value 2. This requires students to find the average of the two middle data points to find the median. It is also important to discuss counting strategies for reliably finding the middle of the data set, both in list format and in line plot format. It is also important to discuss the meaning of a median of 1.5 siblings per family.

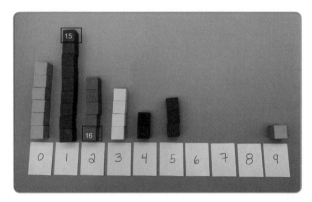

6. Return to the discussion in Step 3 to talk about the relative advantages and disadvantages of median and mode as descriptors of data sets in general and the specific data set in use. Guide the discussion with questions like these:

   » *If you summarize the data with the mode, 1, how will you explain what that means? Whose families does it describe well, and whose families are not described well by this value?*

   » *If you summarize the data with the median, how will you explain what it means? Whose families does it describe well, and whose families are not described well by this value?*

Why This Manipulative?

This activity can be done with any sort of counter. It is helpful for students to work by hand with modest data sets in order to see what is happening when computers calculate measures of central tendency for a data set. Activities like this can be done with virtual manipulatives as long as appropriate annotation tools are available.

Developing Understanding

As students develop understanding of central tendency, work with data sets that include outliers. This allows students to see how changing a single value to an outlier impacts the different measures of central tendency. It is also interesting to look at data sets with different distributions to see how this impacts measures of central tendency.

Featured Connection

Use the Caption Your Picture strategy to support students connecting their physical representations of the data with graphic and numeric summaries. Students can draw a line plot representing their data set and then numerically summarize the data with median and mode values.

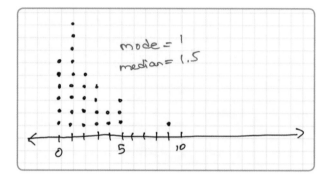

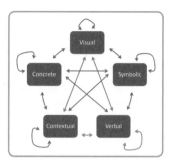

Source: Lesh, Post, & Behr (1987).

Notes

_____

_____

_____

_____

_____

_____

_____

_____

_____

_____

_____

_____

_____

Notes

Materials

- Unit cubes, a handful per student
- Activity sheet (one for each student)

Organization (physical)

- **Getting Started:** Distribute a bag of squares or cubes to each group of students.
- **Winding Down:** Rebag and collect the squares or cubes.

Mathematical Purpose

Students understand what the mean represents (a leveling out of quantity across a group) and where the formula for calculating mean (add them all up and divide by the number of items) comes from.

Activity 4.11 Resources

- *Median and Mode Data* Activity Sheet

 To access resource visit resources.corwin.com/ MasteringMathManips/ 4–8

Manipulative Illustrated

- unit cubes

Steps

1. As with Activity 4.10, it is helpful to work with data generated by and about the students in the class. Each student represents a data point in the data set and should take the number of cubes for that data point. If you are using the sample sibling data provided, students will hold anywhere from 0 cubes (an only child) to 9 cubes, representing the largest family in the sample.

2. Ask students to share what they know about the idea of "average" or a mean. Remind students that there are three measures of central tendency that can describe a typical value. Today's lesson is about calculating the mean value. If everyone had the same number of cubes right now, for the data set at hand, how many cubes would each person have?

3. In order to answer the question, circle around the room and collect all the cubes in an empty cup or bucket. What do the cubes represent? (They represent all the siblings of all the children in the class.)

4. Pass the container around the room—each student takes one cube each time the container passes by. Continue until all the cubes are distributed. Discuss what is happening using questions like these:

   - *How many cubes does each person have? How does this relate to our prediction from Step 2 about distributing the cubes evenly?*

   - *The cubes can't be cut. What can we do mathematically to represent each person having exactly the same number of cubes? [Divide the total number of cubes by the number of data points.]*

   - *Will each person have a whole number of cubes? What does the fractional part of the mean represent in this situation?*

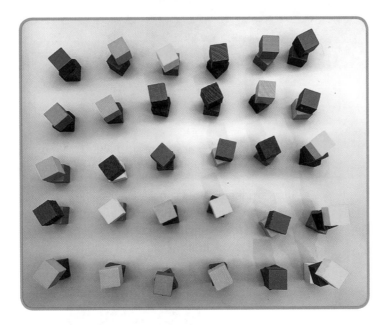

5. Support students to connect this activity and the formula for calculating mean. When we pool all the cubes in the container, we are adding them all up. When we redistribute them evenly, we are dividing by the number of data points in the sample. As the cubes from the sample data are distributed, 27 students will have 2 blocks (representing 2 siblings), and 3 students (shown at the bottom of the right-hand column) will have 3 blocks (representing 3 siblings). What does this mean of 2.1 mean in the context of siblings where a fraction of a sibling does not make sense?

Why This Manipulative?

This activity can be done with any type of counter. The physical materials help students see what is happening when we "add them all up and divide by *n*." If linking cubes are used, it can be easier to redistribute cubes by passing from those with more to those with fewer to get a more even distribution. This approach does not represent the formula as literally but reinforces the idea of mean as a theoretically even distribution.

Developing Understanding

As students develop understanding of central tendency, work with data sets that include outliers. This allows students to see how changing a single value to an outlier impacts the different measures of central tendency. It is also interesting to look at data sets with different distributions to see how this impacts measures of central tendency.

Featured Connection

This activity uses the Build the Equation strategy to connect the abstract formula for calculating the mean with the physical representation of the work.

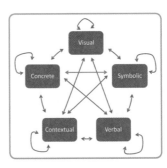

Source: Lesh, Post, & Behr (1987).

Materials

- Virtual or concrete square tiles or cubes

Organization (virtual)

- **Getting Started:** Ensure students can access and use the virtual tool. Review annotation tools, the process for taking screenshots, and other important supports.

- **Winding Down:** Use screenshots to save student work.

Mathematical Purpose

In this activity, students use the idea of area to estimate the **square root** of numbers between **perfect squares**.

Manipulative Illustrated

- Didax Virtual Color Tiles: www.didax.com/apps/color-tiles/

Steps

1. Activity 4.9 used unit squares to build square numbers. This activity extends this thinking to estimate square roots.

2. Show students a 4×4 square. Discuss the vocabulary of squares and square roots so that students are comfortable with the language "four squared is sixteen" and "four is the square root of sixteen." Use multiple examples as required, returning to Activity 4.9 if necessary.

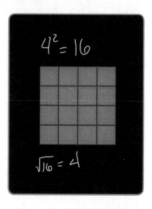

3. Ask students to estimate the square root of 20. Support them using questions like these:

   - *The answer has to be between two whole numbers. What are they? How do you know?*

   - *Is the square root of 20 closer to 4? Closer to 5? In the middle? How do you know?*

4. Have students use their cubes to build a 4×4 square of one color and then add 4 additional squares to the outer row in another color. The full square is 16, and the 4 squares of the second color get to 20, the value at hand. The 4 "extra" squares are the beginning of the extra L of squares that build up from a 4×4 to a 5×5 square. What fraction of that L shape do the 4 squares represent?

5. The full *L* would have 9 squares in it, so the 4 "extra" squares mean 20 is $\frac{4}{9}$ of the way from 16 to 25. The square root of 20 is approximately $4\frac{4}{9}$ or 4.44. The actual square root of 20 is approximately 4.47.

6. Repeat the activity to approximate other square roots.

Why This Manipulative?

This activity builds on the relationship between geometric squares and algebraic squaring.

Developing Understanding

This activity does not give precise values because the denominators are restricted to the odd number interval between the two adjacent squares. This yields a reasonable approximation but not the exact value. Talk with students about the idea of spreading the area of those four "extra" squares around two sides of the 4 × 4 square. What fraction would it be? Counting squares gives an estimate of the fractional part created.

Featured Connection

Use the Caption Your Picture strategy to explain why this is a reasonable approach to estimating square roots. Encourage students to explain the intervals between square numbers and the idea of estimating the partial row this activity uses.

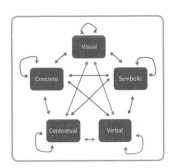

Source: Lesh, Post, & Behr (1987).

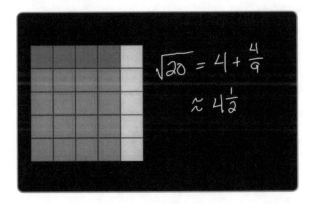

MODELING THE PYTHAGOREAN THEOREM

| 3 | 4 | 5 | 6 | 7 | 8+ |

Materials

- Square tiles (either 1 centimeter or 1 inch)
- Activity sheet (one for each student)

Organization (physical)

- **Getting Started:** Distribute 25 inch tiles or 169 centimeter tiles or cubes (for the 5–12-13 triangle).
- **Winding Down:** Collect the tiles and return them to home storage.

Mathematical Purpose

In this activity, students model the Pythagorean theorem by creating three squares around a **right triangle**. While this is not a formal proof of the theorem, this hands-on experience helps students believe that the theorem works and helps them see what it means to square each side of the triangle.

Activity 4.13 Resources

- *Pythagorean Theorem Models Activity Sheet* (pages with 3–4-5 [scaled for 1-inch tiles] and 5–12-13 [scaled for 1-centimeter tiles] triangles)

 To access resource visit resources.corwin.com/ MasteringMathManips/ 4–8

Steps

1. Distribute unit squares (either 1 inch or 1 centimeter) and the appropriate model from the activity sheet. Write the Pythagorean theorem on the board and show students where the three sides of the triangle are located on their figure. Point out that the **hypotenuse**, side c, is always opposite the right angle in the triangle. Label the sides a, b, and c, making sure students recognize that correctly labeling the hypotenuse as c is essential. Sides a and b are interchangeable labels.

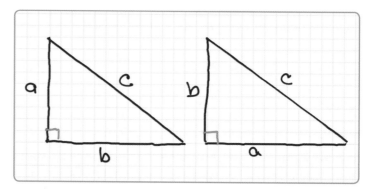

2. Building from other work modeling square numbers (see Activity 4.9), have students use their unit squares to construct the squares adjacent to the legs of the triangle.

3. If the theorem is true, this should be enough unit squares to create a square adjacent to the hypotenuse. Ask students to test this with their materials.

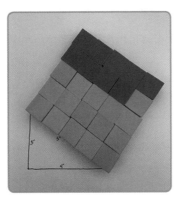

4. Provide additional right triangles for additional modeling.

Why This Manipulative?

This activity builds on the relationship between geometric squares and algebraic squaring to illustrate the Pythagorean theorem.

Developing Understanding

Students gain experience with the meaning of the Pythagorean theorem from this activity. While not a formal proof, seeing the formula work with tangible materials can give students faith in the truth of the formula. This will help as students move to working with right triangles in the coordinate plane calculating slope and distance. (See Activity 7.6 for these applications.) This also gives students practice with identifying the parts of a right triangle, particularly distinguishing the hypotenuse and the legs.

Featured Connection

This activity uses the Build the Equation strategy to connect the abstract formula with the physical model students have created using triangles and squares.

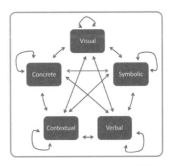

Source: Lesh, Post, & Behr (1987).

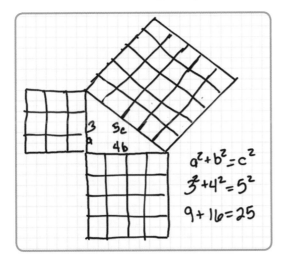

CLOSING REFLECTION: UNIT SQUARES AND CUBES

How do I use unit squares and cubes in my classroom now? What concepts do I use them to teach?

_____

_____

_____

_____

_____

_____

_____

_____

_____

_____

_____

What new ways have I found to use unit squares and cubes to better support student understanding?

_____

_____

_____

_____

_____

_____

_____

_____

_____

_____

_____

What are my goals to make unit squares and cubes a more regular part of my instruction?

_____

_____

_____

_____

_____

_____

_____

_____

_____

_____

_____

Chapter 5

Algebra Tiles and Two-Color Counters

UNDERSTANDING ALGEBRA TOOLS

Algebra tiles, Algeblocks®, and other related tools are manipulatives designed to represent algebraic **expressions** and equations. At a minimum, there are pieces to represent a constant unit (1), a variable (typically x), and the square of the variable (x^2). Depending on the set you have, there may be a second variable and/or third power terms such as x^3 or y^2x. Pieces are typically named by their area (or volume), so the unit square is 1×1 while the variable piece is a rectangle of dimensions 1 by x. The square variable is indeed a square, x by x in dimension. In addition to representing these basic building blocks of expressions and equations, these tools have a way to show the sign of the term, positive or negative, either by color or by position on a work mat.

These manipulatives are proportional in the way that the variable pieces relate to one another. Ideally, they are not proportional in the sense that the variable term is not an even multiple of the unit. If the variable term is "4 and a bit" units long, it's easier to remember that these tools are not base-ten materials or Cuisenaire® Rods, and we have to do math, not just compare pieces, to find the value of x.

If the pieces use color to designate sign, they typically follow the convention that the negative value has a red color. The positive side may be a single color, or it may be a different color for each shape, depending on the manufacturer and set you have.

Two-color counters (small circular disks that are red on one side and typically white or yellow on the other) are included in this chapter because they are often used for initial introductions to integer operations.

Algebra tools are especially useful for teaching these ideas:

- Integer operations
- Writing expressions and equations
- Combining like terms

- Adding and subtracting polynomials
- Multiplying and factoring polynomials
- Solving one-and two-step equations

Introducing Algebra Tools to Students

Students are likely familiar with two-color counters; they may not be familiar with the convention of using the red side to represent a negative value. As you re-introduce them, encourage students to focus their exploration on how their use of the tool might change from representing quantities to now representing both quantity and sign.

As you introduce algebra manipulatives, use the *Notice and Wonder Thinking Routine* (described in the introductory chapter) to encourage students to explore the tools. Students may notice the color(s) and shapes of the pieces as well as how they do or do not fit together. Encourage potential connections to base-ten blocks; these will be useful in understanding how the algebra tools work for multiplication.

Key Ideas With Algebra Tools

- Be careful to use a variety of values for x and y. Some students believe that x must always be less than y if the x-rod is shorter than the y-rod. Using a wide range of values for both helps students see the value as the result of mathematics, not connected to the length of the rod.

- Algebra tools do not lend themselves well to fractional values. Once students understand the process, provide a problem where students will encounter a fraction (e.g., $3x = 10$), and support students to use their reasoning skills and the abstract processes they have used to script their work with manipulatives to find the solution. The process of forming 3 groups (dividing by 3) or multiplying by $\frac{1}{3}$ still works, even though the tool itself will not partition evenly.

- Build on the connections between base-ten materials and algebra tools. Students will find, for example, that their physical or sketched representations of $(x + 1)(x + 3)$ and 11×13 look quite similar. They will also find the same product if they substitute 10 as the value of x. In some ways, students have been doing algebra all along but with the value of x restricted to 10 in the early years.

Things to Consider About Algebra Tools

- Consider how you will name the pieces. Carrying the term *unit* over from work with base-ten blocks is good for the small square or cube that represents ±1. Do you want to label the variable term(s) x (and y) or simply variable 1 and variable 2 so the letter can change depending on the problem students are solving? The non-red side of each piece in an algebra tile set is typically unique to that value or shape so it can also be used to identify pieces.

- Consider how you want to refer to the red side of the pieces. For constants, references to "positive 1" or "negative 1" are appropriate. For variables, the idea of "the opposite of x," treating the negative sign as a toggle switch, is more appropriate given that $-x$ could have a positive value. These references might change as students move from working with integer operations to variables and algebraic expressions.

- Most algebra tools use two colors to represent signs. A few have pieces all the same color and use mats to identify the sign. The activities in this chapter include both varieties of tools so you can see how they behave.

- Algebra tools typically work well for small integer values; fractions are a challenge. Use the tools with friendly numbers and then challenge students to reason about fractions when they are ready.

Alternatives to Commercial Algebra Tools

Two-color counters can easily be made by cutting small squares or circles from paper or craft foam. You can glue two sheets together for the two-color effect. Macaroni or large lima beans can be spray-painted red on one side as another easy substitute.

Homemade algebra tiles can be created fairly easily using a table in a text file or spreadsheet. Create a reasonable dimension for your variable rod (1 by x) and then create two sizes of squares, one for each dimension. The smaller squares are the units, and the larger squares represent x^2. There are also dies for die-cut machines, which will cut algebra tiles.

Working With Virtual Algebra Tools

Virtual algebra tools continue the benefit of an endless supply of all the pieces. As you look at virtual tools, consider whether the pieces flip to change signs or if there are separate pieces for positive and negative. Either one will work, but students will think differently with the two different models. When creating arrays, it is helpful if the pieces snap together. Also consider whether work mats are available and how much annotation students can make directly in their workspace. Screenshots can be annotated, of course, but it is helpful to be able to annotate the workspace directly.

Notes

_____

_____

_____

_____

_____

_____

_____

_____

Notes

Materials

- Small unit cubes (10–15 per student or pair of students)
- Work mat designating positive and negative zones for each student or pair of students

Organization (physical)

- **Getting Started:** Distribute a bag of unit cubes and a work mat to each student.
- **Winding Down:** Return the unit cubes (in the correct count) to the bag and stack the work mats.

Mathematical Purpose

In this activity, students represent integer values and **absolute value** using unit cubes and a work mat. Students are learning to attend both to value and to sign in representing numbers; this is a major change after the exclusively positive world of elementary mathematics. This activity illustrates representing signed numbers and absolute value with single-color counters and a mat.

Activity 5.1 Resources

- Signed Numbers Mat

 To access resource visit resources.corwin.com/ MasteringMathManips/ 4–8

Manipulative Illustrated

Algeblocks (hand2mind)

Steps

1. Ask students to represent a small positive number, +5 for example, with their cubes. Students should easily count the 5 cubes; notice where they place them on the mat. Some students may notice the signed sections of the mat while others will simply drop the counters and wonder why they are doing kindergarten math again.

2. Ask students to change their representation from +5 to −5 on the mat. Discuss what changed using the following questions:

   - *Did the quantity of cubes change? How did you know to keep the quantity the same or change it? Why did you make any change you made?*

   - *Did their location change? How did you know to keep the location the same or change it? Why did you make any change you made?*

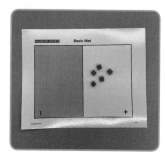 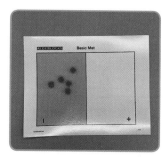

3. In this representation, the location of the cubes changes from the right (positive) side of the mat to the left (negative) side of the mat. The quantity of cubes does not change.

4. Ask students to represent several more positive and negative values, pointing out each time the number of cubes and the position on the mat. Include some positive/negative pairs (like ±5) in your examples.

5. When presenting positive/negative pairs, vary the sign of the starting value and ask students how they can quickly change the sign, or find the opposite, of the value on their mat. Encourage them to realize they do not have to recount but can simply slide the cubes to the other side of the mat.

6. To define and illustrate absolute value, ask students to focus on what is common between the representations of positive/ negative pairs of numbers. It will be helpful to have sketches of several representations available to students. (The "Featured Connection" section gives suggestions for creating sketches.) Support students to see that the number of cubes is constant; only their location changes. Tell students that this quantity

(or distance from zero, when represented on a number line) is the *absolute value*, represented by | | around the number. Absolute value is the quantity or distance without direction, without representing the sign. A handful of cubes represents an absolute value until placed on the mat. Placement on the mat gives a sign or direction to the quantity.

Why This Manipulative?

Positive and negative values can be represented by many tools. Because this activity highlights the connection to absolute value, use a single-color tool with a mat to determine whether the sign is positive or negative. With this manipulative, students see the distinction between quantity (the number of cubes and the absolute value) and sign (location on the mat) clearly. If you do not have Algeblocks, use unit cubes from another source (ideally all the same color) and create signed mats. The physical manipulatives are helpful for working with integer values. Discuss rational numbers (fractional values) when transitioning to a number line representation in the "Featured Connections" section.

Developing Understanding

The transition to signed numbers is a meaningful change for students because it attaches a second attribute (sign or direction) to familiar quantities. The use of familiar unit cubes as counters helps students focus on these two attributes of a signed number (quantity and sign) separately. Quantity is the familiar element, represented by a familiar tool. Sign is the unfamiliar element, represented by location on the mat. As students move to pictorial representations, sign will be represented by direction from 0 on the number line.

Featured Connection

Use the Make a Sketch strategy to connect this physical representation to a number line as a pictorial representation. The physical model of cubes on a mat illustrates quantity and sign as two components of a number. On the number line, quantity is the distance from zero, and sign is the direction.

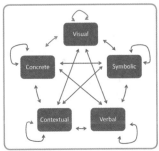

As students create physical models of signed numbers, ask them to sketch the models on the board or on paper. These literal sketches are useful in Step 6 of the activity, discussing absolute value.

Source: Lesh, Post, & Behr (1987).

Once students are comfortable drawing pictures of their physical models, ask them to think about representing signed numbers on a number line. Talk about the elements of a number line, the zero point and incremental steps to the left and right. The right side of the number line is familiar to students from their elementary work with what they now know are positive values. Encourage students to compare their physical models or sketches of positive numbers with those same values marked on the number line. They should notice that all positive numbers are to the right of zero and the number of steps to the right corresponds to the number of cubes. Ask students to discuss how they might represent negative values on the number line and support them to reason that the distance will still correspond to the quantity while the negative sign means they will be to the left of (or below) zero. Share with students that negative fractional values (rational numbers) can also be represented on the number line in this way, with the quantity showing the distance from zero and the sign telling direction.

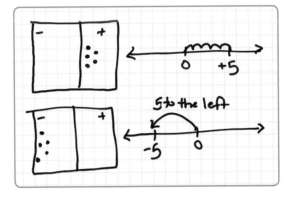

Materials

- Virtual two-color counters or physical two-color counters, approximately 20 per student or per pair

Organization (virtual)

- **Getting Started:** Ensure students can access and use the virtual tool. Review annotation tools, the process for taking screenshots, and other important supports.

- **Winding Down:** Use screenshots to save student work.

Mathematical Purpose

In this activity, students use an active addition model to add positive and negative integers. Addition is understood as the action of putting counters into the collection on the desk. Students work with a series of examples to understand the patterns that occur with addends of the same sign or addends of different signs.

Manipulative Illustrated

- Didax Two-Color Counters: www.didax.com/apps/two-color-counters/

Steps

1. Ask students to represent +3 add +5 (read "positive three add positive five") with their counters. Support students to share their thinking using the following questions:

   - *Where do you see the two addends in your representation?*

   - *How do we know that the values are positive?*

   - *How did you act out addition as you built the representation? Where do you see the sum of these values?*

   Look for a representation where the two addends are clearly distinguished and all counters are on the positive (non-red) side. Confirm the sum of +8 and ask students to describe how they built their model. Emphasize an active notion of addition, first placing three counters on the positive side and then placing an additional five counters, also on the positive side. Repeat with an additional example or two if necessary.

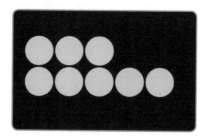

2. Ask students to add pairs of negative numbers in the same way. To add −2 plus −4, for example, first place two counters on the negative side and then place four more counters on the negative side. There are six counters, all negative, so the sum is −6. Repeat with additional examples, supporting discussion with questions similar to those in Step 1 and encouraging students to see the generalization that the sum of two integers with the same sign is the sum of the values with the sign carried along. The model highlights the fact that there are more of the same piece when adding two numbers of the same sign.

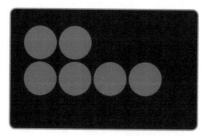

3. Ask students to represent +3 add −5 with their counters. Encourage them to follow the same pattern of placing three counters on the positive (yellow) side and then placing an additional five counters on the negative (red) side. Observe that there are still eight counters on the mat and ask what the sum is. Give students time to discuss their thinking with a partner then lead a class discussion guided by these questions:

    *   *What do you think the sum is? Why?*

    *   *Explain what each counter or group of counters on the mat represents in the problem.*

    *   *Where is −2 on the mat? Why are there more counters there if this is the sum? What do those "extra" counters represent?*

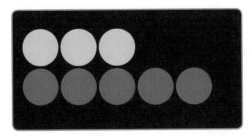

4. Support students to understand that a pair of counters, one of each color, has a value of zero. We call these **zero pairs**. Use a number line to help students understand why the pair has a value of zero. Each member of the pair represents a step right or a step left. One step in each direction (a pair of counters) means the location is unchanged in the end. This represents a change of zero. If you have a floor number line in your classroom, have students walk forward and back an equal number of steps to see that they land in the same location where they started.

5. Looking at the problem, there are three zero pairs as each of the three positive counters has a negative counter "partner." Once the zero pairs are identified, the remaining counters have a value of −2 as there are two red counters left.

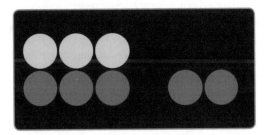

6. Repeat this process with a variety of other signed number addends.

7. Once students are comfortable with this, provide pairs of addends with opposite sign positions, such as +3 plus −8 and −3 plus +8. Encourage students to record their equations in a list so they can notice that both sums have an absolute value of 5 (the difference between 3 and 8) and what the sign is in each case (it matches the addend with the greater absolute value). Finding this pattern, and testing it with other pairs of addends, will help students develop automaticity adding integers and extend their knowledge of basic facts into this realm.

Why This Manipulative?

This work begins with a quick reminder of first-grade addition, focusing now on the two attributes of signed numbers, the quantity and the sign. This activity is designed to help students focus on the role of each part in adding signed numbers. Two-color counters (or the two-color unit pieces from an algebra tiles or similar set) are particularly helpful because it is easy to see each element, one in quantity and one in color.

The most important work here is the idea of a zero pair. Counters make it easy to see the zero pairs and to move them, as pairs, to a nearby area in the workspace so students can see the net sum clearly. It is important not to sweep the zero pairs back into the main collection of counters so students can check their work and still find the original addends in the model.

Developing Understanding

It is important to attend to magnitude in these discussions. While −8 has a greater absolute value than −3, its value is actually less than −3 because it is located to the left of −3 on the number line. As students generalize their findings about addition with unlike signs, help them be careful in their language.

While not all addition situations are active, this approach to addition of integers lays a strong foundation for work with subtraction (in Activity 5.3) and connects with students' intuitive understanding of addition. Once students are confident in their addition skill, provide examples in contexts that include additive comparison (e.g., temperature comparison) or part-part-whole situations (e.g., ionic charge situations) to allow students to use their learning in all contexts where addition is appropriate.

Featured Connection

Use the Make a Sketch strategy to connect concrete and pictorial representations of integer addition. When you reinforce students' ability to use a quick sketch to support computation, students are able to find success even when they do not remember a rule or shortcut they might have seen. Encourage students to build their addends in parallel rows or columns. This makes it easy to identify zero pairs with manipulatives or in a sketch. Students can use the + and − symbols to represent counters in their sketch.

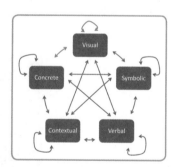

Source: Lesh, Post, & Behr (1987).

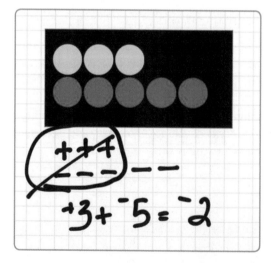

Encourage students to use the Write a Word Problem strategy to identify situations where they will need to add integers. It might be helpful to brainstorm contexts as a class (e.g., altitude, money, ionic charge) before asking students or pairs to write problems for the equations they have solved.

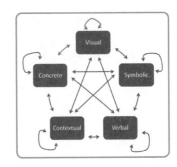

Source: Lesh, Post, & Behr (1987).

Notes

_____

_____

_____

_____

_____

_____

_____

_____

_____

_____

_____

_____

_____

_____

_____

Materials

- (Virtual) algebra tile units (or two-color counters), 20 per student or per pair

Organization (virtual)

- **Getting Started:** Ensure students can access and use the virtual tool. Review annotation tools, the process for taking screenshots, and other important supports.

- **Winding Down:** Use screenshots to save student work.

Mathematical Purpose

In this activity, students learn to subtract integers using the intuitive "take away" model of subtraction. This approach helps students connect subtracting integers with what they already know about subtracting whole numbers or other positive rational values.

Manipulative Illustrated

- Didax Algebra Tiles: www.didax .com/apps/algebra-tiles/

Steps

1. Have students model the action of taking away +3 from +8. They are modeling the subtraction sentence +8 − (+3) = ___. (Read this as "positive eight subtract positive three is what value?") Encourage students to return to Grade 1 thinking to place 8 positive counters and then remove 3 of those positive counters from the mat. Repeat the process with a similar pair of values to reinforce this action.

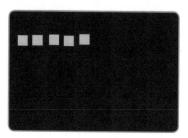

2. Have students model (−8) − (−3) using the algebra tiles. Place 8 negative counters and then move 3 of those negative counters away from the workspace to see the difference of −5. Repeat with other similar examples until students are comfortable with this process.

Discuss how these situations are similar and different using questions such as these:

- *How are the steps you followed similar to what you did in the primary grades when you first learned to subtract?*

- *How are these problems alike? How are they different?*

- *What pattern do you see in the subtraction problems you have solved so far?*

Note that in all of these problems, the signs are the same and the smaller absolute value is being subtracted from the greater absolute value. The next part of the activity expands the range of examples beyond these boundaries.

3. Ask students to model +3 − (−1) ("positive three subtract negative one") using the algebra tiles. Place 3 positive counters and look for 1 negative counter to remove. How could students change the representation, without changing the value, so there is a negative counter to remove?

4. After some discussion, ask students how they might use zero pairs to help them if no one has suggested this strategy or something that would lead to this strategy. Remind students that adding zero does not change addition and subtraction equations. In this case, what would happen if we add zero to the mat in the form of a zero pair (one red counter and one not-red counter)?

5. Ask students to add at least one zero pair to their problem representation and check that the value has not changed. Now take a single negative counter from the mat. What is the result? After cleaning up extra zero pairs, for students who added more than one, the students should see a value of +4.

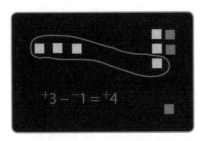

$$^+3 - {}^-1 = {}^+4$$

6. Practice a few more subtraction problems where the signs are different using this approach. Students can either add zero pairs as needed or begin the problem with a "bank" of 3 − 5 zero pairs already on the mat. Keep the difficulty low for now as the focus is on the process. Acknowledge that while this is how students first learned about subtraction, the model is not efficient with all rational values.

7. Provide students with pairs of related problems to model with the counters. +3 − (−1) is paired with +3 + (+1). (−4) − (−2) is paired with (−4) + (+2). Have students keep sketches of their work, captioned by equations, so they can see the pattern of adding an **additive inverse** instead of subtracting. See an example of this in action in the "Featured Connection" section.

Why This Manipulative?

The use of counters reinforces the intuitive model of subtraction as takeaway. This helps establish a connection to students' prior knowledge of subtraction as well as connecting to the model used for integer addition. The model crashes (Morrow-Leong et al., 2020) and becomes inefficient when we subtract terms with opposite signs, or when the subtrahend has a larger absolute value than the minuend. This provides a useful access point for transitioning to a more abstract approach using **inverse operations**, a model that is robust enough to work for any subtraction computation.

Developing Understanding

It is important for teachers to support students as they connect subtraction of negative values with their early whole-number subtraction learning because the work of the operation has not changed. Students are extending the range of values they can confidently subtract, and finding the limits of a model or tool can help build this understanding. You can expand the range of situations more by providing examples where the signs are the same but the greater absolute value is being subtracted from the lesser absolute value—for example, +3 − (+8) or (−2) − (−5).

Pay attention to the vocabulary you use when reading subtraction equations. Using the term *minus* for both the subtraction operation and the negative value can be confusing to students. It is much clearer to read 3 − (−1) as "three subtract negative one" than "three minus minus one." This makes the verb (*subtract*) clearly different from the adjective (*positive* or *negative*).

It is important to recognize that while +3 − (−1) is computationally equivalent to +3 + 1, it is not functionally the same in context. An ion shedding an electron (subtracting a charge of −1) is not the same as an ion gaining a proton (adding a charge of +1), even though the new net charge is the same.

Featured Connection

Use the strategy Name Your Model to connect concrete or visual and abstract representations. By recording the number sentence for each model built, students can see the pattern of equivalent solutions when adding the additive inverse. This allows them to recognize that integers allow them to use mathematical structure to create an equivalent addition expression from a given subtraction expression.

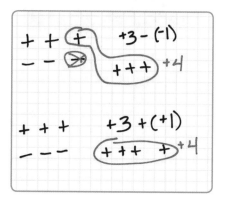

Encourage students to use the Write a Word Problem strategy to identify situations where they will need to add integers. It might be helpful to brainstorm contexts as a class (e.g., altitude, money, ionic charge) before asking students or pairs to write problems for the equations they have solved.

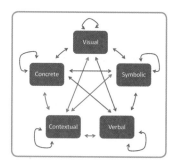

Source: Lesh, Post, & Behr (1987).

Notes

_____

_____

_____

_____

Notes

Materials

- Two-color counters

Organization (physical)

- **Getting Started:** Distribute the algebra tiles sets in bags; students should only remove the unit pieces.

- **Winding Down:** Return the units to the bags, counting and visually sweeping the desk and floor to be sure all pieces have been returned.

Mathematical Purpose

In this activity, students use an equal groups model to represent integer multiplication. The negative sign is interpreted to mean "a negative value" or "the opposite of," depending on the role it takes in the problem.

Activity 5.4 Resources

- *Multiplying Integers* Activity Video

 To access resource visit resources.corwin.com/ MasteringMathManips/ 4–8

Manipulative Illustrated

- Two-color counters

Steps

1. Ask students to use their units to create a model of 3 groups where each group includes 2 counters. Building from what they learned in Grade 3, they should easily find the product to be 3 × 2 = 6.

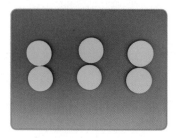

2. Ask students to model 3 groups where the value of each group is (−2). Discuss what has changed using the following questions for guidance:

   - *How does the model change? Why is this change important?*

   - *What is the product now? How do you know?*

   - *What number sentence would you write? [3 × (−2) = (−6)]*

   If it is helpful to your students, encourage them to think about this product as repeated addition: (−2) + (−2) + (−2) = (−6).

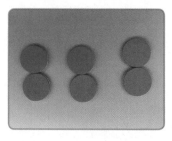

3. Repeat this activity with other small factors, keeping the number of groups positive for now and varying the value of each group. In this context, the value of the group is positive or negative, but the number of groups is always positive. Support students to see that if both factors have a positive sign, the product has a positive sign. If one factor has a negative sign, the product has a negative sign.

4. Ask students to predict the sign of the product (−3) × 2. Using the commutative property, it should be straightforward to see that the product is the same as 2 × (−3) or (−6). From a meaning perspective, the original number sentence represents (−3) groups, a term that may not make sense.

Talk with students about the idea that (−3) can also mean "the opposite of three," where opposite refers to the additive inverse. From this perspective, (−3) × 2 can be read as "the opposite of 3 × 2" or "the additive inverse of 6" or (−6). From an action perspective, (−3) × 2 means to make 3 groups of +2 and then flip the 3 groups over to find the additive inverse, or opposite, of the value. This is modeled in the accompanying video. Practice this until students are comfortable with the process.

5. With this understanding in mind, explore the product of (−3) × (−2). In this case, it is helpful to think of this expression as "the opposite of three groups when each group has a value of negative two." This long-winded description shows the efficiency of mathematical notation and can be readily modeled with the unit tiles. Students should create 3 groups, each including 2 negative (red) tiles. They then flip over all the tiles to find the opposite. The resulting product is +6, seen visually in the absence of red tiles. Repeat the process with other combinations of small factors to help students develop fluency with this interpretation of multiplying negative factors.

Why This Manipulative?

The units from algebra tiles (or two-color counters) are helpful tools for modeling both meanings of the negative symbol incorporated here. By placing them red or not-red side up, students show the sign of the number, an adjective-like descriptor indicating the "negative" kind of 3 in the same way an adjective tells the reader to focus on the yellow dress. By flipping them over, to show the opposite side, students signal the operator interpretation of the negative symbol, toggling between a value and its additive inverse (Stephan & Akyuz, 2012). Making sense of multiplication where both factors are negative is a challenging topic, most straightforward when these two interpretations of the negative sign are used for the two purposes of the factors in an equal groups structure.

Developing Understanding

Not all multiplication situations are equal groups situations, and the interpretation of negative values varies depending on the context. The use of an equal groups structure here is designed to support students' emerging understanding of how the product of two negative factors could be positive. This helps develop computational fluency; it does not eliminate the need to understand the meaning of individual multiplication situations when the computations appear in context.

As with subtraction, be careful with the language used to express these number sentences. Using different terms to represent the three meanings of the negative sign (*negative*, *subtract*, or *opposite*) helps clarify for students the sometimes confusing use of the same symbol for three different mathematical ideas.

Featured Connection

This lesson incorporates the Name Your Model strategy for connecting physical representations with symbolic representations. As the video shows, students hear verbal descriptions of mathematical operations, create physical models of those operations, and then name the models with symbolic equations.

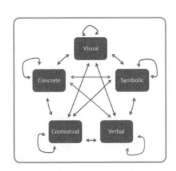

Source: Lesh, Post, & Behr (1987).

Materials

- Algebra tiles, one set per student or per pair

Organization (physical)

- **Getting Started:** Distribute algebra tiles in bags.
- **Winding Down:** Return tiles to bags, counting and scanning the desk and floor for stray pieces.

Mathematical Purpose

In this activity, students learn to represent variable expressions, using algebra tiles. This serves two purposes: (1) It helps students understand the naming of algebra tile pieces, and (2) it helps students understand the idea of "combining like terms" in algebra.

Manipulative Illustrated

Algebra Tiles, Combination Set (EAI Education)

Steps

Note: Students are familiar with the unit squares from their work with integers. This experience has also familiarized students with the use of the red side to represent negative values and the not-red side to represent positive values.

1. Have students pull one piece of each size or shape from the set of algebra tiles they are working with. In the set illustrated, this includes six pieces. Following the model of work with base-ten blocks, these pieces can be named as units, rods, and flats. Unlike base-ten blocks, there are two rods and three flats. How will these be distinguished?

2. Just as base-ten blocks were named by their volume, these algebra tile pieces are named by their area. The small unit square is defined with an area of 1 square unit and a side length of 1 unit. Ask students to use the unit to estimate the length of the longer side of each rod. They will find the lengths are not an even multiple of the unit square. This is typical of many sets of algebra tiles and reminds students that these lengths are variables to be determined. For this activity, call the shorter rod (orange) the *x*-rod (area 1 unit by *x* units) and the longer rod (green) the *y*-rod (area 1 unit by *y* units). Given these dimensions, what is the area of each of the three flats? The purple flat has an area of x^2, the blue flat has an area of y^2, and the teal flat has an area of xy.

3. Ask students to build the expression $3x + 2$. There should be 3 orange rods and 2 yellow unit squares since all the terms are positive. Try several more examples:

   - *What would $2y - 1$ look like? How do you know? [2 green rods and 1 red unit]*

   - *What would $x^2 - 2x + 1$ look like? How do you know? [1 purple flat, 2 red (orange) rods, and 1 yellow unit]*

   - *Is there more than one way to build an expression when working with algebra tiles? There is often more than one way to build a number with base-ten blocks.*

Continue to provide practice modeling expressions within the parameters of your course until students are comfortable with the pieces.

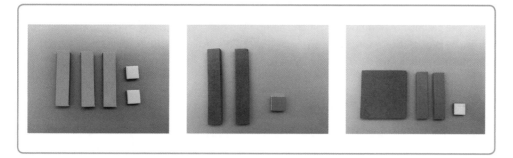

4. Ask students to build the following expression: $3x - 2 - 4x + 1$. Discuss the model guided by these questions:

- *What do students notice about the expression and the model they built?*
- *Are there zero pairs embedded in the representation? Why are they important?*
- *What is the value of the model after the zero pairs are accounted for?*

This act of identifying zero pairs and "cleaning up" the expression is called combining like terms in algebra.

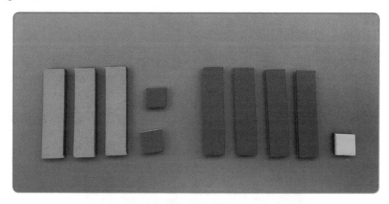

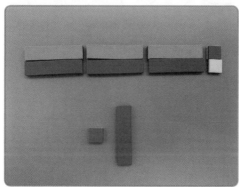

5. Continue to practice building, recording, and combining like terms until students are confident. One fun way to do this is to have the students take a random handful of pieces and spill them onto the table. Following the pattern of the pieces, create an expression of at least 3 terms and then combine like terms using zero pairs to simplify the expression. Adjust the parameters of the task to suit the algebra tile set available to you and the expressions your students are expected to work with.

Why This Manipulative?

Algebra tiles are particularly helpful to students when learning to combine like terms. Many students confuse $2x$ and x^2, seeing an x and a 2 in each case. By understanding that the algebra tile pieces are named by area and seeing the difference in size and shape between the x and x^2 pieces, this confusion can be reduced. The design of algebra tiles means that zero pairs are only formed between pieces represented by the same size and shape.

Developing Understanding

Algebraic expressions can be complex to read and understand. This activity helps students make sense of algebraic terms by connecting the abstract symbols with physical objects in the algebra tiles set. It will help students to both write the expressions on the board and say them aloud as students build and describe their models. This emphasizes the connection across representations. Encourage students to read and write their expressions carefully so they build a strong connection between the symbols and the physical tools.

Featured Connection

This activity features the Build the Equation strategy to connect symbolic and physical representations when students are given algebraic expressions and asked to build them using algebra tiles. As your students read expressions, build models, create expressions (by spilling pieces), and write expressions, encourage them to identify each term of the symbolic expression in the physical model and to identify each.

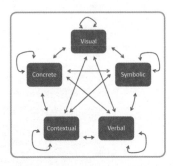

Source: Lesh, Post, & Behr (1987).

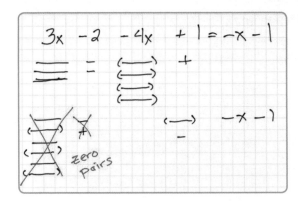

Notes

_____

_____

_____

_____

Notes

Materials

- Virtual algebra tiles or one set of algebra tiles per student or pair

- Activity sheet (one for each student)

Organization (virtual)

- **Getting Started:** Ensure students can access and use the virtual tool. Review annotation tools, the process for taking screenshots, and other important supports.

- **Winding Down:** Use screenshots to save student work.

Mathematical Purpose

In this activity, students transition from working with expressions to solving algebraic equations. The activity models core strategies for solving one-step equations involving addition and subtraction using a single variable.

Activity 5.6 Resources

- *Solving Addition Equations Activity Sheet*

 To access resource visit resources.corwin.com/ MasteringMathManips/ 4–8

Manipulative Illustrated

- Mathsbot Virtual Algebra Tiles: https://mathsbot.com/ manipulatives/tiles

Steps

> Jay'la had some basketballs. She gave 2 basketballs away, and now she has 3 basketballs left. How many basketballs did Jay'la have?

1. Read the problem and discuss the situation with students using questions like these. Acknowledge that this feels like a very elementary problem (and it is!) but it also has a purpose, so hang in there with the discussion.

    - *What is happening in the story?*

    - *How can you represent this as a number sentence or equation?*

    - *How do you know what operation to use in the equation?*

    - *Where is each part of the story in your equation?*

    Support students to understand that Jay'la started with 5 basketballs. Now that the solution is clear, students will learn to use algebra to represent and solve situations like this.

2. Ask students to identify the unknown, the element of the story to be figured out. This can be called *x* and represented by the yellow rod. It's not possible to subtract 2 (remove two units) from the variable, so we use the algebraic equivalent and add (–2) to the same side of the equation. The other side of the equation has +3, representing the 3 basketballs remaining.

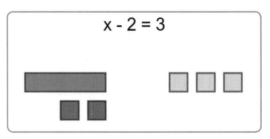

3. Because we are working with an equation, we must keep it balanced. Algebraically, this means we must act on each side in the same way. Our goal is to isolate the variable, to have the variable alone on one side of the equation. In order to accomplish this, we must add +2 to both sides in order to create two zero pairs on the left. This leaves five on the right, representing the 5 basketballs Jay'la started with. Students can check their work by substitution.

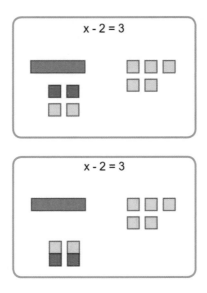

4. Repeat this process for the other problems on the activity sheet.

Why This Manipulative?

Algebra tiles allow students to see the action of each step in solving simple equations. They see the groups or the zero pairs and can follow the action of the notation with the blocks. While different algebra tools represent positive and negative values in different ways, the idea of creating zero pairs as a first step toward isolating the variable is a universal principle.

Developing Understanding

These problems are deliberately written so that students can reason about the answer by using known facts and understanding the problem situations. As algebra students, the approaches shown in this example should work for any values, not just those friendly to mental math. The goal is always to isolate the variable. When adding or subtracting, this typically means creating zero pairs by adding an inverse.

Featured Connection

Use the Name Your Model strategy to record algebraic steps that correspond to each step used with the Algeblocks. Students may need to sketch their algebra tiles models as an intermediate connection.

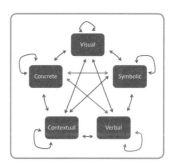

Source: Lesh, Post, & Behr (1987).

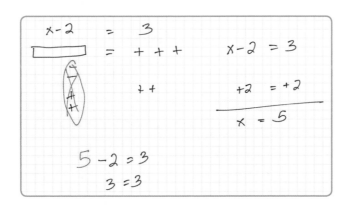

Materials

- Virtual algebra tiles or one set of tiles per student or pair
- Activity sheet (one for each student)

Organization (virtual)

- **Getting Started:** Ensure students can access and use the virtual tool. Review annotation tools, the process for taking screenshots, and other important supports.
- **Winding Down:** Use screenshots to save student work.

Mathematical Purpose

In this activity, students transition from working with expressions to solving algebraic equations. The activity models core strategies for solving multiplication equations using a single variable.

Activity 5.7 Resources

- *Solving Multiplication Equations Activity Sheet*
- *Solving Multiplication Equations Activity Video*

online resources ↖ To access resources visit resources.corwin.com/ Mastering MathManips/4–8

Manipulative Illustrated

- Mathsbot Virtual Algebra Tiles: https://mathsbot.com/ manipulatives/tiles

162

Steps

> Peter bought 3 toys for $9. What was the cost of each toy?

1. Read the problem and discuss the situation with students using questions like these:

   - *What is happening in the story?*
   - *How can you represent this as a number sentence or equation?*
   - *How do you know what operation to use in the equation?*
   - *Where is each part of the story in your equation?*

   Support students to understand that Peter paid $3 for each toy. Now that the solution is clear, students will learn to use algebra to represent and solve situations like this.

2. Create a model for the problem, using three green rods to represent that each of the three toys has the same cost and 9 units to represent the total cost. Model division by separating the three rods and creating three groups with the 9 units. Record this work as dividing both sides by 3 or multiplying both sides by 1/3.

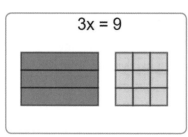

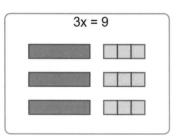

3. Repeat this process for the other problems on the activity sheet.

Why This Manipulative?

Algebra tools allow students to see the action of each step in solving simple equations. They see the groups and can follow the action of the notation with the blocks. The problems in this activity are chosen to give students experience with both ways signs are used in multiplication. In the second problem, the dive of 45 feet can be represented as −45 for the total amount. In the fourth problem, the term (−2)x represents "the opposite of 2x."

Developing Understanding

These problems are deliberately written so that students can reason about the answer by using known facts and understanding the problem situations. As algebra students, the approaches shown in this example should work for any values, not just those friendly to mental math. The goal is always to isolate the variable. When multiplying or dividing, this typically means constructing equal groups.

Featured Connection

This activity can be seen as an instance of the Build the Equation strategy. For the first two word problems, students should be able to write an equation to represent their understanding. They then build that equation using algebra tools and act out their reasoning to find the solution. Students are supported to focus on the reasoning because the values are friendly enough that students are confident of the answer from the beginning. The video shows the solution to Problem 4 on the activity sheet.

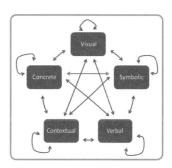

Source: Lesh, Post, & Behr (1987).

Notes

_____

_____

_____

_____

_____

_____

_____

_____

_____

Materials

- Algeblocks units
- *x*-rods and *y*-rods
- Sentence mat
- Activity sheet (one for each student)

Organization (physical)

- **Getting Started:** Distribute the required Algeblock pieces to each student or pair of students. A small bag including 15 units and 5 of each variable is sufficient for examples with less difficult computation.

- **Winding Down:** Count and return the pieces to the bag. Return each bag to its larger tub of all Algeblock pieces.

Mathematical Purpose

In this activity, students transition from working with expressions to solving algebraic equations. The activity models core strategies for solving two-step equations using a single variable.

Activity 5.8 Resources

- *Solving Two-Step Equations* Activity Sheet

 online resources To access resource visit resources.corwin.com/ MasteringMathManips/ 4–8

Manipulative Illustrated

- Algeblocks (hand2mind)

Steps

> Kyndall bought 2 tickets to the movie and 1 snack pack. The snack pack cost $7, and he spent a total of $15. How much did each ticket cost?

1. Read the problem and discuss the situation with students using questions like these:

   - *What is happening in the story?*
   - *How can you represent this as a number sentence or equation?*
   - *How do you know what operations to use in the equation?*
   - *Does it matter which operation you do first? Why or why not?*
   - *Where is each part of the story in your equation?*

   Support students to understand that Kyndall paid $4 for each ticket. Now that the solution is clear, students will learn to use algebra to represent and solve situations like this.

2. Create a model for the problem. Ask students to identify the unknown, the element of the story to be figured out. This can be called *x* and represented by the yellow rod.

3. The balance at the bottom of the work mat reminds students to keep the two sides of the equation balanced. Algebraically, this means we must act on each side in the same way. Our goal is to isolate the variable, to have the yellow rod alone on one side of the equation. In order to accomplish this, we must first subtract 7 from both sides. These pieces are set to the side to show they have been subtracted.

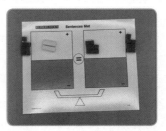

4. Then we can create two groups to find the cost of each ticket.

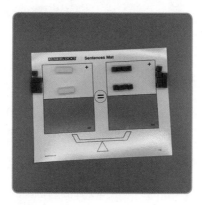

5. Repeat each of these steps with the other problems on the activity sheet.

Why This Manipulative?

Algebra tools allow students to see the action of each step in solving simple equations. They can follow the action of the notation with the blocks. In this example, it is possible to subtract 7 from both sides. This (adding or subtracting a given value from both sides) is not a universal strategy. Creating zero pairs is the universal strategy, and students should have practice with both methods.

Developing Understanding

This problem is a start-unknown situation. Students first account for the cost of the snack pack and then can figure out about the tickets. By presenting in context first, students are able to reason about the process. Then they can apply what they have figured out to bare equations. These problems are written to introduce added complexity of signed values. Please adjust the tasks to meet the learning needs of your students. Students should realize that the goal is always to isolate the variable. When adding or subtracting, this typically means creating zero pairs. When there are multiple copies of a variable, form groups to find the final value.

Featured Connection

Students can use the Caption Your Picture strategy to caption a series of sketches showing the steps to solving a two-step equation. By creating a series of images and captioning them, students engage more actively with the reasoning they need to solve a multi-step equation.

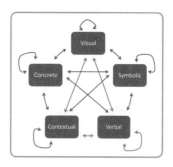

Source: Lesh, Post, & Behr (1987).

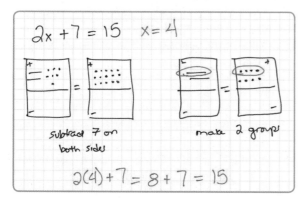

Materials

- Algebra tiles (physical or virtual)
- Multiplication mat (with physical tiles)
- Activity sheet (one for each student)

Organization (virtual)

- **Getting Started:** Ensure students can access and use the virtual tool. Review annotation tools, the process for taking screenshots, and other important supports.
- **Winding Down:** Use screenshots to save student work.

Mathematical Purpose

In this activity, students use the distributive property to multiply a **monomial** and a binomial.

Activity 5.9 Resources

- Multiplication Mat
- *Multiplication Problems* Activity Sheet

 To access resource visit resources.corwin.com/ MasteringMathManips/ 4–8

Manipulative Illustrated

- CPM Education Algebra Tiles: https://technology.cpm.org/ general/tiles/

Steps

1. Ask students to describe the connection between multiplication and area. Students might say that you multiply to find area or that you can draw pictures of multiplication using an area model. This lesson develops the idea of this connection.

2. Ask students to draw a rectangle and label one dimension 3 and the other dimension $x + 2$. (These are the factors in Problem 1.) How can students find the area of the rectangle? What algebra tile pieces fit in the space exactly? Give students time to explore and find the area of the rectangle. Discuss their thinking using the following questions:

   - *Do you have to find the entire area at once? Why or why not?*

   - *Are there parts of the area you can figure out in your head? How can you mark those in your work?*

   - *Could you use algebra tiles to help you figure out the area? Are there different options for doing this?*

   Show the students how to sketch a recording of their work.

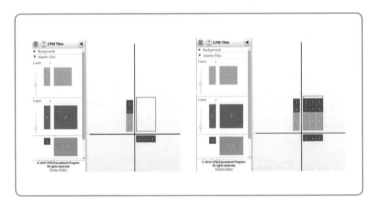

3. Part of the complexity of algebraic multiplication is the role (and meaning) of negative factors. The second example includes a negative factor so students can explore this. In this context, the factor of (−2) can be interpreted as "the opposite of two times . . ." In this way, students can see that 2 multiplied by x is $2x$, and this problem asks for the opposite of that. See Activity 5.4 for additional support about this idea.

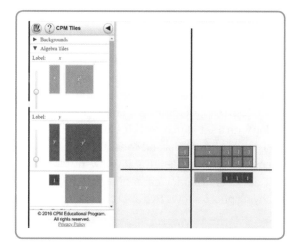

4. In the third example, the monomial factor is a variable. This is where students are reminded that $x * x = x^2$, not $2x$. If students see that the form of the product (the area) matches the form of the factors (the side lengths), they are able to catch mistakes like this themselves.

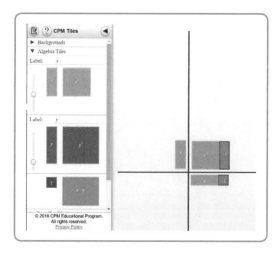

Why This Manipulative?

Algebra tiles are useful for multiplication because the structure of the pieces means the seams where two blocks come together will always match. $x * x = 2x$ is a common mistake; visually this does not work with algebra manipulatives because two variable rods do not cover the same area as an x by x square.

Developing Understanding

This approach to multiplication mirrors the experience students have with base-ten blocks, area models, and open arrays as they learn about multiplication of whole numbers (one-digit by two- or three-digit numbers) and the distributive property. The algebra tools allow students to work confidently by providing a structure and visual imagery to support the difference between x^2 and $2x$. This learning will be extended in Activity 5.10 when students multiply two binomials (using the same approach Activity 1.7 shows for multiplying two two-digit numbers) and learn a general approach to multiplying algebraic expressions.

Featured Connection

Use the Make a Sketch strategy to teach students to connect their physical models with visual representations. If students follow the same structure they were taught for base-ten materials, they will use a dot for a unit, a line segment for a variable, and a square for a squared variable. If students are working with a set of materials featuring both x and y, they will need to be careful and consistent that their two segments are different lengths. It will also be important to use color or another indicator of negative values. The accompanying photo shows two approaches.

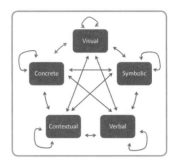

Source: Lesh, Post, & Behr (1987).

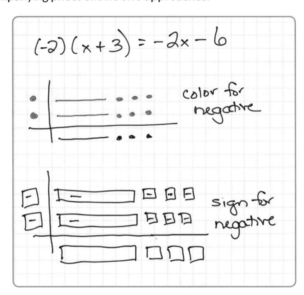

Notes

_____

_____

_____

_____

_____

_____

_____

_____

Notes

Materials

- Algebra Lab Gear, one set per student or pair of students

Organization (physical)

- **Getting Started:** Distribute the materials.

- **Winding Down:** Repackage and gather the materials.

Mathematical Purpose

This activity extends Activity 5.9 to multiply two binomials and model the "double-distributive" nature of this product. The lesson also teaches the open array, a more general representation for multiplying any two expressions.

Activity 5.10 Resources

- *Multiplying Two Binomials* Activity Video

online resources ⬦ To access resource visit resources.corwin.com/ MasteringMathManips/ 4–8

Manipulative Illustrated

- Algebra Lab Gear (Didax)

Steps

1. This lesson builds on two previous experiences. Looking back several years, students are building from what they know about multiplying two two-digit numbers. The video from Activity 1.7 illustrates this strategy and could serve as a review. This activity also extends student experience in Activity 5.9 using algebra tools to multiply a monomial and a **binomial**.

2. Remind them of base-ten multiplication with an example from Activity 1.7 if appropriate. Use the following questions to guide a discussion:

   - *How is this problem similar to those you have solved before?*

   - *Do you have to find the entire area at once? Why or why not?*

   - *Are there parts of the area you can figure out in your head? How can you mark those in your work?*

   - *Could you use algebra tiles to help you figure out the area? Are there different options for doing this?*

   Support students to share their thinking and create a representation similar to the one shown. The orientation of the factors, in general, does not matter.

3. Following the principles used for other distributive-property and area-based models, students can multiply each part of each factor separately and build a representation of the product. Encourage students to sketch each representation they create using the structure illustrated in earlier lessons in this chapter.

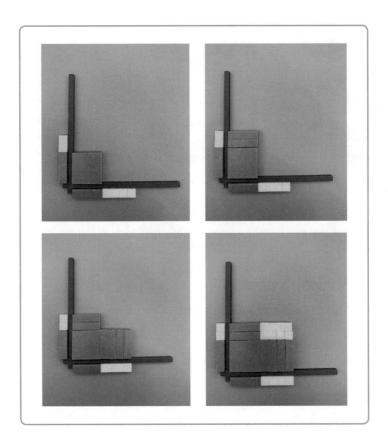

4. Support students to solve $(x + 1)(x + 3)$ using the same strategy. Provide additional examples where all terms are positive until students are confident of the structure.

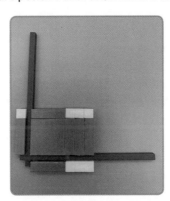

5. Students must extend their thinking in two ways, to expressions where the variable has a coefficient other than 1 and to situations where one or more terms is negative. Provide examples such as these to support these extensions. For the negative value examples, algebra tiles are used with the frame.

   » $(2x + 2)(x + 1)$

   » $(x - 2)(x + 1)$

   » $(x - 2)(2x - 1)$

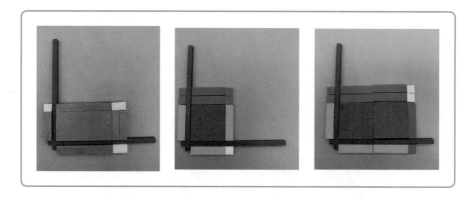

6. Support students to transition to an open array approach to multiplying polynomials. This is shown as the "Featured Connection" for this activity.

Why This Manipulative?

The area-based structure of algebra tools embeds the attributes of the distributive property into the tools. Because their structure is similar to that of base-ten blocks, these tools also support the connection between multi-digit multiplication and polynomial multiplication. Open arrays and partial product strategies work well for both contexts. The video accompanying this lesson parallels the video accompanying Activity 2.6 so students can see both base-ten multiplication and algebra tile multiplication in action.

Note that these models assume students understand the sign rules for multiplication (see Activity 5.4). Students should know before beginning to multiply expressions when a product is positive and when it is negative.

Developing Understanding

Multiplication as an operation accomplishes the same functions and, generally, works the same way no matter what form the factors take. By investing the time to connect binomial (and, ultimately, polynomial) multiplication to base-ten multiplication (see Activity 1.7), students can see these connections and understand the structural linkages of mathematics more fully.

Featured Connection

Use the Name Your Model and Create a Diagram strategies to transition from sketches as a more literal visual representation to open arrays as a more general representation, which works for multiplying any two polynomials.

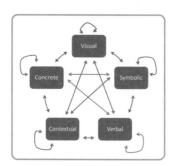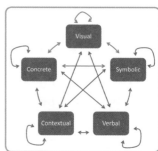

Source: Lesh, Post, & Behr (1987).

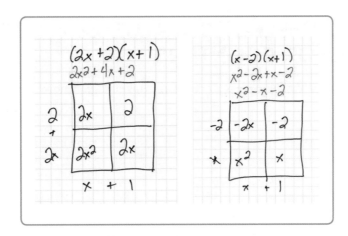

Rather than sketching all the manipulative pieces, students use the distributive property structure and an open array diagram to represent the partial products and then sum them to find the product. This has the added advantage of making negative terms easier to manage. Factoring, by extension, becomes using the open array model in reverse.

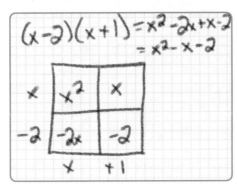

Notes

_____

_____

_____

_____

_____

_____

_____

_____

CLOSING REFLECTION: ALGEBRA TILES AND TWO-COLOR COUNTERS

How do I use algebra tiles and two-color counters in my classroom now? What concepts do I use them to teach?

_____

_____

_____

_____

_____

_____

_____

_____

_____

_____

_____

What new ways have I found to use algebra tiles and two-color counters to better support student understanding?

_____

_____

_____

_____

_____

_____

_____

_____

_____

_____

_____

_____

What are my goals to make algebra tiles and two-color counters a more regular part of my instruction?

_____

_____

_____

_____

_____

_____

_____

_____

_____

_____

_____

CHAPTER 6
Geometric Strips and Solids

UNDERSTANDING GEOMETRIC STRIPS AND SOLIDS

This chapter includes lessons using two categories of geometry manipulatives. Geometric strips are plastic strips that attach together using brads or snapping connections. A set of strips typically comes in a variety of colors and lengths. They may or may not have connections other than at the ends of the strips. In most cases, the lengths of the strips and the locations of connectors are intentional. The pieces are likely not proportional in a traditional sense.

Geometric solids are sets of three-dimensional figures (either hollow or solid) designed to illustrate the various categories of three-dimensional shapes: cubes, prisms, **pyramids**, **cones**, **spheres**, and/or **cylinders**. Some hollow sets may have inserts to show **altitude**, **slant height**, or **cross sections** (e.g., cutting a circle, ellipse, or parabola from a cone), potentially making them useful even into high school. Some geometric solid sets are available with corresponding nets. In some cases, the various shapes within the set are built from the same units (e.g., the circular base of a cone is the same diameter as the sphere).

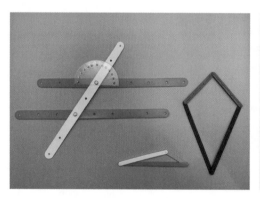 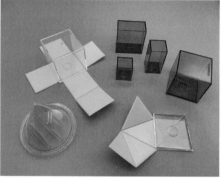

Geometric strips and solids can be used to develop these concepts:

- Classification of **polygons**
- **Attributes** of polygons
- Transformations
- Angle measurement and relationships
- Parallel and perpendicular relationships
- Volume
- Surface area

Introducing Geometric Strips and Solids to Students

Use the *Notice and Wonder Thinking Routine* (described in the introductory chapter) to introduce geometric strips or solids to students. You will likely introduce each at a different time given that they address different areas of the curriculum.

As students explore geometric strips, they may notice the various colors and lengths of the strips. They may experiment with connecting strips and wonder what shapes they can create. They may even try to create three-dimensional shapes with the strips. Listen to the vocabulary students use to assess their use of terms such as side, **vertex**, or various types of angles.

As students explore geometric solids, they may build composed shapes from the blocks. They may notice the relationships between the various pieces or count their faces, edges, and vertices. If the pieces are hollow and fill materials are available, they may fill the shapes and pour from one to another, wondering about volume.

Key Ideas With Geometric Strips and Solids

- This chapter uses geometric strips to teach angles as **rotation**. Use fraction circle wedges to look at angles as wedges of a circle and make the connection to 360 degrees.

- Working with geometric strips means all figures are technically line segments, even when the strips are representing rays (as with angles) or lines (as with **parallel**, **perpendicular**, and **transversals**). Take time with students to make this distinction as a limitation of the model.

- Geometric solids are easily found from a variety of sources. It is helpful to have shapes where the sides have a relationship to one another. For example, the cone and cylinder in Activity 6.16 have the same circle as the base and the same height. This means they can be used to illustrate the $\frac{1}{3}$ relationship for volume.

- A variety of materials can be used for measuring volume; water, sand, rice, and small beans are most common.

- If you have a set of hollow related cubes and rectangular prisms (a small cube, and then three figures where one, then two, then all three dimensions are doubled), it is possible to spray the inside of the shapes with cooking spray and fill them with extra-thick gelatin. Pop the shapes out and cut them with dental floss to see that the volume of the large cube (where all three dimensions are doubled) is 8 times the volume of the small cube.

Things to Consider About Geometric Strips and Solids

- Think about how your strips connect as you consider what shapes to model with them. Connectors at the center of strips help with partitioning sides or angles.

- If your strips connect with brads, consider how you will manage these materials.

- If your solid figures do not have nets, think about how you might create nets for them.

- If your three-dimensional figures are not hollow, think about how you might use displacement to explore volume. If your figures are hollow, think about what fill material is most appropriate for your classroom. Water, sand, or rice are materials typically used.

Alternatives to Commercial Strips and Solids

Geometric strips can be replaced by toothpicks or skewers connected with gumdrops or bits of clay. Straws connected by pieces of chenille stems (pipe cleaners) can work as well.

Depending on your activity, you may need to be careful that all pieces are cut to the same length and connect in the same way. Straws and chenille stems are typically easier for accuracy.

There are dies available for die-cut machines that will cut nets for many solid figures. If these are cut from card stock and assembled carefully, they can be reasonably sturdy. If one face is omitted, they can even be filled with sand or rice to explore volume. Sand is more likely to leak if the edges are not firmly taped.

Sets of children's blocks often include a variety of three-dimensional shapes. They may not address the full range of solid figures in the curriculum but can be a good start. Everyday objects may also approximate a number of three-dimensional shapes.

Working With Virtual Strips and Solids

As of this writing (spring of 2021), we have not found virtual resources that can be used for the activities in this chapter. While there are some online resources that allow for work with premade nets and solids, we have been unable to find digital resources that are reasonable substitutes for physical manipulatives for these activities.

Notes

_____

_____

_____

_____

_____

_____

_____

_____

_____

_____

_____

Notes

Materials

- Geometric strips, one set per pair or trio of students

Organization (physical)

- **Getting Started:** Distribute one set of materials to each pair or trio of students.
- **Winding Down:** Rebag the strips and return the materials to home base.

Mathematical Purpose

In this activity, students create and name polygons based on the number of sides each figure has.

Manipulative Illustrated

- AngLegs® (hand2mind)

Steps

1. Each student takes three strips from the bag and uses them to make a triangle. If the three strips will not make a triangle, set the group aside and draw another three strips.

2. Have a class gallery walk to look at all the triangles students have created. Guide the discussion using questions like these:

   - *What makes all the figures triangles? Why doesn't it matter that the angle sizes and side lengths are different?*

   - *How are they alike, and how are they different? Can you arrange the shapes you have made into groups? What makes each group distinctive?*

   Ask students to identify and sketch several different triangles to show the full range of possible shapes within the triangle family.

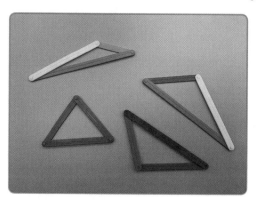

3. Depending on lesson goals, the triangles can be classified by sides or angles into a variety of groups.

4. Repeat the activity for **quadrilaterals** with four strips. After students build their quadrilaterals, observe and discuss the variety of quadrilaterals constructed using questions like these:

   - *What makes each of these shapes a quadrilateral? Why doesn't it matter that the angles and sides vary across the figures?*

   - *How are they alike and different? What do you notice about sides and angles? Can you arrange the shapes you have made into groups? What makes each group distinctive?*

   Ask students to identify and sketch several different quadrilaterals to show the full range of possible shapes within the quadrilateral family.

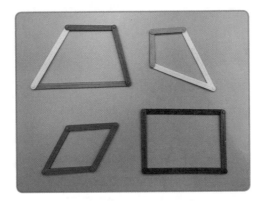

5. Depending on lesson goals, the quadrilaterals can be classified into a variety of groups.

6. This activity can be extended to polygons with more sides.

Why This Manipulative?

Connecting strips are a flexible tool for creating two-dimensional shapes. The variety of side lengths gives a wide range of possible figures to create.

Developing Understanding

Many students develop misconceptions about shapes because so many of the examples they see are the same form (e.g., **isosceles triangles** with base parallel to the bottom of the page). By using a random draw of strips and examining the variety of shapes made, students can better identify the essential characteristics of a given polygon.

It is possible to pull a set of strips that cannot make a triangle. For older students, investigating when this happens is an interesting extension to this activity.

For both triangles and quadrilaterals, students can sort and classify the shapes they make by angles or sides. This continues to build their understanding of the attributes of various shapes and begins to help students understand how different shapes are related.

Featured Connection

Use the Make a Sketch strategy to help students connect physical models with sketches of the figures. Teach students the notation for indicating sides the same length and for noting right or congruent angles.

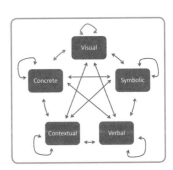

Source: Lesh, Post, & Behr (1987).

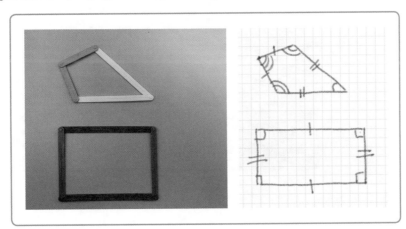

Materials

- Geometric strips

Organization (physical)

- **Getting Started:** Distribute one set of materials to each pair or trio of students.

- **Winding Down:** Rebag the strips and return the materials to home base.

Mathematical Purpose

In this activity, students explore the attributes of triangles and quadrilaterals with a focus on the sides.

Manipulative Illustrated

- EAI Exploragons®

Steps

1. Each pair or trio should build six to eight triangles based on random draws of three strips from the bag. As in Activity 6.1, students can draw a new set if a triangle cannot be made.

2. Use the following questions to observe and classify the triangles:

   - *Are there any triangles where all sides are the same length? What else do you notice about these triangles?*

   - *Are there any triangles where exactly two of the sides are the same length? What else do you notice about these triangles?*

   - *Are there any triangles where each side is a different length? What else do you notice about these triangles?*

3. As students discuss each category of triangle, provide the appropriate names: **equilateral**, isosceles, and **scalene**.

4. A similar activity can be completed with quadrilaterals. Here are questions to use in observing and classifying the quadrilaterals based on side lengths:

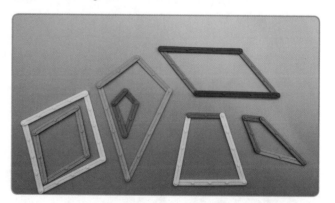

- *Are there any quadrilaterals with all four sides the same length? What else do you notice about these quadrilaterals?*

- *Are there any quadrilaterals with side lengths in two pairs (two of length x and two of length y)? What else do you notice about these quadrilaterals?*

- *Are there any quadrilaterals with exactly one pair of sides the same length? What else do you notice about these quadrilaterals?*

- *Are there any quadrilaterals with no sides the same length? What else do you notice about these quadrilaterals?*

5. As students discuss each category of quadrilateral, provide the appropriate names and relationships for the shapes in focus for the lesson.

Why This Manipulative?

Connecting strips are a flexible tool for creating two-dimensional shapes. The variety of side lengths gives a wide range of possible figures to create. The fact that the same color piece is typically the same length makes these tools particularly useful for examining shapes in terms of side length.

Developing Understanding

This activity reflects at least two lessons of work, one on triangles and one on quadrilaterals. Classifying quadrilaterals is much more complex as there is more to consider than just side length. Activity 6.3 looks at the angles in shapes; it is teacher's choice about when to discuss parallel sides for quadrilateral figures.

Featured Connection

Use the Caption Your Picture strategy to create a glossary of shapes discussed. For each term, students should sketch and label at least two different examples.

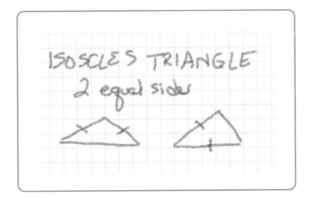

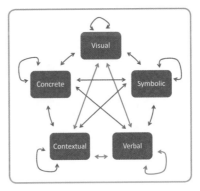

Source: Lesh, Post, & Behr (1987).

Materials

- Geometric strips with protractors

Organization (physical)

- **Getting Started:** Distribute one set of materials to each pair or trio of students.
- **Winding Down:** Rebag the strips and return the materials to home base.

Mathematical Purpose

In this activity, students explore the attributes of triangles and quadrilaterals with a focus on the angles.

Manipulative Illustrated

- AngLegs® (hand2mind)

Steps

1. Each pair or trio should build six to eight triangles based on random draws of three strips from the bag. As in Activity 6.1, students can draw a new set if a triangle cannot be made.

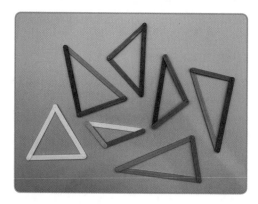

2. Use the following questions to observe and classify the triangles:

   - *Are there any triangles where all angles are the same? What else do you notice about these triangles?*

   - *Are there any triangles where exactly two of the angles are the same? What else do you notice about these triangles?*

   - *Are there any triangles where each angle is a different size? What else do you notice about these triangles?*

   - *Are there any triangles with a right angle? What else do you notice about these triangles?*

3. As students discuss each category of triangle, provide the appropriate names: equilateral, isosceles, **acute**, **obtuse**, and right. Point out that some names are still associated with side length even though this lesson is about angles.

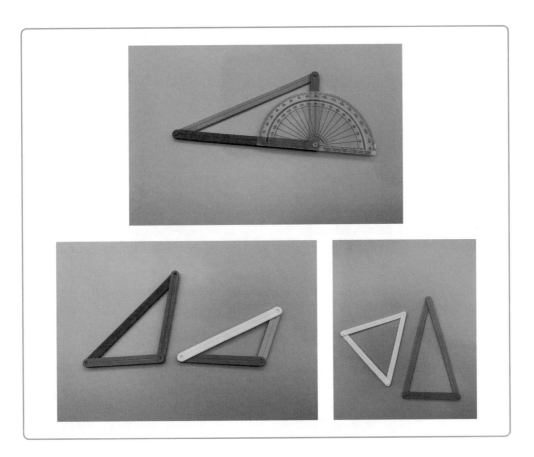

4. A similar activity can be completed with quadrilaterals. Here are questions to use in observing and classifying the quadrilaterals:

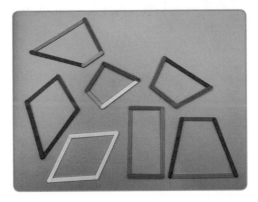

- *Are there any quadrilaterals with all four angles the same? What else do you notice about these quadrilaterals?*

- *Are there any quadrilaterals with two pairs of matching angles? What else do you notice about these quadrilaterals?*

- *Are there any quadrilaterals with one pair of matching angles? What else do you notice about these quadrilaterals?*

- *Are there any quadrilaterals with angles the same? What else do you notice about these quadrilaterals?*

5. As students discuss each category of quadrilateral, provide the appropriate names and relationships for the shapes in focus for the lesson.

Why This Manipulative?

Connecting strips are a flexible tool for creating two-dimensional shapes. The variety of side lengths gives a wide range of possible figures to create. Use the included protractor to measure the angles in a shape (see Activity 6.6 for more information).

Developing Understanding

As with Activity 6.2, this lesson reflects at least two lessons of work, one on triangles and one on quadrilaterals. Classifying quadrilaterals is much more complex as there is more to consider than just angle congruence. It is teacher's choice about when to discuss parallel sides for quadrilateral figures.

Featured Connection

Use the Caption Your Picture strategy to create a glossary of shapes discussed. For each term, students should sketch and label at least two different examples.

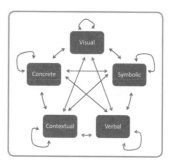

Source: Lesh, Post, & Behr (1987).

Notes

_____

_____

_____

_____

_____

_____

Notes

Materials

- Geometric strips
- Centimeter grid paper

Organization (physical)

- **Getting Started:** Distribute one set of materials to each pair or trio of students.
- **Winding Down:** Rebag the strips and return the materials to home base.

Mathematical Purpose

In this activity, students review the area of a rectangle and reason about the area of a **parallelogram**.

Manipulative Illustrated

- Didax Geostix

Steps

1. Take four strips, two orange and two yellow, and make a rectangle. Place the rectangle on the grid paper and find the area of the rectangle. Be sure to keep the angles right angles while working.

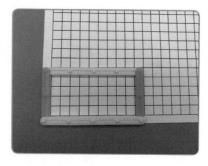

2. Slide the top of the rectangle to one side, creating a non-rectangular parallelogram. Ask students to estimate the area of this shape.

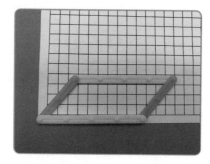

- *How is this shape the same as the rectangle? How is it different?*
- *Is the area of the new shape greater than, less than, or about the same as the area of the rectangle just calculated? What is your reasoning?*

3. Use the grid to estimate the area of the parallelogram, revising the earlier prediction as necessary.

4. Add two additional geometric strips to the figure as shown.

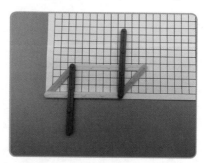

Look at the two triangles created. Ask students what they notice about the new figure:

- *What do you notice about the triangles the extra strips create?*
- *Is it possible to figure out the area of this shape by reasoning about the area of the parts? How would you do that?*
- *Is it possible to rearrange the parts of this figure to make another shape whose area you know how to find? How would you do that?*
- *How can you use your observations to figure out a strategy for finding the area of a parallelogram without counting squares?*

5. Support students to identify the attribute of height as something different from the length of the side of the figure. In the case of a rectangle, height and the length of the vertical side are the same; this is not true for all parallelograms.

6. Test the conjecture with additional figures.

Why This Manipulative?

The hinged joint on the geometric strips makes them ideal for this activity. It is easy for students to see that the side lengths have not changed but the angles have. By placing the figure on grid paper, the change in area is straightforward to estimate.

Developing Understanding

When students first learn to find the area of a rectangle, they are finding the area for a special case of parallelogram, one with four right angles. This activity helps students transition from the special case to the general case as they understand the idea of height in a figure with non-perpendicular sides.

Featured Connection

Use the Build the Equation strategy to help students summarize their experience with this activity. Share the formula for the area of a parallelogram and ask students to build a model showing the elements of the formula. The sketch here is an example based on the image in Step 4.

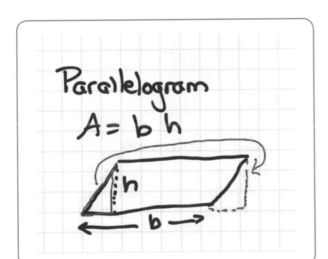

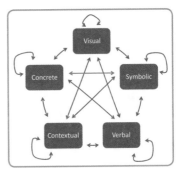

Source: Lesh, Post, & Behr (1987).

Materials

- Geometric strips
- Centimeter grid paper

Organization (physical)

- **Getting Started:** Distribute one set of materials to each pair or trio of students.
- **Winding Down:** Rebag the strips and return the materials to home base.

Mathematical Purpose

In this lesson, students reason about the formula for the area of a triangle. The work begins with right triangles and is then generalized to other triangles.

Activity 6.5 Resources

- *Exploring Area: Triangles* Activity Video

 online resources: To access resource visit resources.corwin.com/ MasteringMathManips/ 4–8

Manipulative Illustrated

- EAI Exploragons®

Steps

1. Have students take three strips (green, orange, and purple) and create a right triangle. Place the triangle on grid paper and count squares to approximate the area.

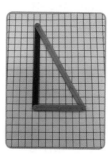

2. Ask students to explore with additional strips to see if they can see the triangle as part of another shape. (To make the exploration more structured, ask them to use additional strips of the same three colors.)

3. Support students to create a rectangle partitioned along one diagonal into two matching right triangles. Use the following questions to guide the discussion:

   - *What shape did you create that includes the triangle? What do you know about that shape?*

   - *What is the relationship between the area of the triangle and the area of the rectangle?*

4. Repeat the process with additional examples until students gain confidence.

5. Have students take three different strips (yellow, green, and purple) and create another triangle. Challenge students to find a rectangle or parallelogram related to this triangle.

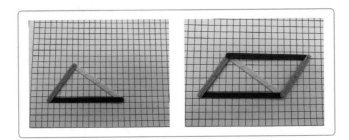

6. Return to the idea of height discussed when learning about the area of a parallelogram in Activity 6.4. Triangles also have height, and this height is useful in finding the area of any triangle.

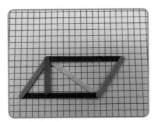

7. Share the formula for the area of a triangle, identifying each component of the formula in the models students have built. Work with additional examples until students gain confidence.

Why This Manipulative?

Because multiple strips can be stacked on a given connector, these pieces are ideal for showing extensions to figures and finding various relationships. At times, the use of paper tracings can support students further.

Developing Understanding

This activity is designed to help students reason about the area of triangles. It may make sense to teach this lesson in two parts, one for right triangles and one for general triangles. Both cases apply the same principle, but the rectangle is easier to see in the case of right triangles.

Featured Connection

Use the Make a Sketch and Name Your Model strategies to record student work for this lesson. Students should show both a right triangle example and a non-right triangle example so they reinforce both aspects of the formula.

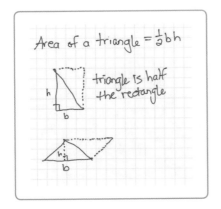

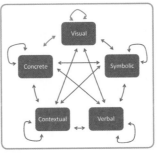
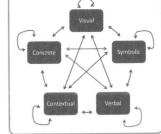

Source: Lesh, Post, & Behr (1987).

Materials

- Geometric strips with protractors
- Activity sheet (one for each student)

Organization (physical)

- **Getting Started:** Distribute one set of materials to each pair or trio of students.
- **Winding Down:** Rebag the strips and return the materials to home base.

Mathematical Purpose

In this lesson, students learn to read a protractor by thinking about angles as the amount of rotation from one location to another.

Activity 6.6 Resources

- *Angles as Rotation* Activity Sheet

 To access resource visit resources.corwin.com/ MasteringMathManips/ 4–8

Manipulative Illustrated

- AngLegs® (hand2mind)

Steps

1. Distribute an activity sheet to each student. Ask students to estimate the size of each angle shown, marking whether it is acute, right, or obtuse. This will help students self-assess as they read the protractor.

2. Distribute two different-colored strips and a snap-on protractor to each student. Show students how to attach the protractor to the two strips so there are three layers at the single connection point. The protractor typically goes on top, as shown in the photo.

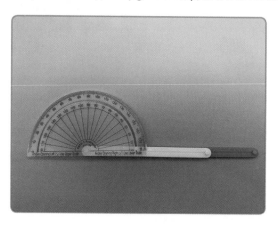

3. Have students place the assembled pieces on the first angle diagram. Remind students that one leg should stay fixed on the starting place (the red leg in the picture) while the other leg will rotate below the protractor. Use one hand to hold the protractor and base leg steady while using the other hand to rotate the second (yellow) leg to the indicated angle. Encourage students to count aloud in increments of 10 degrees as they rotate the leg. Use a wet-erase marker to indicate 10-degree increments on the protractor if desired. Remind students to measure the angle based on the raised line segment in the center of the geometric strip.

4. Repeat the process with several angles until students are comfortable reading the protractor. It is possible to tape the base leg down if that helps students coordinate the parts of the model.

Why This Manipulative?

Using a rotation approach to measuring angles makes it easier for students to see what they are measuring. The fact that the legs and protractor snap together makes it straightforward to keep the pieces aligned when learning to use the tool.

Developing Understanding

Rotation or turn is one of two understandings of angle. The second is the idea of angle as a wedge of space between two rays. It is often easier to learn to use a protractor with the rotation idea of an angle, as shown in this activity. Once students understand this idea, they can use the protractor to measure wedge angles such as those at the center of fraction circle wedges or those created in polygons made with geometric strips.

This activity presumes students have some familiarity with the idea of right, acute, and obtuse angles. While they may not know the specific measurements associated with each, having some idea of relative size, using the corner of a piece of paper as a benchmark, is helpful when beginning to use the protractor. As students gain confidence and experience, encourage students to estimate angle size using 45 degrees or 30 and 60 degrees as benchmarks to improve their measurement skills.

Featured Connection

Use the Make a Sketch strategy to record the angles and their measurements. Encourage students to sketch the semicircle of a protractor over their angle to remember how the tool is positioned for use.

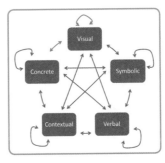

Source: Lesh, Post, & Behr (1987).

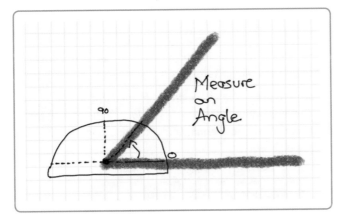

Notes

_____

_____

_____

Materials

- Geometric strips with protractors

Organization (physical)

- **Getting Started:** Distribute one set of materials to each pair or trio of students.

- **Winding Down:** Rebag the strips and return the materials to home base.

Mathematical Purpose

In this activity, students explore parallel lines and transversals cutting across them. This activity can be used to teach perpendicular lines as well.

Manipulative Illustrated

- EAI Exploragons®

Steps

1. Each student should have three long strips, two in one color and one in a second color.

2. Create two perpendicular line segments using two strips, as shown. Measure the angle to confirm it is 90 degrees.

3. Create two parallel line segments, shown in orange. Discuss what makes the segments parallel. Add a transversal, shown in blue, and ask students what they notice and wonder about the figure. Guide the discussion with questions like these:

   - *What does it mean that the orange strips [line segments] are parallel?*

   - *If we moved the blue strip to a different position, but kept it perpendicular, what would change? What would stay the same? Try it to test your conjectures.*

   - *What do you notice about the angles formed by the orange and blue segments? What do you think would stay the same if the blue segment were not perpendicular to the orange ones? What would be different?*

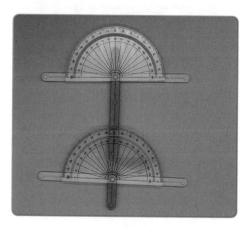

4. Attach a protractor (or two) to the figure and measure the angles around a point where the transversal cuts the parallel lines. Discuss the figure using these questions:

- *How do these angles around a single point relate to each other?*
- *How do they relate to the angles at the corresponding point on the other parallel segment? [It can help to tape the segments down to keep them stable while measuring.]*

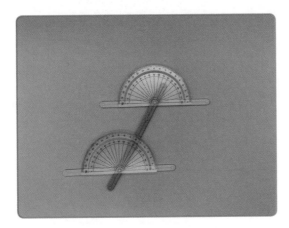

5. Discuss the relationships of **supplementary angles**, of **vertical angles**, and of **corresponding angles** in the figure. Test the relationships with other figures.

Why This Manipulative?

These linear strips are excellent for representing line segments and showing relationships. If you are working with physical strips, a version with connections along the length of the strips is helpful for making a stable diagram.

Developing Understanding

This activity is not intended as a formal proof of the angle relationships for parallel lines with a transversal. Rather, these tools provide experience for students creating these figures and measuring to find the angle relationships and notice a pattern. Because geometric understanding is developed through experience, not through age and maturation, providing hands-on experiences for key geometric ideas is critical for student learning.

Featured Connection

Use the Create a Diagram strategy to label the figure with the terms discussed.

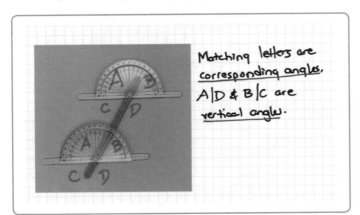

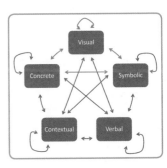

Source: Lesh, Post, & Behr (1987).

Materials

- Geometric strips with protractors

Organization (physical)

- Getting Started: Distribute one set of materials to each pair or trio of students.
- Winding Down: Rebag the strips and return the materials to home base.

Mathematical Purpose

In this activity, students build and measure pairs of **complementary** and supplementary angles.

Manipulative Illustrated

- Didax Geostix

Steps

1. Each student should use two long geometric strips of the same color to form a right angle.

   A single long strip with connectors along the length can be used to represent a straight angle. If the strips you have only connect at the end, connect two to form a straight angle. Form a right angle to explore complementary angles; form a straight angle to explore supplementary angles.

2. Add a strip of a different color to the base and place a protractor on top. Use one of the intermediate connectors on the straight angle.

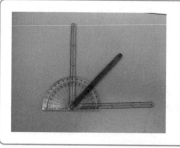 

3. Position the different strip to form an angle. Sketch the figure and record precise measurements for each angle. Check that the sum is 90 or 180 degrees as a check for accurate measurements.

4. Reposition the strip to form a smaller angle and repeat the measurement process. Discuss the patterns students might find using these questions:

   - *What happens to the other angle as the first one gets smaller?*
   - *What will happen as the first angle gets larger? Test the conjecture.*
   - *For supplementary angles, what happens when the first angle is obtuse? Why does this happen?*

Why This Manipulative?

Geometric strips with a connected protractor make measuring angles a relatively straightforward process. Remind students to measure the angle using the ridge down the center of the strip and to place the protractor on top of the stack of strips for easy visibility. Strips with intermediate connectors are easier for creating a straight angle; the additional strip and protractor can be linked to the center connector as shown.

Developing Understanding

This activity gives students experience reasoning about complementary and supplementary angles. Students practice finding the sum of 90 or 180 along with predicting what happens to one angle of the pair as the other angle changes size. Encourage students to estimate angle size (using 45 degrees or 30 and 60 degrees as benchmarks) to improve their measurement skills.

Featured Connection

Use the Name Your Model strategy to create a glossary of terms discussed. For each term, students should include both a sketch and an equation related to the term.

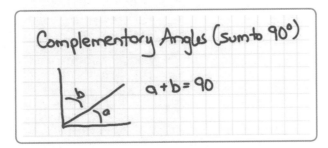

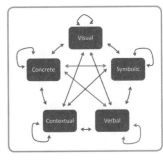

Source: Lesh, Post, & Behr (1987).

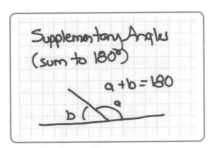

Notes

_____

_____

_____

_____

_____

_____

_____

_____

Materials

- Geometric strips with protractors

Organization (physical):

- **Getting Started:** Distribute one set of materials to each pair or trio of students.
- **Winding Down:** Rebag the strips and return the materials to home base.

Mathematical Purpose

This activity models **dilation** of triangles to create **similar figures**. Students can see the change in length and use the protractor to confirm that the angles have not changed.

Manipulative Illustrated:

- EAI Exploragons®

Steps

1. Have students create an equilateral triangle with three strips of the same color.

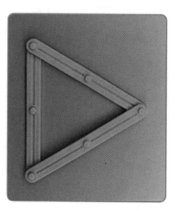

2. Have students use more strips of the same color to extend this triangle so each side is twice the length.

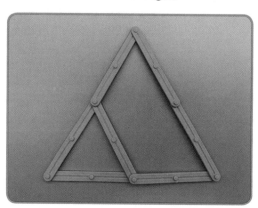

3. Use the protractor to measure the angles of the triangle. Discuss what is the same and what is different about the two figures:

   - *What happened to the side lengths? Did they change? Why or why not?*

   - *What happened to the angle measurements? Did they change? Why or why not?*

4. Create a different triangle (either isosceles or scalene) and then use additional strips to double (or triple) the side lengths.

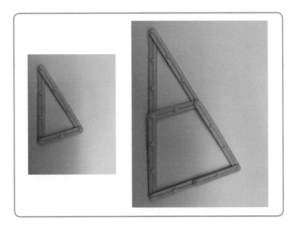

5. Use the protractor to measure the angles of each triangle. Again, discuss what is similar and what is different about the two figures.

6. Share the mathematical definition of similarity with students (corresponding angles are congruent, side lengths are proportional). Talk about how the two examples so far meet the definition. Guide the discussion with questions like these:

   • *How do you know the angles are the same measurement, especially if the shape does not have all angles the same? How do you know which measures to compare?*

   • *What is the ratio between the sides of the first figure and the sides of the second? Did each side change length by the same factor? How do you know?*

7. Create a quadrilateral and extend its side lengths to be twice as long. Use questions like those in Step 6 to discuss whether the two figures are similar.

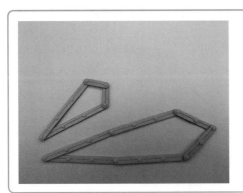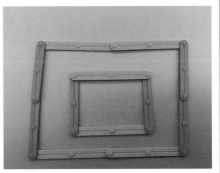

8. Continue exploring additional examples to build student understanding, experience, and confidence. Incorporate the vocabulary term *dilation* into the discussion. The idea of a zoom function on a monitor or photocopy machine can be a good context for what happens when we dilate a figure by changing its scale by a constant ratio.

Why This Manipulative?

Geometric strips make construction of polygons easy. This activity uses the fact that strips of the same color are the same size to scale figures in an easily visible way. Snapping the larger and smaller figures together makes it easier to confirm corresponding angles.

Developing Understanding

Similarity can be a challenging topic for students because the mathematical definition of the term is more precise than the everyday usage of the term to mean "almost alike." If students need to compare the two meanings, use the strips to create another triangle that is almost alike and talk about how the pairs of figures are not mathematically similar. This non-example can help students solidify understanding of the vocabulary. In the accompanying image, the blue side is slightly longer than the double-green side.

Featured Connection

Use the Caption Your Picture strategy to create a glossary entry for *similar*. Students should include two sketches, an example and a non-example.

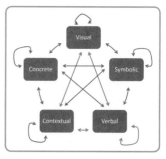

Source: Lesh, Post, & Behr (1987).

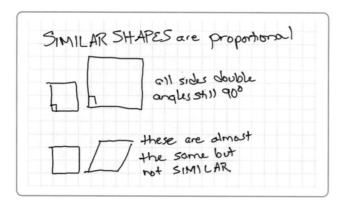

Notes

_____

_____

_____

Notes

Materials

- Geometric strips with protractors

Organization (physical)

- **Getting Started:** Distribute one set of materials to each pair or trio of students.

- **Winding Down:** Rebag the strips and return the materials to home base.

Mathematical Purpose

This activity gives students experience practicing **rigid transformations** (flips, slides, and turns *or* **reflections**, **translations**, and **rotations**) to transform a shape by changing its position in one way.

Activity 6.10 Resources

- *Modeling Rigid Transformations* Activity Video

 To access resource visit resources.corwin.com/ MasteringMathManips/ 4–8

Manipulative Illustrated

- Didax Geostix

Steps

1. Use the strips to build two identical scalene triangles. Tell students they will be using these to model three different transformations. These are called rigid transformations because they change the location and/or orientation of the shape without changing the sides and angles of the shape. Dilations (Activity 6.9) are not rigid transformations because the sides of the shape change.

2. Place the triangles on top of each other to ensure the orientation is the same. Do not connect the snaps. Slide one triangle away from the other without lifting it off the table. This is a translation or slide transformation. Practice other slide transformations, both directed by the teacher and chosen by the students. Students can specify both the direction of a slide and the distance to slide the figure.

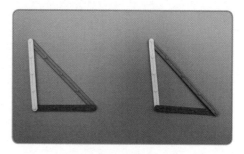

3. Return the shapes to their stacked position and connect one vertex to serve as a pivot point. Rotate the upper figure to another position. This is a rotation or turn transformation. Practice other rotation transformations, both directed by the teacher and chosen by the students. Add a protractor to the top of the stack to measure the amount of rotation if desired.

Return the shapes to their stacked position, unconnected. Lift the upper shape by one vertex and flip it over to the opposite side as if turning the page of a book (see the accompanying video). This is a reflection or flip transformation. Practice other flip transformations using the other two edges of the triangle.

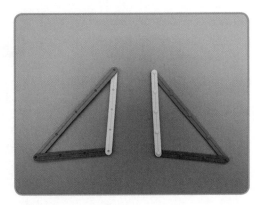

4. Repeat the activity with other triangles and other polygons if desired. Discuss student observations using questions like these:

   • *As you make a transformation, does the shape itself change? Why or why not? If the shape doesn't change, what does change?*

   • *How would you describe the change of each transformation? What mathematical vocabulary is helpful to be precise in these descriptions?*

Why This Manipulative?

Rigid transformations are best modeled with triangles as these figures maintain their shape most clearly when handled. Students can build a variety of triangles to get a sense of how the transformations generalize. It is also possible to do this activity with quadrilaterals or other shapes. The transformations are easiest to see if the shapes are irregular. It can be helpful to add diagonals to the shapes to keep them stable when handled. The red and yellow kite pictured is stabilized by the dark strip.

Developing Understanding

This activity builds initial experience with rigid transformations and allows students to connect the vocabulary with hands-on experiences. It pairs nicely with the transformation lessons in Chapter 7 (Activities 7.8 and 7.9). These activities with geometric strips are less coordinate focused and are useful as first experiences with rigid transformations. Activity 6.11 provides experience using the language of transformations to describe how a shape changes position.

Featured Connection

Use the Caption Your Picture strategy to create a glossary entry for each rigid transformation. Students should include a sketch along with a description of key elements for each transformation.

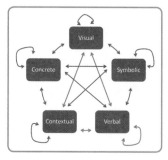

Source: Lesh, Post, & Behr (1987).

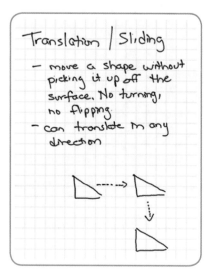

Notes

_____

_____

_____

_____

_____

_____

_____

_____

_____

_____

_____

Notes

Materials

- Geometric strips with protractors
- Activity sheet (one for each student)

Organization (physical)

- **Getting Started:** Distribute one set of materials to each pair or trio of students.
- **Winding Down:** Rebag the strips and return the materials to home base.

Mathematical Purpose

In this activity, students gain experience mapping or describing the path to transform a shape from one position to another.

Activity 6.11 Resources

- *Mapping Congruence With Transformations* Activity Sheet

 To access resource visit resources.corwin.com/ MasteringMathManips/ 4–8

Manipulative Illustrated

- EAI Exploragons®

Steps

1. Select one of the figure pairs on the activity sheet. Build two copies of the shape and position them on the table to match the locations/positions on the drawing.

2. Each transformation on the activity sheet is two steps. Identify the two transformations used to move from the left figure to the right figure. Students should be prepared to justify their response. Guide the discussion with questions like these:

   - *Using only translations, rotations, and reflections, how can you move one triangle so that it is positioned on top of the other triangle?*

   - *Is there more than one way to make the transformation?*

3. Repeat with the other transformations on the page.

4. Challenge students to describe the transformations in both directions (left to right and right to left).

   - *How are the instructions different if you start with the other shape? Why is this the case?*

5. Discuss the idea of congruence, two shapes that are identical in size and shape but may not be identical in position or orientation. One way to verify that shapes are congruent is if one can be transformed to the other using only rigid transformations.

6. Use the strips to build two identical scalene triangles. Lay one triangle on the table and drop the other triangle nearby from a height of 30–50 centimeters (12–18 inches). Write the steps to transform from the placed triangle to the dropped triangle. Repeat several times for additional experience.

Why This Manipulative?

The figures included on the activity sheet are fairly rigid and can be repositioned easily. Students continue to build understanding through hands-on experiences with transformation. In this activity, distance and direction are approximate when describing transformations. If there are two translations, for example, it is helpful to note sliding right for a longer distance and up for a shorter distance as this gives a basis for reflecting on measurements when working on the coordinate plane as in Activities 7.4 and 7.8.

Developing Understanding

This activity moves from understanding the actions associated with each rigid transformation to building a sense of congruence as modeled by rigid transformations. Students know the figures are congruent because they built two of the same figure, but they develop practice mapping from one orientation to another through these activities.

Featured Connection

Use the Create a Diagram strategy to record the steps to transform from one position to the other. Students can do this by sketching and labeling each step along the way. Students might also create and narrate a video of their transformations; this would be closer to the Caption Your Picture strategy.

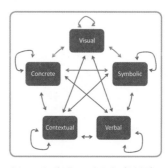

Source: Lesh, Post, & Behr (1987).

Notes

_____

_____

_____

_____

ACTIVITY
6.12

ANGLE SUM AND
EXTERIOR ANGLES FOR
TRIANGLES

| 3 | 4 | 5 | 6 | 7 | 8+ |

Materials

- Geometric strips with protractors

Organization (physical)

- **Getting Started:** Distribute one set of materials to each pair or trio of students.

- **Winding Down:** Rebag the strips and return the materials to home base.

Mathematical Purpose

In this activity, students explore the angles in triangles. They model the sum of the interior angles of a triangle as well as looking at the relationship between interior and exterior angles.

Manipulative Illustrated

- AngLegs® (hand2mind)

Steps

1. Build three identical scalene triangles. Lay them out side by side (oriented the same way) and clearly identify each of the three distinct angles.

2. Connect the three angles together in one stack, aligning the sides of the triangles. Discuss the resulting figure using questions like these:

   - *What do you notice about the figure? What does it tell you about the angles in the triangle?*

   - *Is this true for every triangle? How can you convince yourself (or a friend or a skeptic) that this is always true?*

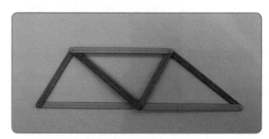

3. Repeat the activity using a variety of other triangles, including isosceles and equilateral triangles. Work with your students to justify their conjecture using appropriate strategies for the standards being addressed.

4. Build a triangle and add an extra strip at each vertex so the figure looks a bit like a pinwheel.

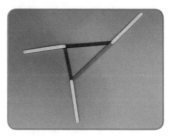

5. Use the protractor to measure each interior and exterior angle of the triangle. Discuss findings using questions like these:

- *What do you notice about each angle pair? Why do you think this is true?*

- *What do you notice about the size of the exterior angle and the measurements of the two opposite interior angles? Why do you think this is true?*

Why This Manipulative?

Connecting strips and protractors make it easy to create and work with a wide range of triangles quickly. The standard strips mean the initial three figures are congruent and save the mess of cutting and tearing paper triangles.

Developing Understanding

This activity is not a formal proof of the sum of the interior angles of a triangle. Where appropriate, this hands-on experience can serve as the foundation for a more formal proof. It can also provide an opportunity for a thoughtful conversation about what constitutes proof in mathematics and creating a careful argument.

Featured Connection

Use the Caption Your Picture strategy to summarize what students have learned about triangle angles in this activity. Student sketches should be labeled and captioned to explain the relationships among the angles in the figure.

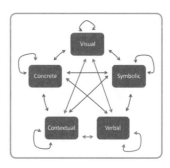

Source: Lesh, Post, & Behr (1987).

Notes

_____

_____

_____

_____

Materials

- Geometric solids
- Activity sheet (one for each student)

Organization (physical)

- **Getting Started:** Distribute three to five related shapes to each group of students.
- **Winding Down:** Collect the shapes and return them to home base.

Mathematical Purpose

In this activity, students use geometric solids to create a **composed shape**. They use their knowledge of finding the volume of each basic shape to find the volume of the composed shape.

Activity 6.13 Resources

- *Identifying Composed Figures* Activity Sheet

 To access resource visit resources.corwin.com/ MasteringMathManips/ 4–8

Manipulative Illustrated

- Didax Geometric Volume Shapes

Steps

1. Distribute three to five shapes to each student or group. Ask students to use two or three shapes to create a composed figure.

2. Ask students to describe the process they would use to find the volume of the composed figure. Guide the discussion with questions like these:

   - *What measurements do you need? Why these particular values?*
   - *How will you use those measurements?*
   - *Is there more than one way to find the volume?*
   - *What is the minimum information you need to find the volume?*

3. Students can build shapes for each other to find the volume as a next level of challenge. Finally, students can locate pictures of composed shapes (e.g., in pictures of buildings) and describe how they would find the volume of the overall figure.

Why This Manipulative?

For this activity, it is helpful for the solids to be related sizes. This means that the **base** of a cylinder has the same diameter as the flat side of a hemisphere or the base of a circular cone. It means prisms have the same (or related) rectangular faces. This allows solids to interact smoothly, creating figures similar to what we see in architecture or other real-world settings. Depending on your instructional purpose, you may wish to distribute deliberate groups of shapes or a more random collection.

Developing Understanding

This activity is not designed to teach the volume formulas. Other lessons in this book (Activities 4.1 and 4.2) support this foundational knowledge. The focus of this activity is to build students' capacity to think strategically about composed shapes so they can readily identify component figures to find the volume by deconstructing the overall figure. Estimations are quite reasonable for calculating volume in this context given the focus on composing and decomposing shapes.

Featured Connection

Use the Caption Your Picture strategy to sketch the composed figure and identify the component parts. This same strategy can be used with pictures of real-world objects or buildings to extend the work beyond shapes from the shape assortment. The activity sheet for this lesson provides a sample image students can use for this work.

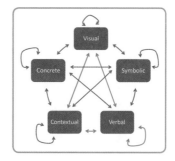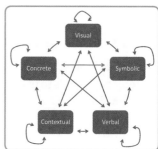

Source: Lesh, Post, & Behr (1987).

World Image by iStock/Leontura

The Build a Word Problem strategy can be used here to explore real-world contexts where students would need to know the volume of a composed figure. One common context is air-handling situations—HVAC systems, whole-house humidifiers, or air purification systems.

Notes

_____

_____

_____

Materials

- Geometric solids
- Construction paper
- Damp sponge

Organization (physical)

- **Getting Started:** Distribute geometric solids to each student or small group. Distribute construction paper and a damp sponge if students will be using this strategy to support their thinking.
- **Winding Down:** Dry the solids, put the damp sponges away, and return the solids to their home base.

Mathematical Purpose

In this activity, students explore the idea of a **net**, a flat shape that can be folded to cover a three-dimensional figure. This sets the stage for Activity 6.15 focusing on **surface area**.

Manipulative Illustrated

- Relational GeoSolids®
  (hand2mind)

Steps

1. Distribute shapes to each group of students. Have each student select one shape and ask students to imagine the shape dipped in paint and then the paint peeled off to create a flat covering for the shape.

Guide the discussion with questions like these:

- *What shapes will we see in the peeled paint? The peeled paint figure is an example of a net, a two-dimensional covering of a three-dimensional shape.*
- *Where does each face of the solid figure appear in your peeled paint net?*
- *How are you sure you have accounted for all of the faces?*

2. Ask students to sketch or trace the shapes they expect to see in their net. Shapes can be dipped in water and used to stamp figures on construction paper. Trace the damp images for a more permanent record. (The images are easiest to see on medium colors of paper.)

3. As students work, encourage them to think strategically about how the various faces of the solid figure are connected. Use questions like these to guide the discussion:

- *Which flat shapes will be adjacent to other flat shapes in the net?*
- *Can you create a figure to cut and fold into the three-dimensional shape?*

4. Provide students with time to sketch, cut, and fold nets for a variety of shapes.

5. Encourage students to keep both nets that "work" and those that do not work. For example, any net of a cube will have six squares for the six faces. Not all arrangements of the six faces will fold into a cube. Students may enjoy exploring the distinctions between these groups.

Why This Manipulative?

A set of solid figures allows students to imagine the process of creating a net (working from three- to two-dimensional) rather than always working to fold a three-dimensional figure from a two-dimensional net. Some figures are more challenging than others; this activity is typically easiest with prisms and pyramids. Finding the rectangle in a cylinder can be challenging for some students. The variety of included figures enables students to progress from simpler figures (like a cube, where the greatest challenge is in thinking about how to position the squares relative to each other) to more complex figures such as a cone or hemisphere.

Developing Understanding

This activity uses the idea of painting a figure and then peeling the paint to introduce the idea of a net. Teachers may want to use precut nets to fold solid figures as an alternate way of introducing the concept of a net to students. It is important that students have experience moving both directions between two- and three-dimensional figures. This supports their developing spatial reasoning and provides greater flexibility in their thinking.

Encourage students to cut out and fold their nets, without concern for connecting tabs. While pieces may not fit together perfectly, students can see which parts of their model are accurate and which require more refinement to correctly develop a net for a given shape.

Featured Connection

Use the Create a Diagram strategy to draw both the solid figure and the net, showing how the parts of one relate to the parts of the other.

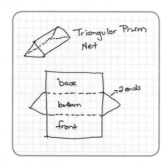

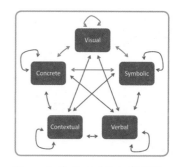

Source: Lesh, Post, & Behr (1987).

Again, students may use the Write a Word Problem strategy to envision situations where they need to think about what a three-dimensional figure would look like if flattened out. Any situation where surface area is useful (e.g., painting a house or wallpapering a room) is appropriate. Digital cutting tools may also require this thinking in order to create the pieces for a three-dimensional model.

Materials

- Geometric solids

Organization (physical)

- Getting Started: Distribute three to five shapes to each group of students.
- Winding Down: Collect the shapes and return them to home base.

Mathematical Purpose

In this activity, students move from the general work of sketching a net to using a more precise figure to calculate surface area.

Manipulative Illustrated

- EAI GeoModel® Shapes

Steps

1. Activity 6.14 helped students understand what form a painted net for a three-dimensional figure might take. This activity asks a related question: How much paint do we need?

2. Discuss the idea of surface area with students. Focus on the fact that this is still area (a two-dimensional measurement) now applied to a three-dimensional shape. The surface area is the total area across all surfaces of the figure.

3. If necessary, return to Activities 6.4 and 6.5 to review area for parallelograms and triangles.

4. Students can use a premade (commercial or die-cut) net, sketch a net for a new figure, or use a net created in Activity 6.14. Working on grid paper or using careful measurements will create a more precise surface area calculation. Ask students to calculate the area of each component shape in the net in order to find the surface area of the shape. Students can record their calculations in the appropriate section of their sketched net to ensure they have included all component faces. The accompanying image is the triangular prism net created in Activity 6.14.

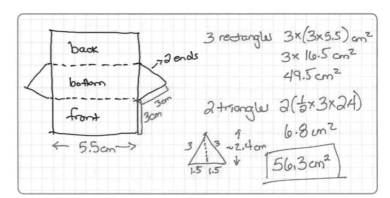

5. For some figures, students will need to think about how to identify the measurements needed. For example, one dimension of the rectangular section of a cylinder's net is the circumference of the circle on each end. This value may be easier to calculate than to measure.

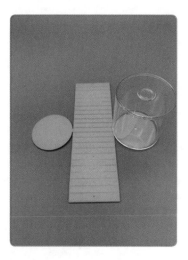

Why This Manipulative?

Surface area can be an abstract concept for students, and it is easy to miss a face when reasoning about the computation. Use solid figures to create nets and then calculate surface area so students can see where the formulas come from. Shapes with premade nets can serve as a check for student-made nets. Students can create their own nets and calculations, then check them against the premade figures. For more difficult figures (like the cylinder), the premade net is helpful because these can be challenging to visualize. To help students move directly from concrete to abstract, provide removable stickers so students can mark each face as they include it in the surface area calculation.

Developing Understanding

Formulas are typically quite abstract for students. Just as students use unit squares and cubes to develop initial understandings of area and volume, creating nets for solid figures and finding the surface area develops foundational understanding of surface area. Individual teachers can decide how much precision to look for in this activity.

Featured Connection

Use a variation of the Build the Equation strategy to have students sketch a solid figure and record the process they would use to calculate surface area for the figure. While students are not literally building the elements of the equation, they are matching the components of the figure to the elements of their calculation. The image in Step 4 of this activity is an example.

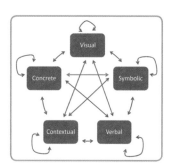

Source: Lesh, Post, & Behr (1987).

Encourage students to use the Write a Word Problem strategy to consider contexts in which knowing surface area is important. In some cases, partial surface area is enough; solar panels on the roof of a house is an example of this.

Materials

- Hollow geometric solids in related sizes
- Filler material (sand, rice, water, etc.)

Organization (physical)

- **Getting Started:** Distribute shapes to groups of students.
- **Winding Down:** Return the shapes to their home base.

Mathematical Purpose

In this activity, students estimate the relationship between the volume of a known figure (a cube or rectangular prism) and the volume of an unknown figure, a cone or pyramid, cylinder, or sphere.

Manipulative Illustrated

- Relational GeoSolids® (hand2mind)

Steps

1. To explore the volume of a cylinder, have students consider both a square prism and a cylinder where the side length of the square prism is the same as the diameter of the circular end of the cylinder.

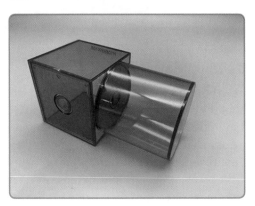

Review the ideas of area developed with unit cubes in Activities 4.1 and 4.2. For the prism, the volume is the area of the first layer multiplied by the height. Discuss students' thinking guided by questions like these:

- » *How are the cylinder and cube alike? How are they different?*
- » *Is the cylinder's volume greater than, less than, or about the same as the volume of the cube? How do you know?*
- » *How does considering base and height help you reason about the volume of the cylinder?*
- » *Can you figure out the area of the base of the cylinder? How would you do that? If not, what if you use an estimated value or a variable?*
- » *What do you know about the height of the shape?*

2. This approach will not work for cones or pyramids because the area of the cross section changes with the height of the figure. Compare a cylinder and right circular cone with the same diameter of the circular base and the same height. Discuss their volumes using the following questions:

- » *How are the cylinder and cone alike? How are they different?*
- » *Is the volume of the cone greater than, less than, or about the same as the volume of the cylinder? Why do you think that?*
- » *What fraction of the volume of the cylinder is the cone?*

Have students predict and then use filling materials to test their conjecture. If possible, test with cones and cylinders of various sizes.

3. Compare a rectangular pyramid with a **right rectangular prism** of the same overall dimensions. Does the $\frac{1}{3}$ relationship still hold with these figures? Again, test using fill materials. Share the relevant formulas and find both the volume of the larger figure (the cylinder or prism) and the $\frac{1}{3}$ fraction in the formula.

4. Compare a sphere with a cube of similar proportions (side length either the diameter or radius of the sphere). How do the volumes of these figures relate? Test with filling material and compare the results to the formula for finding the volume of a sphere. Can students identify the various elements in the formula in their model?

Why This Manipulative?

Volume formulas, as with many formulas, can feel abstract to students. By relating the volume of less intuitive figures to the volume of more intuitive figures, students can see where the elements of the formula come from and where the basic idea of volume (cross-sectional area × height) appears. Hollow solid figures allow for this exploration.

Developing Understanding

In this activity, students pour filler material to reason about the relationships between the volume of figures they can easily visualize and those they cannot readily see. By connecting this concrete experience to abstract formulas, students are better able to understand and apply the formulas when needed.

Featured Connection

This activity is a variation of the Build the Equation strategy when students connect their physical experiences pouring filler materials to the components of the standard volume formulas for various three-dimensional shapes. Students can experience the fact that three fills of the cone will fill the related cylinder, for example.

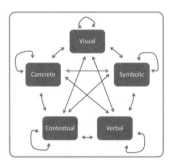

Source: Lesh, Post, & Behr (1987).

Notes

_____

_____

_____

_____

_____

_____

_____

_____

_____

_____

CLOSING REFLECTIONS: GEOMETRIC STRIPS AND SOLIDS

How do I use geometric strips and solids in my classroom now? What concepts do I use them to teach?

_____

_____

_____

_____

_____

What new ways have I found to use geometric strips and solids to better support student understanding?

_____

_____

_____

_____

_____

What are my goals to make geometric strips and solids a more regular part of my instruction?

_____

_____

_____

_____

_____

UNDERSTANDING GEOBOARDS

Geoboards are a family of tools designed to help students think about shapes. The flat board has pegs arranged in a grid, and students use rubber bands to create shapes on the board. The traditional geoboard has an array of 25–100 pegs arranged in a square grid. Some boards have pegs in an approximately circular arrangement on the back of the board. Other boards have pegs arranged in an **isometric grid**. Finally, there are "pegboards" that have holes where students can insert pegs and transparent **axes** to create a coordinate grid on the board. This variation is helpful for plotting points or working with simple coordinate geometry.

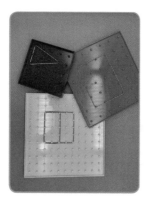 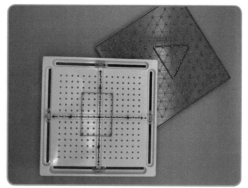

Geoboards are most effective for teaching the following ideas:

- Representing data using graphs (especially line plots and linear functions)
- Representing shapes and attributes
- Coordinate geometry, including transformations

Introducing Geoboards to Students

For many teachers, the use of rubber bands is nerve-wracking. Remind students about the appropriate use of mathematical tools before you distribute materials, and trust your own ability to distinguish a band that slips from a band intentionally aimed at a target. Some teachers provide a fixed number of bands to each student to limit the risk.

Use the *Notice and Wonder Thinking Routine* (described in the introductory chapter) to support students exploring the board. Students may notice the quantity of pegs or the arrangement of the pegs. They may explore the number of squares they can find on the board or whether they can make certain shapes. How many different types of triangles can they make? Is there any triangle they cannot make?

Key Ideas With Geoboards

- Some coordinate boards have removable axes while others are fixed. Removable axes make line plots easier but are more pieces to keep up with. If the axes are removable, be careful of the order in which you put the axes on the board. They are typically designed for one to go first and one to go second.

- Axes will be more stable if there is a peg at each end. It is straightforward to peg the origin and then points 5 and 10 units away. This allows the pegs both to stabilize the axes and to provide count guidance as the student is plotting points.

- Depending on the color of the boards, dry spaghetti can be hard to see. It can be colored with a marker to make it easier to see on a light-colored board.

Things to Consider About Geoboards

- There are many different kinds of geoboards, each supporting different kinds of mathematical thinking. Explore using a variety of geoboard tools to support the full range of your standards.

- Depending on how you place bands on the geoboard, the side of a shape might not be a single segment, but the two sides of the stretched band. It is worth talking to students about this as a limit of the tool so they understand that the side of a shape created on the geoboard might not look exactly like the shape we sketch or create with other tools.

- Consider how you will manage the bands. Set your classroom expectations and manage the materials in ways that support your students successfully using the tool.

- Recognize that if you use the "circular" side of the geoboard, you will actually get a many-sided polygon, not a true circle, when stretching a band around the pegs.

Alternatives to Commercial Geoboards

Geoboards can be constructed from squares of plywood or foam-core board with strong pins or small nails arranged on the appropriate grid. It is helpful to use a paper template to place the pins or nails consistently when creating homemade boards.

Working With Virtual Geoboards

Students can use virtual geoboards for many of the same experiences. The way students construct shapes might be different, tracing around the perimeter rather than stretching a band from one vertex. Shapes might also appear differently, with single-edge segments rather than the double-edge segments that bands can create.

MULTIPLYING FRACTIONS WITH AREA MODELS

Materials:

- Virtual geoboard resource or geoboards
- Bands in at least three colors

Organization (virtual):

- **Getting Started:** Ensure students can access and use the virtual tool. Review annotation tools, the process for taking screenshots, and other important supports.
- **Winding Down:** Use screenshots to save student work.

Mathematical Purpose

In this activity, students create an area model for multiplying fractions.

Manipulative Illustrated

- Toy Theater Virtual Geoboard: https://toytheater.com/geoboard/

Steps

1. This activity will model the product $\frac{1}{2} \times \frac{3}{4}$.

2. Have students loop a 2 × 4 rectangle on the board. This is the only use of this color band (blue). This rectangle represents the whole for this multiplication problem. The area of this rectangle is defined to be the whole.

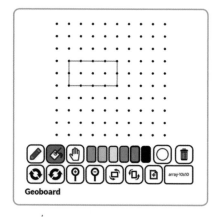

3. Ask students to find the area of the rectangle. Discuss their thinking using these questions:

   - *How did you find the area of the rectangle? Can you confirm your finding by using another method?*

   - *How many squares are inside the rectangle? How does the number of squares relate to the dimensions of the rectangle?*

4. Ask students to use a band in a second color (orange) to ring the lower half of the rectangle.

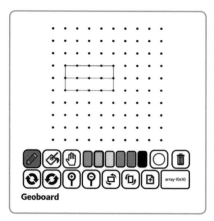

Guide their thinking using questions like these:

- *What fraction of the rectangle's area is inside this new ring? How do you know?*
- *What are the dimensions of this smaller rectangle? How do they relate to the dimensions of the larger rectangle?*

5. Use a band in the third color (green) to ring $\frac{3}{4}$ of the rectangle, building from the longer side. Guide students' thinking using questions like these:

- *What fraction of the rectangle's area is inside this new ring? How do you know?*
- *What are the dimensions of this smaller rectangle? How do they relate to the dimensions of the larger rectangle?*
- *What part of this figure represents $\frac{1}{2} \times \frac{3}{4}$? How do you know?*
- *What is the area of the rectangle representing $\frac{1}{2} \times \frac{3}{4}$? How do you know?*

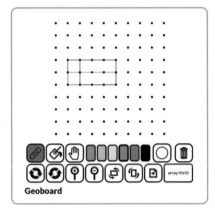

6. The product is represented inside the rectangle bounded by the second and third color bands. Ask students to count the number of squares in the smaller bounded rectangle (the numerator of the product) and to count the number of squares in the whole rectangle. Students should see that the number of squares in the smaller rectangle is the product of the numerator and the number of squares in the whole rectangle is the product of the denominators.

7. Repeat this activity with a variety of other factors to build student confidence in the process.

Why This Manipulative?

This activity can be done with 5-pin or 11-pin geoboards. A wider range of denominators can be modeled with an 11-pin board. This activity is more difficult to describe in writing than to build in practice; do not be discouraged by the number of steps listed.

Developing Understanding

Area is a common model for understanding multiplication. It helps students understand multiplication generally to see this model used with a variety of numbers, including whole numbers, fractions, and decimals. Using this approach helps students see how multiplying both numerators and denominators contributes to finding the product.

This is not the time to create equivalent fractions or be concerned about simplifying fractions. Students will see what is happening in the model if they leave the products as they appear. For example, multiplying $\frac{3}{8} \times \frac{4}{6}$ should be left as $\frac{12}{24}$ so students can see the underlying structure.

Featured Connection

Use the Caption Your Picture strategy to help students connect the physical model built on the geoboard with the symbolic representation of fraction multiplication.

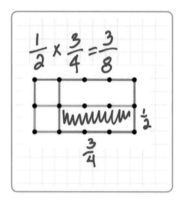

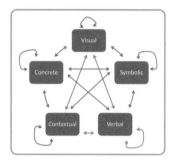

Source: Lesh, Post, & Behr (1987).

Notes

_____

_____

_____

_____

_____

_____

_____

_____

_____

_____

Notes

_____

_____

_____

_____

_____

_____

_____

_____

_____

_____

_____

_____

_____

_____

_____

_____

_____

_____

_____

_____

_____

Materials

- Coordinate board with axes and pegs (bands are not needed)
- Sticky notes or wet-erase marker
- Activity sheet (one for each student)

Organization (physical)

- **Getting Started:** Distribute materials to students.
- **Winding Down:** Gather materials and return to home base.

Mathematical Purpose

In this activity, students create a line plot based on a data set.

Activity 7.2 Resources

- *Line Plot Measurement Data* Activity Sheet

 To access resource visit resources.corwin.com/ MasteringMathManips/ 4–8

Manipulative Illustrated

- XY Coordinate Pegboard (hand2mind)

Steps

1. Review the elements of a line plot with students. Share a data set with students and begin to build the line plot.

2. Place a horizontal axis on the board and use one color of peg to anchor either end.

3. Use sticky notes or a strip of construction paper to label the axis. Benchmark points can be marked with pegs along the axis.

4. Use the second color peg to mark the data points from the data set. Discuss the data distribution. If appropriate, identify the median and mode of the data.

Use questions like these to guide the discussion:

- *What do you notice about the data? What do you wonder about the data?*
- *Is there a way to find the value "in the middle" of these data? How might you do that? Why did you choose the method you chose?*
- *If you summarize the data with the mode, how will you explain what that means? How does it describe the data well? What are the weaknesses of describing the data this way?*
- *If you summarize the data with the median, how will you explain what it means? How does it describe the data well? What are the weaknesses of describing the data this way?*

5. This activity can be repeated with other data sets, including the sibling data from Activity 4.10.

Why This Manipulative?

Students are often anxious when creating graphs. The images are complex, and a small mistake can mean re-creating a great deal of work when starting over. When students create graphs on the pegboard, the stakes for errors are lower, and students can focus first on creating and understanding the graph and second on drawing the graph on paper.

Developing Understanding

Line plots are an effective way of representing frequency distributions of data. This activity develops students' understanding of creating line plots and interpreting data represented within the line plot.

Featured Connection

Use the Create a Diagram strategy to support students moving from the physical representation created on the coordinate pegboard to visual representations drawn on grid paper or plain paper. You can see a sample line graph from this "roll of a die" data in Activity 4.8.

Students can also use the Write a Word Problem strategy to identify situations and questions where line plots can be helpful in making sense of data.

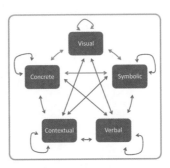

Source: Lesh, Post, & Behr (1987).

Materials

- Coordinate pegboard with axes, pegs, and bands, stored in a gallon bag

Organization (physical)

- **Getting Started:** Distribute the pegboards.
- **Winding Down:** Repackage materials and return to home base.

Mathematical Purpose

In this activity, students learn to plot points in a coordinate plane. The instructions graph a triangle in the first quadrant. Alternate data points are provided for graphing a quadrilateral in four quadrants for older students.

Manipulative Illustrated

- Didax XY Axis Pegboard

Steps

1. Distribute the coordinate boards and place the axes on the board to indicate the first quadrant. Use pegs to anchor the axes at the origin and the remote ends of the axes.

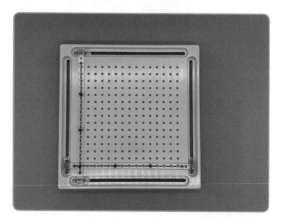

2. Write the first set of coordinates on the board (2, 3) and discuss the meaning of the coordinates. Guide students to locate this point and place a peg there.

3. Repeat the process for two additional points (8, 4) and (4, 7). Loop the triangle with a band and discuss the shape. Guide the discussion with these questions:

   - *How do you know where to place each vertex? Why is it important to read the coordinates the same way every time?*

   - *What shape have you created? How do you know?*

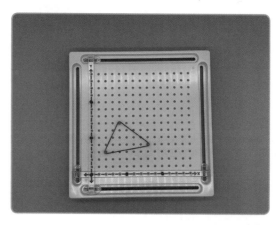

4. Repeat the process with additional points and shapes as desired.

5. For work in four quadrants, place the axes for four quadrants and use the points (2, 3), (−4, 2), (−3, −4), and (4, −2). Loop the quadrilateral with a band and discuss the shape.

Why This Manipulative?

Students are often anxious when creating graphs. The images are complex, and a small mistake can mean re-creating a great deal of work when starting over. When students create graphs on the pegboard, the stakes for errors are lower, and students can focus first on creating and understanding the graph and second on drawing the graph on paper. While the pegboard is not friendly to randomly selected coordinates, it is a powerful tool for helping students develop confidence and competence in graphing.

It is also important to recognize that the coordinate range for the pegboard is small. Fractional values are not friendly unless you choose values and set up the axes carefully. This is an excellent tool for working with small integer coordinates to understand what happens when points are plotted on a graph. Challenge students to use a dry- or wet-erase marker to show you where they would like to plot a fractional coordinate as readiness for working on graph paper directly.

Developing Understanding

Plotting points is an essential skill for students to master. This activity is designed to help students learn to plot points while reducing the anxiety often created by graphing on grid paper. Support students to understand the meaning of coordinate points (horizontal position, vertical position) and the connection between the value of coordinates and location on the plane.

Featured Connection

Use the Create a Diagram strategy to support students moving from the physical representation created on the coordinate pegboard to visual representations drawn on grid paper or plain paper. Challenge students who are ready to reverse this process, creating a shape on the pegboard and then recording the coordinates of the vertices.

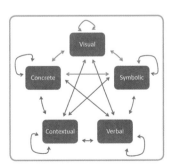

Source: Lesh, Post, & Behr (1987).

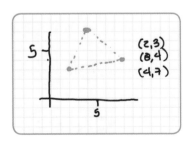

Materials

- Coordinate pegboard with axes, pegs, and bands, stored in a gallon bag

Organization (physical)

- **Getting Started:** Distribute the pegboards.
- **Winding Down:** Repackage materials and return to home base.

Mathematical Purpose

In this activity, students learn to calculate the distance between points that are aligned vertically or horizontally.

Manipulative Illustrated

- Didax XY Axis Pegboard

Steps

1. Using the pegboard set up for first-coordinate graphing, peg and loop a rectangle with the following coordinates: (2, 2), (7, 2), (2, 5), and (7, 5).

2. Ask students to determine the length of each side of the rectangle. Encourage students to use at least two different strategies to find and confirm the length of each segment. Discuss their work using these questions:

   - *Is each side a different length? How many side lengths did you have to calculate?*
   - *How long is each side? How do you know? Can you confirm that length with another method?*
   - *How can the coordinates help you find the side length?*
   - *Do you need to use both coordinates or only one? Why?*

3. Model or ask a student to model using coordinates to calculate side length for the rectangle. Be sure to discuss the meaning of the coordinate that remains the same as well as the calculation of the distance as the difference between the coordinates. In general, the idea of direction is not important in finding the length of a segment (although context may create exceptions), so using absolute value is appropriate for these questions.

4. Repeat the activity with other first-quadrant rectangles.

5. Where appropriate, repeat the activity with four-quadrant rectangles. Use these coordinates for the first example: (3, 2), (−4, 2), (−4, −3), and (3, −3).

As you discuss the distance between these points, you can use similar questions to those in Step 2. Also include the idea of absolute value. Typically, students compute the distance across an axis in two chunks—how far to 0 and then how far beyond 0.

Why This Manipulative?

As with many graphing activities, the coordinate board relieves students' stress around graphing and provides concrete experiences with marking locations on the coordinate plane. Working with the pegboard, where distance can be counted as well as calculated, allows students to develop confidence in the process, which serves them well when values are not friendly to modeling on the coordinate board.

Developing Understanding

This activity extends early understanding of distance on the number line to distance in two directions, parallel to either axis. It is an intermediate step along the way between one-dimensional distance and finding distance between any two points on the plane.

For students who are ready, this lesson can be generalized to the distance formula (for the distance between any two points) by using the Pythagorean theorem. If the graph is on a 1-centimeter or 0.5-inch square, then a ruler can easily be used to measure the approximate distance to confirm calculations.

Featured Connection

Use the Caption Your Picture strategy to support students connecting the physical representation of distance (the sides of a rectangle) with the abstract representation of calculating distance based on coordinates.

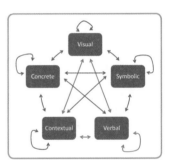

Source: Lesh, Post, & Behr (1987).

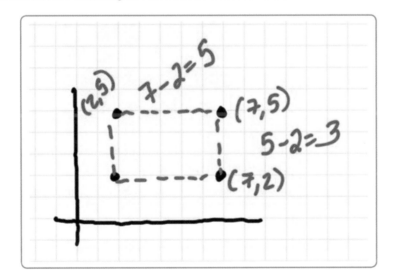

Notes

_____

_____

_____

Materials

- Coordinate pegboard with axes, pegs, and bands, stored in a gallon bag
- Sticky notes

Organization (physical)

- **Getting Started:** Distribute the pegboards.
- **Winding Down:** Repackage materials and return to home base.

Mathematical Purpose

In this activity, students develop understanding of proportional relationships by graphing.

Manipulative Illustrated

- XY Coordinate Pegboard (hand2mind)

Steps

The highway department can paint lines on 3 miles of road each day. How many miles of road can be painted in 2 days? In 3 days?

iStock/zhaojiankang

1. Review the problem with students and discuss the context to develop their understanding.

2. Distribute the coordinate boards to students and set the boards up for first-quadrant graphing. Use sticky notes to label the axes based on the information in the problem.

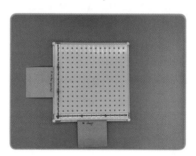

3. Ask students to consider the situation described in the problem. Guide the discussion with questions like these:

    - *How many miles of highway can be painted in one day? How would this point be indicated on the graph? Use a peg to plot this point.*

    - *How many miles of highway can be painted in two days? Where is this point located on the graph?*

    - *What are the coordinates of this point? What does each value mean in the context of the problem?*

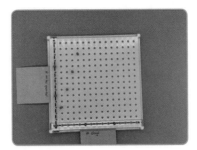

- *Place other points on the graph and explain the meaning of their coordinates.*
- *What does the origin (0, 0) mean in the context of this situation?*
- *How much road could be painted in $1\frac{1}{2}$ days? Where is this point on the graph?*

4. Once students understand the graph, have students record their graph on grid paper as part of their answer to the questions in the prompt.

5. Repeat with other proportional situations to build student confidence and skills.

Why This Manipulative?

As with many graphing activities, the coordinate board relieves students' stress around graphing and provides concrete experiences with marking locations on the coordinate plane. The coordinate board does not lend itself to fractional values, but students benefit from estimating values for straightforward fractions in context.

Developing Understanding

Proportional relationships are a critical understanding in middle school. Students must be able to move back and forth across contextual, visual, and symbolic representations of a problem situation. This exercise gives students practice interpreting a graph of a proportional situation.

Featured Connection

Use the Make a Sketch strategy to connect the physical graphs created on the coordinate board to a more traditional graph on grid paper. Students should create a graph and indicate at least two points on the graph. For those points, students should describe the meaning of each point in terms of the problem context. This supports students both to construct graphs confidently and to make sense of data presented in graphical form.

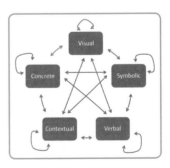

Source: Lesh, Post, & Behr (1987).

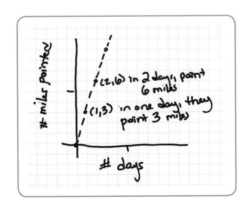

Students can also use the Build the Equation and Write a Word Problem strategies to reverse this activity. Starting with an equation for a proportional relationship ($y = kx$), students can build the equation on the pegboard and create a word problem context represented by the equation.

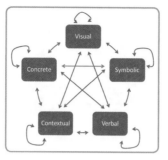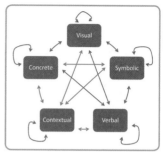

Source: Lesh, Post, & Behr (1987).

Notes

_____

_____

_____

_____

_____

_____

_____

_____

_____

_____

_____

_____

_____

_____

Notes

Materials

- Coordinate pegboard with axes, pegs, and bands, stored in a gallon bag

Organization (physical)

- **Getting Started:** Distribute the pegboards.

- **Winding Down:** Repackage materials and return to home base.

Mathematical Purpose

In this activity, students explore **slope** and build their understanding of similar triangles in the context of slope. This activity assumes students have some familiarity with the concept of slope and how it is represented in a linear equation.

Manipulative Illustrated

- XY Coordinate Pegboard (hand2mind)

Steps

1. Distribute the coordinate boards and set them up for four-quadrant graphing. Ask students to graph the line $y = x - 2$ on the board, extending the full range of the board.

2. Discuss the slope of the line with the class. Guide the discussion with the following questions:

   - *What is the slope of this line? How do you know?*

   - *Where do you see the slope in the equation? Where do you see it in the graph?*

   - *Is the slope the same everywhere on the line? How do you know?*

3. Add an additional peg to the board and use a band to create a slope triangle. This is a right triangle whose hypotenuse is a segment of the line, as shown in white in the image. Use the coordinates on the board to check the slope using these two points.

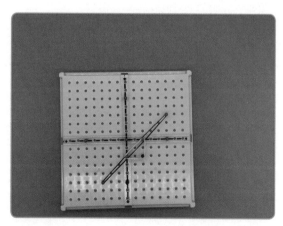

4. Now create another slope triangle in a different size and/or orientation. The image shows two examples.

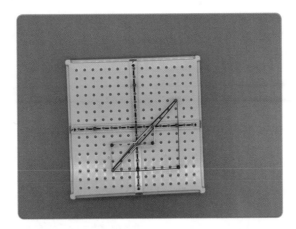

5. Ask students to select two of the slope triangles and determine whether the triangles are similar.

6. Once students have determined that their own triangles are similar, partner them with another student to see if all four slope triangles are similar. Guide the discussion using these questions:

   • *How do these triangles help you measure slope? Does it matter which triangle(s) you use? Why or why not?*

   • *Do you think all the slope triangles for a given figure are similar? Why or why not?*

   • *How do you know when two figures are similar? How can you determine if these triangles are similar?*

   • *How many figures must be tested to make this determination?*

7. Have students record their thinking in their math journals, sketching a graph of the line, at least two different slope triangles, and evidence that the triangles are similar.

8. Repeat with additional examples as appropriate for the students.

Why This Manipulative?

Graphing a line on the coordinate board makes it easy to construct a variety of slope triangles, both above and below the line. If students wish to test another case, they can easily create new triangles.

Developing Understanding

This activity brings two important ideas together—slope and similar figures. Because slope is a ratio (rise over run), the triangles must be similar in order to have a constant slope. Help students understand this idea by creating equivalent ratios with triangles of various sizes. Be careful to support students working correctly with signed numbers, especially if their two slope triangles are on opposite sides of the line.

Featured Connection

Use the Create a Diagram strategy to connect the physical graphs created on the coordinate board to a more traditional graph on grid paper. Students should create a graph and indicate at least two slope triangles on the graph. Use equivalent ratios to show that the slope triangles are similar.

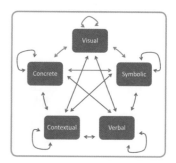

Source: Lesh, Post, & Behr (1987).

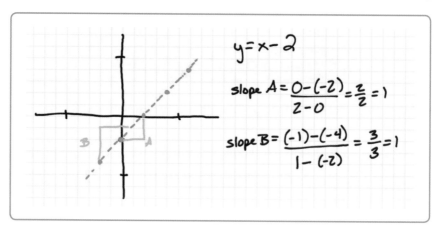

$$y = x - 2$$

$$\text{slope } A = \frac{0-(-2)}{2-0} = \frac{2}{2} = 1$$

$$\text{slope } B = \frac{(-1)-(-4)}{1-(-2)} = \frac{3}{3} = 1$$

Notes

_____

_____

_____

_____

_____

_____

_____

_____

_____

_____

_____

Notes

Materials

- Virtual geoboard resource or physical geoboards (5-pin, 11-pin, or isometric)
- Bands
- Dry spaghetti (several pieces per group)
- Activity sheet (one for each student)

Organization (virtual)

- **Getting Started:** Ensure students can access and use the virtual tool. Review annotation tools, the process for taking screenshots, and other important supports.
- **Winding Down:** Use screenshots to save student work.

Mathematical Purpose

In this activity, students create a shape and identify **lines of symmetry** in the shape.

Activity 7.7 Resources

- *Lines of Symmetry* Activity Sheet

 To access resource visit resources.corwin.com/ MasteringMathManips/ 4–8

Manipulative Illustrated

- Math Learning Center Virtual Geoboard: https://apps. mathlearningcenter.org/ geoboard/

Steps

1. Review the idea of symmetry with students. Use the following questions to guide the discussion:

   - *What does it mean for a shape to be symmetric?*
   - *Can a shape have more than one line of symmetry?*
   - *Find an object in the room with at least one line of symmetry. Show the object and line of symmetry, explaining how you know the object is symmetric.*

2. Open the virtual manipulative and ask students to construct one of the shapes on the geoboard. Indicate all the lines of symmetry they see.

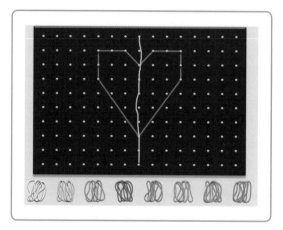

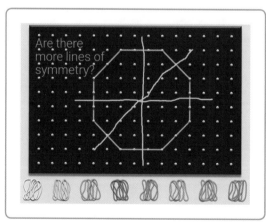

3. Transfer the line(s) to the handout, cut out the shape, and fold on the lines. Check to see if the halves of the shape match by holding the folded paper up to a window.

4. Students could also print their work and fold it to test for symmetry.

5. Repeat with additional shapes to help students build experience and confidence.

6. Challenge students to create a shape with symmetry. The specific terms given to students can vary based on the learning goals of the lesson.

Why This Manipulative?

This activity can be completed with any geoboard. There is more flexibility in the 11-pin board because more shapes can be created. The isometric board allows different shapes and rotational symmetry based on 60 degrees rather than 90 degrees on the square board. If you are working with a physical geoboard, pieces of dry spaghetti are a good tool for testing lines of symmetry. On a virtual geoboard, make sure the tool you are using allows annotation so students can mark the line(s) of symmetry they find.

Developing Understanding

Students develop their understanding of symmetry through experience. By building the figures, students notice design features and shapes that suggest symmetry. For example, the V shape at the bottom of the triangle is an indicator of a potential line of symmetry.

Featured Connection

When students transfer their line of symmetry from the geoboard to the image (Step 3), they are using the Make a Sketch strategy to move their thinking from concrete representations to visual representations or from one visual representation (the virtual geoboard) to another (the image on the activity sheet).

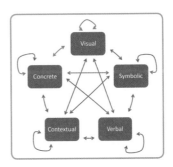

Source: Lesh, Post, & Behr (1987).

Notes

_____

_____

_____

_____

_____

_____

_____

Materials

- Coordinate pegboard with axes, pegs, and bands, stored in a gallon bag

Organization (physical)

- **Getting Started:** Distribute the pegboards.
- **Winding Down:** Repackage materials and return to home base.

Mathematical Purpose

In this activity, students practice translating a polygon on the coordinate plane. This activity focuses on how coordinates change when a shape is translated.

Manipulative Illustrated

- Didax XY Axis Pegboard

Steps

1. Set up the coordinate board for four-quadrant graphing. Make a triangle with vertices at (2, 1), (4, 2), and (3, 4).

2. Ask students to create a new triangle, the result of translating the original triangle 6 units to the left. Discuss what happens using the following questions:

   - *What are the new coordinates of the vertices?*
   - *Did both coordinates change? If not both, which one changed? Why?*

3. Ask students to predict where the triangle will be if it is translated 7 spaces down.

   - *Will one or both coordinates change? If only one, which one?*
   - *How will one or both coordinates change?*

   After predicting the new coordinates, have the students build this third triangle on the coordinate board.

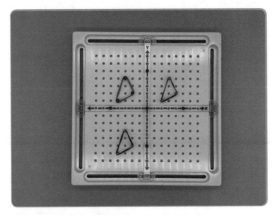

4. Repeat the activity with additional shapes, varying the starting points and translation instructions.

5. Have students sketch one figure on grid paper, labeling the original coordinates as well as the transformed coordinates.

Why This Manipulative?

Students can slide a paper figure on grid paper or simply draw the figures, but the experience of translation is more active when students deliberately count and place pegs for the transformation of each vertex. The coordinate board makes this a straightforward activity for students.

Developing Understanding

Transformations are important tools for spatial reasoning as well as for coordinate geometry. Understanding how translations impact the graph of a figure prepares students for many future areas of study, including predicting the graphs of quadratic functions.

Featured Connection

This lesson uses the Name Your Model strategy to help students connect their physical graph on the coordinate board with the more traditional graph on paper and the systematic way coordinates change with translation. By recording coordinates and their changes, students are supported to see how the action of translation impacts location on the plane.

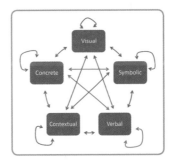

Source: Lesh, Post, & Behr (1987).

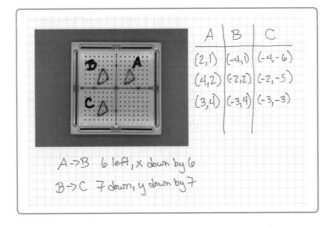

Materials

- Coordinate pegboard with axes, pegs, and bands, stored in a gallon bag

Organization (physical)

- **Getting Started:** Distribute the pegboards.
- **Winding Down:** Repackage materials and return to home base.

Mathematical Purpose

In this activity, students practice reflecting a polygon on the coordinate plane. This activity focuses on how coordinates change when a shape is reflected.

Manipulative Illustrated

- Didax XY Axis Pegboard

Steps

1. Set up the coordinate board for four-quadrant graphing. Make a triangle with vertices at (2, 1), (4, 2), and (3, 4).

2. Ask students to build a second triangle. The second triangle should show what the original triangle would look like when reflected over the y-axis. Discuss the meaning of reflection and be certain students know which axis is the y-axis.

3. After students build the second triangle, have them record the coordinates of the two figures. Discuss their findings using these questions:

   - *How do the coordinates change when the figure is reflected across the y-axis?*

   - *Why do you think the coordinates change in this way?*

   - *How do the changed coordinates represent the idea of reflection?*

4. Repeat the activity by asking students to reflect the original figure over the *x*-axis. How is this figure different from the original figure and from the reflection over the *y*-axis? What happens to the coordinates this time?

Why This Manipulative?

The coordinate board makes the work of creating reflections easier for students by lowering the consequences for making a mistake. If students do not create the reflection correctly the first time, it is easy to remove the pegs and try again.

Developing Understanding

This experience focuses on what happens to coordinates when a figure is reflected over the *x*- or *y*-axis. If you wish to challenge students further, reflect across other horizontal or vertical lines, including those that pass through the figure.

Featured Connection

This lesson uses the Name Your Model strategy to help students connect their physical graph on the coordinate board with the more traditional graph on paper and the systematic way coordinates change with translation. By recording coordinates and their changes, students are supported to see how the action of translation impacts location on the plane.

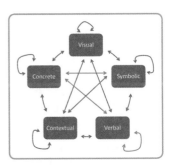

Source: Lesh, Post, & Behr (1987).

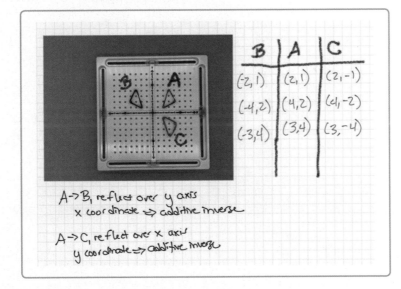

Materials

- Isometric board and bands
- A small irregular shape (e.g., red pattern block)
- Activity sheet (one for each student)

Organization (physical)

- **Getting Started:** Distribute the boards and bands along with a small asymmetric shape.
- **Winding Down:** Repackage materials and return to home base.

Mathematical Purpose

In this activity, students use an isometric geoboard to model rotation.

Activity 7.10 Resources

- *Rotation on the Geoboard* Activity Sheet

 To access resource visit resources.corwin.com/ MasteringMathManips/ 4–8

- Image in "Featured Connection" created with Toy Theater geoboard tool: https://toytheater .com/geoboard/

Manipulative Illustrated

- Isometric Geoboard

Steps

1. Distribute the geoboards and bands, along with the activity sheet. If students have never worked with an isometric geoboard, give them a few minutes to explore the board. Encourage them to notice how the board is similar to and different from a traditional geoboard. Support students to notice that each peg is the same distance from all the other pegs. This board is built on a 60-degree grid rather than the 90-degree grid of the coordinate plane.

2. Ask students to select a figure from the activity sheet and use a band to create the figure on their board.

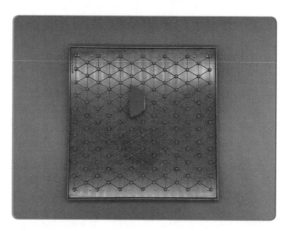

3. What will happen when the figure is rotated 120 degrees clockwise from a selected vertex? Have students place their finger on one vertex to indicate the point of rotation and use a different-color band to make the new figure.

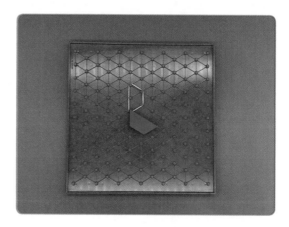

4. Discuss what happens using the following questions:

   - *How is the figure the same as the original figure? How is it different?*

   - *How did you know how far to rotate the figure? Where is the 120-degree rotation on your board?*

   - *What happens if you make the same rotation from a different vertex? Test your conjecture on your board.*

5. Return to the starting position and rotate it 60 degrees counterclockwise from a selected vertex. Discuss the findings using similar questions.

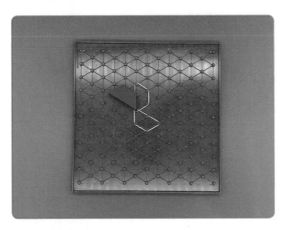

Why This Manipulative?

Rotations can be difficult to visualize. The isometric board makes rotations in 60-degree increments easy to accomplish. This allows students to think about what happens to figures (particularly asymmetric figures) as they are rotated.

Developing Understanding

The shapes students are asked to rotate are deliberately irregular. This allows students to notice what happens to the orientation of a shape as it is rotated. The trapezoid, for example, points in the opposite direction when it is rotated 180 degrees. If this same activity were completed with an equilateral triangle, the rotation would be much more difficult to see.

Challenge students to see if there is more than one way to accomplish a given transformation. For example, can a slide plus a reflection be used to transform the triangle with the same result as the 180-degree rotation?

Featured Connection

Use the Make a Sketch strategy to record both the original figure and the rotated figure. This guides students to move from working with physical representations (helpful, but not always practical) to working with visual representations.

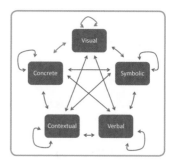

Source: Lesh, Post, & Behr (1987).

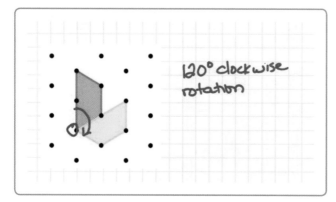

Notes

_____

_____

_____

_____

_____

_____

_____

_____

_____

_____

_____

_____

CLOSING REFLECTION: GEOBOARDS

How do I use geoboards in my classroom now? What concepts do I use them to teach?

_____

_____

_____

_____

_____

_____

What new ways have I found to use geoboards to better support student understanding?

_____

_____

_____

_____

_____

What are my goals to make geoboards a more regular part of my instruction?

_____

_____

_____

_____

_____

_____

CHAPTER 8

Continuing the Journey

You, like the teachers in our introductory chapter, have been on a journey of discovering ways to use manipulatives more intentionally. We hope that you've had powerful conversations and found some new favorite activities, and that you feel more comfortable with these tools as part of your mathematics tool kit.

Using manipulatives is not a new instructional strategy, although new manipulatives are being developed and virtual manipulatives are becoming an increasingly important resource for teachers and students. Remember that the power of manipulatives as tools for learning mathematics is in the connections you develop between these concrete representations and other representations of mathematics. The tools themselves are simply that—tools to spur mathematical conversations and discoveries. The deep learning is in translation from one representation to another.

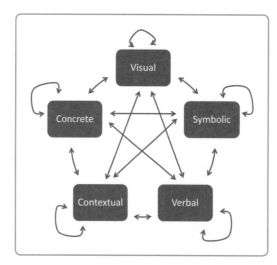

Source: Lesh, Post, & Behr (1987).

As you continue on your journey, we hope you will keep these important ideas in mind:

1. Manipulatives are tools for learning mathematics, for making sense of abstract ideas. As students develop understanding and confidence, they will naturally use manipulatives less and less because the tools become inefficient. Their early work with manipulatives grounds their experiences and serves as a cognitive support for their more efficient work with abstract symbols. The pace of this fading away will vary from student to student.

2. Context is always important. Students can and should connect physical representations, visual representations, and symbolic representations to experiences in their everyday lives. Context is not limited only to working with concrete objects.

3. Manipulatives provide students with an opportunity to act out, think about, and talk about mathematics. That active engagement with the math is our goal, and manipulatives are a tool for creating student engagement. If students can act out a situation, they can talk about it. If they can talk about it, they can write about it. If they write about it, they can develop an equation for it. *That* is how we move from concrete to abstract.

4. While we talk about concrete-pictorial-abstract as if it is a tight sequence of fixed steps, the reality is that learners move back and forth across the phases. They might start building and have an insight about an equation. They write that down and begin working abstractly, only to find a picture helps clarify their thinking. Then, back to the equation they go. Furthermore, students may be thinking abstractly when using concrete tools, or they may be thinking concretely when using pictorial representations (Kamii, 2006).

5. Mathematics is best learned by using and connecting *all* forms of representation. While this book is grounded in physical representations, we have shared a number of strategies for connecting the concrete with the visual, the symbolic, the verbal, and the abstract.

6. Encourage students to use materials creatively and flexibly. If a commercial manipulative is not available, what everyday objects might you substitute? Can you use a manipulative not designed for the problem at hand? What new insights do you gain by thinking about how to use these tools flexibly? What do you get by running up against the limits of the tools?

7. Challenge your students (and yourself) to think deeply about how these tools represent the mathematics and what we can learn from the tools. Learning to represent binomial multiplication with algebra tiles can push your own understanding of the distributive property and what it really means. While you may be quite good at using FOIL (first, outer, inner, last), what new learning happens when you build a model and sketch a picture of an open array?

8. Be open to digital tools and think about how they best support learning. Learners benefit from working with tangible objects to represent important mathematics. Just because this is beneficial does not mean it is always possible. When you use virtual tools, choose carefully to be sure the math is well represented. Push yourself to develop tasks that truly reimagine the work and take advantage of digital features like endless supplies of pieces.

Suggestions for Supporting Families and Caregivers

Now that you and your students have more experience with manipulatives, we encourage you to support families and caregivers in becoming more comfortable with these important tools. The adults in students' lives will need time to explore and understand the tools, both digital and physical versions. Where possible, demonstrate a manipulative activity for them so they can see the power of learning this way. Provide basic tips for navigating and using virtual manipulatives for them so they can support their children at home. You might consider making *brief* video clips (2–3 minutes) that introduce them to the manipulatives and other visual strategies their children will be working on in the coming days.

Families and caregivers will likely share some of your questions about teaching with manipulatives. In the following section, we've addressed just a few of the major concerns we often hear from those supporting students' learning at home. One of the most important things you can do is relate to them, validate their concerns and frustrations, and ease them into realizing that we are not ignoring the ways they learned math in elementary school; we are simply delaying the standard procedures a bit in order to first develop understanding.

This is too complicated and takes too long. Why are you teaching this way?

Do you remember hearing that rhyme, "Mine is not to question why, just invert and multiply"? Many of us learned math by watching our teachers and then copying what they did. We did not focus on understanding, and we certainly weren't invited to ask them "why" questions. Rather, we focused on getting the right answer, and many of us had no idea what kind of magic had just taken place. Unfortunately, many adults have some kind of aversion toward mathematics, and we can't afford to let the next generation fall into that same category.

Much of mathematics is very abstract, and making sense of the symbols is hard. Manipulatives provide us with a way to show students what the symbols represent and ensure that math makes sense to them. While we know it sometimes takes a little longer when we first use manipulatives, our patience is repaid in the long run with greater student understanding. Simply put, time spent helping students understand the math is always time well spent, and manipulatives play a huge role in developing that understanding.

Is it okay if I show my child the way I learned to do it instead?

Please know that the most efficient strategies, known as the standard procedures or standard algorithms, are part of our end game—they are simply not where we begin. One of the things we value in math is that there are many different ways to solve most problems. Having multiple solution pathways helps students become more flexible thinkers. Furthermore, it is so helpful when students become comfortable with many strategies before they learn the most efficient strategies (aka the procedures you and I learned in school). We encourage adults to wait to show traditional algorithms or shortcuts until students are learning about them in the classroom.

I don't know how to help my child with this kind of math. What can I do?

We encourage you to help your child with math by asking questions rather than providing answers. With manipulative activities, the questions are often about how the students represent the math. Here are some general questions you might use to support your child when learning math with manipulatives:

- *Show or tell me the problem you're working on. What parts of the problem make sense to you?*
- *How can you show those parts with your manipulatives?*
- *If this manipulative isn't working for you, is there another one you'd prefer to use?*
- *Where is each part of the problem in the representation you've created?*

I don't have any manipulatives at home, and my child needs help now. What should I do?

Many math problems can be represented with materials you have in your home, especially in your kitchen. Here are just a few ideas to get you started (Wills, 2021).

- Counters: beans, dry pasta, cereal bits, buttons, beads, bottle caps
- Place value, including decimals: *O*-shaped cereal on dry spaghetti noodles, paper clips, beads, string

- Square tiles: cheese crackers, small square bathroom tiles
- Fractions: egg cartons, muffin trays, strips of paper or ribbon

Additional Resources

On the website supporting this book, you will find the following:

- Resources for conducting your own schoolwide manipulative inventory.
- A list of virtual manipulative sites along with the models available on each site, current as of late 2021. If you are looking for a particular tool, this can help you find some good options. Remember, the digital world is always changing, so the site may not look as it did when we first made the list.
- Black-line masters for the activities in this book.

 To view and download resources, please visit **resources.corwin.com/ MasteringMathManips/4–8**

Continuing the Journey

While we've shared many ideas for teaching with manipulatives, there is much more these tools can do. We encourage you to continue exploring these powerful tools as resources in your mathematics classroom. Make manipulatives freely available to your students for their mathematics work. Explore new uses for manipulatives at professional conferences or from other sources. And, like the teachers at the beginning of this book, dig deep into your closets and bookshelves to discover what treasures lie in wait. Bring them to the light of day, explore new ways of bringing math to life for students, and find renewed excitement in teaching for understanding. Your students will thank you … and you'll so enjoy the journey.

GLOSSARY

Absolute Value The distance from 0 on a number line

Active Addition Addition problem situations that include an action such as coming in, moving up, or increasing in quantity

Acute Angle An angle with a measure less than 90°

Additive Comparison Comparison situations where there is a constant difference; answers questions such as "how many more" or "how many fewer"

Additive Inverse A number that, when added to another number, gives a sum of zero

Altitude A line segment connecting a vertex to its opposite side at a right angle

Angle Two rays that share an end point

Area The number of square units needed to cover a surface

Attributes (of shapes) Characteristics of an object such as color, size, thickness, or number of sides/angles

Axes (*x* and *y*) The horizontal number line (*x*-axis) and the vertical number line (*y*-axis) on the coordinate plane; axes are also the lines at the side and bottom of a graph

Bar Model A representation of a word problem or mathematical situation where bars or boxes are used to represent the known and unknown quantities; also known as a *tape diagram*

Base (geometry) The face of a three-dimensional figure or a side of a two-dimensional figure oriented perpendicular to the direction of height

Binomial An algebraic expression with two terms

Complementary Angles Two angles whose sum is 90°

Compose To put a number or shape together using other numbers or shapes

Cone A three-dimensional figure with one curved surface, one flat surface (usually circular), one curved edge, and one vertex

Congruent Equal in size and shape

Coordinates A set of numbers, or a single number, that locates a point on a line, on a plane, or in space

Corresponding Angles Matching angles created when two parallel lines are crossed by a third line (a transversal)

Cross Section A "slice" of a three-dimensional figure created when the shape is cut by a plane

Cylinder A three-dimensional figure with one curved surface and two congruent circular bases

Denominator The number of equal-sized pieces in a whole; the number of members of a set with an identified attribute; the bottom number in a fraction

Dilation Transformation A transformation where all lengths are changed by a common factor

Distributive Property of Multiplication Over Addition Multiplying a sum by a given number is the same as multiplying each addend by the number and then adding the products

Double Number Line A mathematical diagram where two number lines are marked to show the relationship between two values

Equal Groups Multiplication Situation A multiplication situation where there are a number of groups and each group is the same size

Equation A statement using an equals sign (=) showing that two expressions have the same value

Equilateral A polygon with all sides the same length

Exponent The small number placed to the upper right of a number (or variable) indicating how many times the base is multiplied by itself; for example, $2^4 = 2 \times 2 \times 2 \times 2 = 16$ where 2 is the base and 4 is the exponent

Expression A value expressed as numbers and/or variables and operation symbols (such as +, −, and ×) grouped together; one side of an equation; for example, $9y + 7$, $3 + 5$, and 8

Face A flat surface of a three-dimensional shape

Factor As a noun, a number (or expression) that divides without remainders into the number (or expression); as a verb, to break down into terms that multiply to make the quantity to be factored

Groupable vs. Pre-grouped Models for which each group of ten can be made or grouped from the single pieces are "groupable" (e.g., 10 beans in one cup, 10 linking cubes in one tower, 10 straws in one bundle); models for which the ten is already grouped and must be exchanged for 10 single pieces are "pre-grouped"

Height The dimension of a figure perpendicular to the length of the base

Hypotenuse The side of a right triangle opposite the right angle

Interior Angles of a Triangle The three angles inside a triangle

Inverse Operation The partner operation that "undoes" the work of the operation; for example, addition and subtraction, as well as multiplication and division

Isometric Grid A grid where all points are equidistant from all other points

Isosceles Triangle A triangle with two equal sides; the angles opposite the equal sides are also equal

Line of Symmetry A line dividing a figure into two congruent halves

Line Plot A graphical number line display of data using dots (also known as a *dot plot*); a number line with an *X* placed above the corresponding value on the line for each piece of data

Manipulatives Physical objects teachers and students can use to discover and illustrate mathematical concepts

Mean The sum of the numbers in a set of data divided by the number of pieces of data; usually called "average"; arithmetic mean

Median The number in the middle of a set of data when the data are arranged in order; when there are two middle numbers, the median is their mean

Mode The most common value in a data set

Monomial An expression comprised of exactly one term

Multiplicative Comparison A comparison where there is a scale factor, proportional, or "times as many" relationship

Net A two-dimensional representation of a three-dimensional figure that can be folded up into the three-dimensional figure

Numerator The number in a fraction that indicates the number of parts of the whole that are being considered; the top number in a fraction

Obtuse Angle An angle with a measure greater than 90° and less than 180°

Open Array A nonproportional array; the sections are typically filled by quantities represented as numbers

Parallel Lines Lines in a plane that remain the same distance apart and will never intersect

Parallelogram A quadrilateral with two pairs of parallel sides

Partial Product A part of the product in a multiplication calculation, usually based on place value and the distributive property

Partial Quotient A part of the quotient in a division calculation, usually based on place value and the distributive property

Perfect (Square or Cube) Values that are the squares or cubes of whole numbers

Perimeter The distance around a polygon

Perpendicular Lines Lines that are at right angles (90°) to each other

Polygon A many-sided, closed, simple figure whose sides are line segments

Polynomial An expression consisting of one or more terms

Prism A three-dimensional figure with parallel congruent polygons for bases and parallelograms for faces

Proportional Manipulatives Materials where the components are "true to scale"; they have a deliberate mathematical relationship

Pyramid A polyhedron with a polygon for the base and triangular faces that meet at the apex

Quadrant The x- and y-axes divide the coordinate plane into four sections labeled, counterclockwise, I, II, III, and IV, with Quadrant I having all points with positive x- and y-coordinates

Quadrilateral A four-sided polygon

Ratio (part:part and part:whole) A comparison of two quantities

Rectangle A parallelogram with four right angles

Reflection (flip) A transformation that flips the plane over a fixed line

Representation A description or model that demonstrates or presents a mathematical concept or idea

Right Angle A 90° angle, sometimes called a "square" angle

Right Rectangular Prism A prism where all of the lateral faces are rectangles

Right Triangle A triangle with one right angle

Rotation (angle as + turn symmetry) A transformation where a figure turns around a fixed point

Scalene Triangle A triangle with none of the sides the same length

Similar Figures Figures having the same shape but not necessarily the same size; side lengths are proportional

Slant Height The altitude of a face of a three-dimensional figure; the height "running up the face" rather than the height perpendicular to the base

Slope The steepness of a line; the ratio of rise to run

Sphere A three-dimensional figure made up of all points equally distant from the center

Square Root (Cube Root) The number that, when squared (or cubed), makes the number in question

Supplementary Angles Two angles whose sum is 180°

Surface Area The total area of the exterior faces of a three-dimensional figure

Tape Diagram A representation of a word problem or mathematical situation where bars or boxes are used to represent the known and unknown quantities; also known as a *bar model*

Transformation (including rigid) A one-to-one correspondence of points in the plane such that each point P is associated with a unique point P′, known as the image of P; transformations can be dilations, translations, reflections, or rotations

Translation Model The Lesh translation model suggests that mathematical ideas can be represented in five different modes: manipulatives, pictures, real-life contexts, verbal symbols, and written symbols

Translation (slide) A transformation where the original figure is moved to a new location without changing size or orientation

Transversal A line that intersects two or more lines

Unit Whole The portion considered to be 1 when working with fractions

Vertex The common end point of two or more rays or line segments

Vertical Angles Nonadjacent angles with equal measure located across a common vertex

Volume The amount of space contained in a solid; measured in cubic units

Zero Pair A pair of quantities that, when added, sum to zero

Note: Some glossary entries are used with permission from the *Common Core Mathematics Companions,* Grades K–2 (Gojak & Miles, 2015), 3–5 (Gojak & Miles, 2016), and 6–8 (Miles & Williams, 2016).

REFERENCES

Bruner, J. (1960). *The process of education.* Harvard University Press.

Center for Applied Special Technology. (2018). *The UDL guidelines* (version 2.2). http://udlguidelines.cast.org

Dienes, Z. P. (1971). *Building up mathematics* (4th ed.). Hutchinson Educational.

Fetter, A. (2011, April). *Ever wonder what they'd notice?* [Ignite session]. National Council of Teachers of Mathematics Annual Conference, Indianapolis, IN.

Gojak, L. M., & Miles, R. H. (2015). *The Common Core mathematics companion: The standards decoded, grades K–2.* Corwin Mathematics.

Gojak, L. M., & Miles, R. H. (2016). *The Common Core mathematics companion: The standards decoded, grades 3–5.* Corwin Mathematics.

Hattie, J., Fisher, D., Frey, N., Gojak, L. M., Moore, S. D., & Mellman, W. (2017). *Visible learning for mathematics, grades K–12: What works best to optimize student learning.* Corwin Mathematics.

Kamii, C. (2006, April). *Why many second graders think they can't pay for a 6¢ item with a dime* [Session presentation]. National Council of Teachers of Mathematics Annual Meeting and Exposition, Saint Louis, MO.

Karp, K. S., Dougherty, B. J., Bush, S. B. (2021). *The math pact: Achieving instructional coherence within and across grades.* Corwin Mathematics.

Lesh, R. A., Post, T., & Behr, M. (1987). Representations and translations among representations in mathematics learning and problem solving. In C. Janvier (Ed.), *Problems of representations in the teaching and learning of mathematics* (pp. 33–40). Lawrence Erlbaum Associates.

Magiera, J. (2016). *Courageous edventures.* Corwin.

Marshall, A. M., Superfine, A. C., & Canty, R. S. (2010). Star students make connections. *Teaching Children Mathematics, 17*(1), 39–47.

Miles, R. H., & Williams, L. A. (2016). *The Common Core mathematics companion: The standards decoded, grades 6–8.* Corwin Mathematics.

Moore, S. D., Morrow-Leong, K., & Gojak, L. (2020). *Mathematize it! Going beyond key words to make sense of word problems, grades 3–5.* Corwin Mathematics.

Morrow-Leong, K., Moore, S. D., & Gojak, L. (2020). *Mathematize it! Going beyond key words to make sense of word problems, grades 6–8.* Corwin Mathematics.

National Council of Supervisors of Mathematics. (2013, Spring). Improving student achievement in mathematics by using manipulatives with classroom instruction [Position statement]. *Improving Student Achievement Series, 11.* https://www.movingwithmath.com/ncsm-position-paper/

National Council of Teachers of Mathematics. (2020). *Catalyzing change in middle school mathematics.* https://www.nctm.org/Standards-and-Positions/Catalyzing-Change/Catalyzing-Change-in-Middle-School-Mathematics/

Piaget, J. (1971). *The psychology of intelligence.* Routledge & Kegan.

Stephan, M., & Akyuz, D. (2012). A proposed instructional theory for integer addition and subtraction. *Journal for Research in Mathematics Education, 43*(4), 428–464.

Wills, T. (2021). *Teaching from a distance.* Corwin.

Vygotsky, L. (2012). *Thought and language* (E. Hanfmann, G. Vakar, & A. Kozulin, Eds.; A. Kozulin, Trans.; Rev. and expanded ed.). MIT Press. (Original work published 1934)

INDEX

Supporting TEACHERS | Empowering STUDENTS

PETER LILJEDAHL

14 optimal practices for thinking that create an ideal setting for deep mathematics learning to occur

Grades K–12

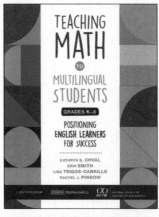

KATHRYN B. CHVAL, ERIN SMITH, LINA TRIGOS-CARRILLO, RACHEL J. PINNOW

Strengths-based approaches to support multilingual students' development in mathematics

Grades K–8

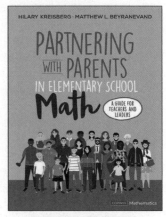

HILARY KREISBERG, MATTHEW L. BEYRANEVAND

Guidance on building productive relationships with families about math education

Grades K–5

BETH MCCORD KOBETT, FRANCIS (SKIP) FENNELL, KAREN S. KARP, DELISE ANDREWS, TRENDA KNIGHTEN, JEFF SHIH, DESIREE HARRISON, BARBARA ANN SWARTZ, SORSHA-MARIA T. MULROE

Detailed plans for helping elementary students experience deep mathematical learning

Grades K–1, 2–3, 4–5

BETH MCCORD KOBETT, KAREN S. KARP

Your game plan for unlocking mathematics by focusing on students' strengths

Grades K–6

JOHN J. SANGIOVANNI, SUSIE KATT, KEVIN J. DYKEMA

Empowering students to embrace productive struggle to build essential skills for learning and living—both inside and outside the classroom

Grades K–12

To order, visit corwin.com/math

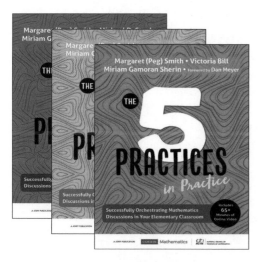

A SAGE Publishing Company

Helping educators make the greatest impact

CORWIN HAS ONE MISSION: to enhance education through intentional professional learning.

We build long-term relationships with our authors, educators, clients, and associations who partner with us to develop and continuously improve the best evidence-based practices that establish and support lifelong learning.

NCTM

NATIONAL COUNCIL OF TEACHERS OF MATHEMATICS

The National Council of Teachers of Mathematics supports and advocates for the highest-quality mathematics teaching and learning for each and every student.